Sender and Sent

Leslie Davison

SENDER AND SENT

A Study in Mission

LONDON
EPWORTH PRESS

First Published in 1969
by Epworth Press
Set in 11/12 *pt. Baskerville*
and printed and bound
by Page & Thomas, The Chesham Press Ltd.,
Chesham, Buckinghamshire

SBN 7162 0122 4

Contents

Foreword

THIS book has grown out of questions raised in the Commission on Evangelism, a sub-committee of the Home Mission Department of the Methodist Church, where we have tried to understand the causes of the drift from faith and why there is so little response to the message of the Church. I hasten to add that while our searching discussions prompted this study, it is in no way the work of the Commission nor are they responsible for its contents and conclusions. Rather their questions provoked me into attempting some sort of provisional answer, drawing from social history and theology a few lessons in the meaning of mission. This study is intended not for scholars and experts, but for interested lay men and women, teachers, class and group leaders, local preachers and lay readers without access to expensive theological and specialist works and who want some clearer idea of what mission really means today.

I have borrowed freely from the works and the summaries of others and I hope I have made due acknowledgement in the text and footnotes. I apologize for any omission or inadequate confession of indebtedness and pray that the authors will regard me as their advocate directing others to read the originals for themselves. I am also aware of how many other scholars should have been referred to, but space and time imposed their limitations. My aim has been to note the main streams of thought and to show their action and reaction within the developing structures of human society. Mission, to be understood, must be seen on a vast canvas. The picture, in spite of its enormous challenge, fills us with hope, for it also discloses the greatness of God.

Acknowledgements

Quotations from the New English Bible—New Testament © 1961 are by permission of Oxford and Cambridge University Presses.

I express my gratitude to my colleagues Sinclair Walker and George Sails whose steady encouragement has held me to this task, to our friend and Treasurer, Lord Rank, whose insistence on the gift of the Spirit stimulates us, and especially to Miss Betty Watkinson, my personal assistant, who has typed the manuscript, some of it several times, in addition to all her other duties and responsibilities in the Department.

And a final word of thanks to Methodism for the privilege of working in the Home Mission Department. If this book can in any way strengthen the hearts and hands of the People of God for mission, how rich is the reward!

Westminster LESLIE DAVISON
February 1969

CHAPTER ONE

INTRODUCTION

The Crisis

WESTERN Christianity in this hectic twentieth century is undergoing the shattering and traumatic experience of massive popular rejection. The drift from the churches which had begun to reveal itself in some denominations in 1906 and 1907 has accelerated in each succeeding decade. Today, worried church leaders, awakening belatedly to the crisis, are anxiously searching for cause and cure. The cry for renewal, reformation, or revival—the choice of term reflects the theological presuppositions of the speaker—comes from every quarter, whether catholic or evangelical, liberal or fundamentalist, radical or traditionalist. Yet in spite of detailed analyses, proclamations and counter-proclamations and a few practical experiments in new methods of mission, nearly everywhere in the West the influence of the Church declines and the number of worshippers decreases.

2. The prevailing mood is one of helpless, sometimes angry, bewilderment, for it is hard for churchmen to understand what is happening. They have at the back of their minds the conviction that Christianity, when properly presented, is irresistible and its ultimate conquest of the world certain. 'The sovereignty of the world has passed to our Lord and his Christ, and he shall reign for ever and ever' (Revelation 11:15). This triumphalism is firmly rooted in Scripture. 'If God is on our side, who is against us?' (Romans 8:31). But the assurance of final victory can easily slide into a superficial and perilous optimism which blinds the Church to her own grievous faults and to impending calamity. The Church has often paid heavily for such false

self-confidence. Ugly facts must be faced resolutely, and the fact is that in the West today the tide of faith is ebbing fast and as yet there is little sign of its turn.

3. Some Christians do not see any problems at all—both diagnosis and cure are obvious. The churches have failed because they are not preaching the 'pure' Gospel and the solution is to return at once to a sound Biblical theology and to the effective methods of traditional evangelism. Blame for the present weakness is attributed to the departure of the Church from the faith 'once and for all delivered'. From such camps comes the cry, 'Back to Wesley!', 'Back to Luther!', 'Back to Paul!' But the past cannot be revived. The stream of time moves only forward. Words change their meaning and emotional overtones, the intellectual and social contours shift from generation to generation. The cultural gulf that separates us from Wesley is in many ways wider than that which separated Wesley from the world of the apostles. The chords that vibrated to Wesley's appeal hang slack today. Those who still present the faith in these traditional forms are no more successful in winning a response from 'secular' man than any other Christian engaged in mission today. In spite of such efforts, often on the huge and expensive scale of 'mass evangelism', the impact on the masses outside the churches is disappointingly small, and the question remains, Why are they so difficult to reach?

4. Some others, far from being disturbed by the drift from faith, regard it as an enheartening sign of the Second Coming of Christ in glory. Prophecy has prepared them for such a development. The Day of the Lord 'cannot come before the final rebellion against God' (2 Thessalonians 2:3). Jesus himself anticipated a withering of faith, 'But when the Son of Man comes, will he find faith on earth?' (Luke 18:8). The Church's business is to proclaim the Gospel 'in season and out of season' (2 Timothy 4:2). The Gospel is always selective, sifting the souls of men. 'Though many are invited, few are chosen' (Matthew 22:14); many prefer the broad road that leads to destruction, few the narrow way that leads to eternal life (Matthew 7:13f). Our duty, therefore, is to preach Christ faithfully and leave the results to God, even though the world rejects our message. The cross has always been a stumbling

block to the proud, and the wisdom of God has seemed foolishness to the world's wise men (1 Corinthians 1:18f). 'The seed' of the Word is sown broadcast, and our job is to go on sowing, even though three quarters of it is unfruitful (Matthew 13:4f.) There is comfort in this thought and a needed corrective to the impatience that wants immediate results every time. Certainly we must leave the results to God when we have done all that we ought to have done. It would relieve our conscience if we were assured that our inability to reach secular man was due entirely to his wickedness and obdurate resistance. But we cannot so easily rid ourselves of the suspicion that the causes of failure lie also in us. Our secular neighbour is as decent, friendly, and generous as any churchman, yet somehow we are unable to talk to him convincingly about our faith.

5. The drift from the churches is all the more perplexing because, on the face of it, there are conditions in the surging life of the West which would seem to be conducive to religious revival. Everywhere there is turmoil and tension as new ideas, inventions and techniques create new standards of living, new values and attitudes. One would imagine that such an age of opportunities and widening horizons, which herald the birth of what could be a brilliant global civilization, would cry out for the unifying vision of the Kingdom of God and that it would welcome the profound insights into human need that the Gospel provides. It is difficult to understand why men and women, caught up in the storm of social change and in such desperate need of the very guidance that Christianity professes to give, should remain so impervious to its appeal. For, in spite of our staggering achievements, the mood of our time is neither buoyant nor gay. Over all human effort hangs the grey cloud of ultimate futility, for secular man has little confidence in the final worth of anything. If he does not himself destroy the planet in one of his periodic outbursts of mass irrationality in nuclear war, it is none the less doomed to perish. Earth is but a tiny speck in the vast ocean of space and the whole human story from beginning to end is only a splutter of flame, which burns for a moment in the immensities of astronomical time, before it expires for ever. To a religious man it would seem that such an age with its aching spiritual vacuum, its unbear-

able tensions, its lack of purpose, its inner emptiness is ripe for a great spiritual awakening. The Gospel can supply a satisfying sense of purpose, it can assure a man that he does not stand alone and deliver him from the finality of death; it can reconcile him to his fellow men, overcoming the barriers of nation, race, and class. Why then is it dismissed as outmoded, irrelevant, and powerless, a relic from the childhood of the race, a spent force without vital word for today? This is the question that baffles and torments. Rarely has there been such a need and such an opportunity for the Gospel, and yet nothing the Church says or does appears to penetrate the indifference of the secular world.

6. Some churchmen have consoled themselves with the thought that many who never darken the doors of a church still retain a considerable measure of faith which could perhaps be revitalized, once the Church learned how to make itself intelligible to them. Some sample surveys show that a surprisingly high percentage of the population, though they do not go to Church, say that they believe in God, and a fair proportion still say their prayers.[1] Such belief and practice is more prevalent in the older age brackets than in the younger. Certainly the churches are still used for the *rites de passage*—christenings, marriages, and funerals which mark the social crises, but an increasing number of people are using lay substitutes for these religious rituals. The evidence of modern art and literature points rather in the other direction and indicates that increasingly people are finding it difficult to attach meaning to the word 'God'. The modern mind is as sceptical of miracles as it is of ghosts and lumps religion with magic and superstition. These doubts and reservations seem more typical of the modern mood than the pale vestiges of ancestral faith which linger on in the memories of the older generation.

7. The gulf between the churchman and the 'outsider', as he is prone to call the non-churchgoer, is immense. The very word reveals the exclusiveness and inturned preoccupation of the 'insider' and his unconscious assumption of superiority. The churchman is often shocked by the sheer lack of accurate information about his faith which he encounters, but his own

[1] *Television and Religion*, A.B.C. Gallup Poll (U.L.P.).

ignorance of the secular world and its motivation is just as great. When he meets someone who can articulate his opposition to Christianity, he discovers to his chagrin that his traditional answers are a far from convincing defence. We are entering a new and more severe phase of the battle between science and religion, though some distinguished theologians who are not scientists, and a few scientists who are not theologians, minimize the differences. But this is to deceive ourselves. Traditional Christian answers are disputed on the telling grounds that they rest on false information about the origin and nature of the universe, and that some Christian doctrines are morally unworthy of a humane society. This kind of criticism cannot be silenced by rebuke. We must show that our faith is not irrelevant, inaccurate, and obscurantist. Unless we give such answers soon our contemporaries will become confirmed in their belief that we are indeed living in the opening stages of the Post-Christian age, in the twilight of faith, and they will leave us among our shadows. Many anxious Church leaders are calling their members to further effort and greater sacrifice. But perhaps what is really needed is a very different kind of effort, the effort to rethink the faith; and a different kind of sacrifice—the sacrifice of our preconceptions and prejudices.

8. The 'Shaking of the Foundations', as Paul Tillich has reminded us, ought not to surprise us.[1] The forces that are beating upon the Church, though they seem so destructive, must be measured and seen for what they are. While some of them are demonic, rising from the dark fears and brutal indisciplines of greed and ignorance, others are the direct or indirect product of Christian teaching. The new partnership between men and women which has been secured only after the emancipation of women from age-long subjection to male domination, the new concern for children, for the sick, the aged, the handicapped, all result from insistence on the ethics of the Family. We are passing through the turbulent change from an authoritarian to an egalitarian conception of society which is affecting every institution—the university, industry, the state, as well as the Church. Today the Church is paying a heavy price for her too close identification with power and

[1]See his *The Shaking of the Foundations* and *The Protestant Era* (Nisbet 1951).

privilege in her recent past. But we ought not to be surprised that the Church is now under judgement by the very forces she helped to create. The chief condemnation is that she failed to renew herself in time. There are those who think it is now too late for her to re-establish her credibility in the eyes of secular Europe. But this would be to misread the nature of the Church. If she will turn, her Lord is always ready to renew her. The price, as always, is humility and obedience to the guiding Spirit.

9. Conflict and change are inevitable whenever humanity begins to move from one form of society to another, and when the established norms of a previous age are left behind. A living Church and a living theology can never remain static. Unless they are always correcting themselves they will eventually crumble before the accumulated pressure of new truth. Ours is such an age and the Church finds itself beset on every side. Many fresh issues must be faced, and many deferred questions can no longer be evaded. Renewal comes out of disruption and struggle. Fierce disagreement, often bitter and prolonged, has characterized all the formative periods of Church history. Usually the eruption is followed by a lengthy time of comparative calm, for human nature does not seem able to sustain the pace of constant revolution, despite Mao Tse Tung's efforts to make it permanent. Time is needed for the new ideas to be digested and institutionalized. Vested interests secure positions of power and resist innovations that would disturb their reign. But the apparent surface stability hides the constant change underneath. So pressure again builds up and a new revolution is born.

10. Karl Marx (1818-1883) is credited with being the first to understand and apply the principles of revolution, yet they were vividly expounded by Jesus when He described the Kingdom of Heaven as yeast working in the dough (Matthew 13:33) and as new unshrunken cloth which will not patch up an old garment but tear a bigger hole, or as rough new wine, still fermenting, which will explode the old bottles (Mark 2:21f). The crisis of today, terrifying as it is, is not disaster; it is a sure sign that the Gospel is still working and that the Spirit has not forsaken us. Jesus expressed the devastating but cleans-

ing effects of His Message in His heartfelt cry, 'I have come to set fire to the earth, and how I wish it were already kindled' (Luke 12:49). Revolutionary thinking, if it is to be more than a petulant protest against the sins of our fathers and grandfathers, needs both a prophetic ability to read what is coming from the signs of the times, and to appreciate the lessons learned long generations ago. While we sift the past, separating the precious from the vile, we also need to examine new ideas no less carefully, for not every suggested change is wise or right. We must not allow ourselves to be panicked by those who want to scrap everything. In revolutionary times advocates of change have short patience with traditionalists and little inclination to listen to the voice of the past. They see only an entrenched conservatism incapable of accepting new ideas, while the defenders of tradition fear lest the hard-won treasures of the past are thrown away by impetuous and hasty iconoclasts. At the moment the exponents are shouting at, rather than talking to, one another, and there is an ungracious tartness and asperity among some of the disputants that springs from the sharpness of their distress. Christians must enter sympathetically into this struggle, seeking to share and understand the concerns felt by the conflicting groups, and helping to create meeting points, for we need one another. If, as some say, drawing a parallel with the convulsions that racked the Church in the sixteenth century, we are in the opening stages of a Second Reformation, then the prayer of all Christians must be that this time we hold on to one another without further fragmentation of the Church.

11. Though we need to listen to each other within the Church, we must be equally open to what the world has to say to us. Today there are vast areas of knowledge and experience, particularly in the new sciences in which churchmen as churchmen have no qualifications. In these fields they are the laymen who must listen to their teachers. They must become sensitive to the real pressure points in modern society, and that is not easy for clergymen who can live, if they choose, within the narrower orbit of church life. Above all we need to recapture the art of listening to what the Spirit has to say to the Churches. Some radicals seem to suggest that He speaks today only through

the mechanics of 'group dynamics'. Others are so suspicious of the claims of religious experience that they can scarcely concede that the Spirit still speaks to individuals at all. So a crop of new questions emerges. How do we listen to God? What is He saying to us today? What is the Gospel? How do we make it intelligible and convincing to secular man? In these pages we offer some reflections on these issues. And first we turn to the source documents of our faith. Christianity is an historical religion; its roots go far back beyond the beginning of civilization in the Near East. Christianity sees itself as the vehicle through which the eternal purpose of God is being fulfilled. It embraces the whole drama of humanity, the tragic story of mankind.

PART ONE

What Mission Has Meant

CHAPTER TWO

Some Old Testament Thoughts on Mission

THE popular word *mission* is not found in Scripture, but that does not mean that the idea is unscriptural. On the contrary, it illustrates the continuing work of the Holy Spirit who leads the Christian community into new truth, revealing the deeper implications of the long-familiar Gospel. The abstract conception of mission is quite modern; the first uses of the word to describe a body of persons sent out by a religious community to convert the heathen appeared, according to the *Shorter Oxford English Dictionary*, about 1622. The Reformers, for all their passionate absorption in the Faith, were aware of no constraint to take the Gospel beyond their national frontiers. We can scarcely comprehend their indifference, for to us a Church without mission seems a contradiction in terms. The nineteenth century saw an immense awakening to the responsibility of the Church to take the Gospel to the whole world with the dynamic zeal of the Early Church. The new concept of mission united several Biblical insights, disclosed their deeper significance and imparted a new energy and purpose to the outreach of the Church. More recent mission experience is causing us to rethink some of the earlier formulations of the theology of mission, and is compelling us to search the Scriptures again, not for proof-texts, but for those insights into the mind of God and the nature of man which have so often proved to be the perennial source of renewal and inspiration.

2. The root idea of mission is sending. Our word comes from the Latin *missio* which translates two Greek words *apostello* and *pempo*—both of which mean 'I send'. The idea has four elements: (a) the Sender, who is someone with a concern; (b) the Message he wants to send which expresses that concern; (c) the

Messenger whom he chooses to convey the Message; and (d) the Recipient who is the object of the Sender's concern.

3. (a) *The Sender.* Mission begins in God. According to Biblical revelation he is the Sender. Mission is a divine activity springing directly from God's own nature. In the current confused debate the sheer uniqueness of the Biblical concept of God is not always appreciated. It is a vigorous protest against the basic assumptions of the all-pervasive Near Eastern culture, that essentially pessimistic world view which saw all things as an endless and essentially meaningless cycle of birth, growth, procreation, death and, perhaps, rebirth. Even the gods were derivative from the primeval chaos and would eventually die when all things would return to chaos once more. Then perhaps the whole meaningless process might begin again. These ideas filtered through even into Greek philosophy and still recur in certain cosmological theories advanced by some modern astronomers, who postulate that the universe began in a mist of sub-nuclear particles and will return to that state to begin the cycle again.

4. The Bible rejects these ideas of cyclic time and finite gods. The declaration 'Before me there was no God formed, neither shall there be after me' (Isaiah 43:10) is an explicit denial of these postulates of Near Eastern religion and philosophy. Not chaos, but the Lord is the First and the Last (Isaiah 44:6). For Hebrew time is linear, not cyclical; it is real, not an illusion. It begins with Creation and it moves through history towards its great culmination in the Day of the Lord when the purposes of Creation will be fulfilled. God is the Lord of history; He works in time and controls, according to His own wisdom, the destinies of all peoples and nations. He alone is the King of all the earth (Psalm 47:2). But He Himself is above and outside time. His years do not fail. He is God from everlasting to everlasting. The human mind cannot comprehend what this means, but neither can it forever repress its longings and aspirations for communion with that life of God (Psalm 42:1).

5. But in making these assertions the Bible preserves a proper reticence and agnosticism about the nature of God. It declares that He cannot be seen or understood by men, but always remains hidden, mysterious, and beyond our command.

Attempts to form any image of Him, either visual or verbal are forbidden and ridiculed. 'To whom then will ye liken God?' (Isaiah 40:18; Exodus 20:4). Hebrew religion has always known that the word 'God' cannot be defined, for He is a deep where all our thoughts are drowned. It is impossible to comprehend God; 'Such knowledge is too wonderful for me' (Psalm 139:6). So when some modern writers tell us that they do not know what the word God means, we can only express surprise that they ever thought they could. How can a finite intellect comprehend God? If we could, God would not be God, but an object amid the plenitude of objects in the universe.

6. But because we cannot comprehend God, it does not follow that there is no God, or that He cannot make Himself known to us. The Scriptures disclose a hidden God who yet seeks fellowship with men. This was His purpose in creating the universe. It was carefully prepared as a home for man who was made 'In the image and likeness of God' (Genesis 1:26; 5:1; 9:6). The likeness does not reside in man's physical being, for God is not a man, but in his capacities as a person. Man is both a reflection of God—a mirror—and a follower of God. It is this unique character of man that thrills the Psalmist when he asks in astonishment, 'What is man that God should always be thinking of him and be willing to visit him?' He answers himself. Because the creating God who formed and ordered the stars, delights in the company of man who also has creative and controlling powers; God has crowned man with glory and honour and put all things under his feet (Psalm 8). 'For thou hast made him a little less than God'—man could be a fit companion for the Lord, and God seeks his companionship. Man's 'humanity' resides in this unique relationship with God. Men can become the friends of God (Exodus 33:11; 2 Chronicles 20:7; Isaiah 41:8). God comes calling for man by name, for He knows and desires the friendship of every man. He uses many ways to introduce Himself—the form of a stranger, a burning bush, a dream, a voice in the night, a hope, a surge of inspiration. The pages of Scripture recount a variety of means by which He knocks and seeks admission, each adjusted to the character of the person concerned. He calls men to seek His face (Psalm 27:8); yet at the same time Scripture asks, 'Canst

thou by searching find out God? Canst thou find out the Almighty unto perfection?' (Job 11:7). He calls, yet remains hidden; He makes Himself known, yet no man can comprehend Him.

7. This paradox of invitation and withdrawal belongs to every age of Biblical revelation, and is exquisitely portrayed in the story of Moses' vision of the Back of God (Exodus 33:11-23). Moses, after long years of companionship with God in the half light of faith, wanted to crown that experience with the full vision of the Beloved. God reminded him, 'Man cannot see my face and live.' If man cannot look upon the sun or into a nuclear furnace without protection, how can he look into the 'face' of God? No created substance could endure the effects of that disclosure. But God understood the desire for closer communion, and went as far as He could to gratify His friend. He hid Moses in the cleft of the Rock, shielding him with His hand while the Glory passed by. Then He withdrew the protecting hand so that Moses could see the retreating Back of God. This ancient story strains at language to express the inexpressible. The unsearchable God, incomprehensible, tenderly makes Himself known up to the limits of human apprehension. We have to use anthropomorphic images like 'hand' and 'back' and 'face' because they convey some hint of what has been experienced, but Scripture itself makes it plain that these are only pictures, analogies, myths, metaphors and symbols of that for which there are no words. What matters, however, is not man's inability to comprehend God, but God's revelation of Himself as One who comes seeking the fellowship of every man.

8. The God of Scripture is never an *It*, however ineffable. The 'I AM' who discloses Himself asserts His personhood; and it is at the level of personal relationship that man experiences Him. When in our western verbalization of experience, we say God is Person, we are not making a definition; we are only using the most adequate picture we have. Martin Buber has reminded us of the pain and distress we feel when others treat us as a thing to be used.[1] We want to be approached as persons who ought to be respected, appreciated and loved for our own

[1]See ch. 12, §11, p. 150.

sakes. When Scripture insists that God is a *He* and not an *It*, it affirms that whatever more the Hidden One is—and He is so much more—He is not less than Person. It is in this realm of the personal, which is the highest that we know, that He is to be understood. In this affirmation, fraught as it is with difficulties, the Bible marks the great gulf that separates it from the impersonal religions of the East. But this is the bedrock foundation of its revelation. There could be no mission unless there was Person, for only a Person can send. Yet the mysterious phrase 'I AM', while affirming Personhood, goes on to affirm the incomprehensible 'THAT I AM' (Exodus 3:14). God can only be measured by Himself. There is no other point of reference, no adjective or description. So when He promises anything He can swear only by Himself (Genesis 22:16; Isaiah 45:23; Amos 6:8).

9. (b) *The Message*. The Message reveals the character of the Sender. It is God's invitation to that fellowship with Himself which was the purpose of Creation. But that invitation as Scripture understands the human story, has been repeatedly refused. The drama of humanity is a tragedy as the world's greatest poets have always known. The Old Testament presents it in the Story of the Fall (Genesis 3:1-21). The modern mind, by its training in the scientific method, immediately questions the historicity of these events and asks, When and where did the Fall take place? In unravelling the story of primitive man no supporting evidence has been discovered. This raises acutely the problem of the authority and reliability of Scripture. It was inevitable that during those ages when the Bible was the only known source of information about the origin of the universe and of the histories of early peoples, that it should be regarded as authoritative. There was no other authority. It was natural to take over the Jewish attitude to the sacred writings and to believe that every word was dictated directly by God and must be absolutely true. But the nineteenth century saw the deciphering of Egyptian hieroglyphics and Babylonian cuneiform and the beginning of the systematic archaeological excavation of ancient sites uncovering the history of the Near East, while palaeontology, anthropology, and geology took the human story back to the dim beginnings

of man, to the appearance of life on the earth, to the formation of the solar system and the birth of our galaxy. Modern man can no longer accept the Biblical account of Creation and the Story of the Fall as literally true. He turns to scientific text-books, not to Genesis, for facts and for the theories that explain the facts. But the Bible also contains facts—religious facts.

10. What then becomes of revelation and what reliance can we place on the Biblical record? We shall return to this question in Chapter Eight. Here we admit that the tendency of many Christians is to be less than frank on this issue. They are caught on the horns of a dilemma, for while they now recognize that the Bible is not a scientific authority, though it once served that purpose, it does reveal in an authoritative way God's dealings with man. It is truth and they do not like to define in what sense it is truth. Thus, when at Utrecht in 1935, Karl Barth was asked by the Dutch pastors, 'Did the serpent actually speak in Paradise?' he replied, 'We should rather inquire what the serpent said.' Brunner remonstrates that this answer was a clever evasion of a question which ought not to be evaded.[1] His stricture is justified and today this is one of the delayed questions which the Church must answer unequivocally and honestly. Yet Barth was right in pointing to the truth they were in danger of missing by their obsession with the problem of verbal inspiration. The temptation has always been the subtle suggestion, 'Ye shall be as gods.' 'Forget God and take command. Live as if He did not exist,' and this is the real nature of what the Bible means by 'sin'. Basically it is a denial of the existence of God. Instead of regarding his dependence on God as the essence of his being, man twists it into a deficiency that robs him of his right to dominate and play the god. He envies God and wants to demonstrate that he is His equal (Genesis 11:1-9).

11. The Story of the Fall is a magnificent example of mythopoetic thought. The word 'myth' has come to mean fictional and untrue, but such popular devaluation completely misunderstands this early and still valid form of reflective thought. Myth, though it uses symbols and is often cast into story form, deals primarily with patterns of socially significant relations involving man as a person. Myths therefore reflect

[1]See ch. 11, §18, p.141.

community experience and actual situations in which every man is caught. They are often very beautiful for they are the product of poetic insight and imagination. In ancient life myth took the place of theology and philosophy. It supplied a sense of identity before there was any sense of history. It could provide the authority for custom and landright when there was no written law or charter. It gathered into itself the experience of a people, their values and aspirations. Very often myth describes regular sequences of events and relationships, such as the cycle of the agricultural year. Repetition of the myth enabled man to express his sense of participation in the pattern and was believed somehow to help in keeping the cycle going. The Story of the Fall belongs rather to the group of myths which account for the origin and continuation of a universal pattern. Its subject is man's alienation from God. It deals with sin, the stages of temptation, the deliberate act of disobedience, defiance, and the subsequent remorse, the sense of estrangement and of the forfeited estate. The pattern occurs every time a man sins, and it has been going on as far back as man can remember. What the Story does is to explain sin to Israel in the terms in which its real nature could be grasped, namely in man's refusal of partnership.

12. We shall return again to this issue of the origin of the universe and of sin when we come to consider the modern criticisms of orthodox theology. Here we are concerned rather to outline the Biblical revelation of the Message. The Bible declares that God has continued to seek man in spite of man's rebellion against Him and rejection of Him. The original invitation still stands. As Johannes Blauw says, 'God does not give up his claim upon man . . . man's view of God may have changed, but God's view of man does not change. When man gives up service, God does not give up man as his servant.'[1] That claim is the relation of the Creator to the creature, and man can evade it only by denying his creaturehood, yet in so doing he dehumanizes himself, for his humanity lies in his 'likeness' to God. And as he dehumanizes himself, he becomes inhuman in his treatment of others, including the animal

[1] 'The Old Testament Basis for Christian Mission' in *The Theology of the Christian Mission*, ed. Gerald H. Anderson (S.C.M. 1961), p. 23.

kingdom and the inanimate world. (Genesis 6:5,11,12.) He brings disaster on himself and on others, and the Message of Invitation becomes the Message of Doom. But it is always presented as an appeal and warning—an appeal for men to turn back to God; a warning that unless they do, they will certainly perish (Ezekiel 18:30-32).

13. The Old Testament vividly presents this relationship between God and man as a *covenant*. Israel had long experience of covenant relations. First, as a nomadic people often separated into small family groups pursuing their own pastoral activities, they were bound to the tribe for mutual help and defence by unwritten obligations which were strictly observed because the life of them all depended on such obedience. Anyone who broke the covenant was a traitor to the whole tribe. Putting his own selfish interest first he had endangered everyone. But in its later history Israel encountered another kind of covenant—the treaty between a paramount lord and a vassal state, setting out the conditions under which self-government was allowed. This form of covenant is not a treaty between equals or a solemn agreement to seek together certain ends; it is a declaration, usually written down, of the terms on which the relationship is to stand. It is not negotiated, for the vassal does not make the conditions, he accepts them. It is God, the Creator, who has made the conditions under which life is to be lived in His universe. In the Old Testament the covenant relation is first recognized in God's merciful action in preserving man through the disaster of the Flood. In the myth the rainbow becomes the lovely symbol by which God reminds not man, but Himself, of 'the everlasting covenant between God and every living creature of all flesh that is upon the earth' (Genesis 9: 8-17). Man receives this covenant and lives under it; he does not negotiate it. But, again, we must emphasize that this too is only an imperfect picture. God is not a paramount king. The picture only helps us to describe a relationship which is beyond our definition. This relationship is offered us by God, and life is full only when we live within it.

14. (c) *The Messenger*. Along with the declaration of the universal covenant the Old Testament discloses the principle of God's election or choice of a Messenger. In every age there

have been men of faith who, like Noah, found grace in the eyes of the Lord, men of humble and obedient heart who gladly recognized and accepted their dependence upon God. While the choice is an immense favour and privilege, it is not made for the sake of the chosen one alone, but for those for whom the Message is intended. That all-embracing purpose is specifically declared in the special covenant God made with Abraham: 'in thee shall all the families of the earth be blessed' (Genesis 12: 1-3). The same universal intent is incorporated into the covenants made with Isaac and Jacob. It appears again in the call and commissioning of Moses. 'Come now and I will send thee' (Exodus 3:10). His task is to bring captive Israel out of Egypt, to bind her in covenant to her God, to prepare her to be the people of God for the sake of the world. The nation is to become the Messenger. 'Ye shall be unto me a kingdom of priests and an holy nation' (Exodus 19:6).

15. The calling of the Messenger always begins in an encounter with God. It is grounded in experience. Apart from such experience little of the Old Testament would ever have been written. That the experience is often mystical we frankly admit, but that does not mean that it is hallucinatory or that it is a mental state achieved only by certain psychological types. The prophetic call is always a crisis of understanding and commitment. The experience is graphically illustrated in the call of Isaiah (Isaiah 6). He sees God as 'high and lifted up'; only the skirts of God fill the Temple, which means that no ecclesiastical structure can contain God. Before that Presence even the seraphim must veil their faces. He hears the Song of Heaven—the 'Holy, Holy, Holy' of adoration of Him who fills earth with his glory. Isaiah's first reaction is an acute awareness of his own and his people's utter unworthiness. In the presence of that holiness his thought and speech and the society in which he lives are all unclean. The sense of sin is followed by an experience of cleansing and pardon as his lips are touched and purged by the purifying fire of the Spirit. These are all symbols of the gracious action of God reconciling man to Himself in self-disclosure and forgiveness. Then, as a forgiven man with a clean heart, Isaiah hears God talking in a divine soliloquy, 'Whom shall I send and who will go for us?'

God's concern is mission; the Sender is looking for a Messenger. Only then comes Isaiah's response, 'Here am I, send me', and the command follows, 'Go!' Thus vision, forgiveness and commission come together in the prophetic consciousness.

16. The Messenger's role, according to the Bible, is never an easy one. He is sent to people who do not want to hear what he has to say, who do not believe his message and who resent his coming. The servant must speak to those who have eyes but cannot see, ears but cannot hear, hearts but cannot understand. He must continue even though his message is rejected, and watch the inevitable consequences of that rejection overtake his people in disaster. The prophet must accept this role if he is to be God's mouth (Jeremiah 15:19). He must identify himself with the message so completely that he cannot repress it, it burns in his bones like fire (Jeremiah 20:9). God's concern must become his concern so that he shares in God's mission, no matter what the cost in loneliness, scorn, and rejection. He realizes that it is not himself but God that is rejected in him (1 Samuel 8:7). The instructive tale of the prophet Jonah emphasizes that the true prophet must care for people, even his enemies and the enemies of his nation, if he is to be God's servant. Though Jonah knew the Message was an invitation to Nineveh to repent before destruction, his hatred of that fierce empire was such that he tried to run away from mission, so that the doom could fall on the detested city. He did not want Nineveh to turn and live. The book teaches that Israel, intended by God to be His servant to the nations, would have to surrender its hate, learn to forgive its persecutors, and go to them with God's invitation, for this is the role of the Servant.

17. It is in the Servant Songs of Isaiah that the role of the Servant of the Lord finds its fullest Old Testament expression (Isaiah 42:1-4; 49:1-6; 50:4-9; 52:13-53:12). The controversy as to whether the Servant of chapter 53 is an individual or the people of Israel is really beside the point. The role belongs to the individual, to the nation and to all mankind, for Servanthood is the completion and maturity of humanity; it is the emergence of the 'image' of God—man in true relationship to his Creator. The nearer a man comes to God, the more fully will he fulfil the role. The Servant's job is to proclaim the

Message, not simply by what he says, but by what he does and is. The task is not merely to restore Israel to her true destiny, but to be 'a light to the Gentiles, that thou mayest be my salvation to the end of the earth' (Isaiah 49:6). He will open blind eyes, set captives free, preach good news to the poor. But in doing so he will alienate those who are blind, but think they see. The gentle, quiet Servant, who gives a second chance to the misfits and failures, who does not break a bruised and broken plant, but supports it; who does not extinguish the dying spark, but blows it to a flame, will be misunderstood, despised and rejected by the powerful and the worldly-wise. In the eyes of the world he will appear contemptible. He will be brutally ill-treated and done to death (Isaiah 50:6-7). Yet by pouring out his soul he will make an offering for sin. By contemplating his innocent suffering the guilty will realize the enormity of their transgression and be healed.

18. Thus the Servant Songs of Isaiah link the death of the Servant with the theology of sacrifice as developed in the Temple services. Behind it lies the age-old conviction that reconciliation is a costly business, something that requires the pouring out of life symbolized in the blood of the victim. The prophets had long known that man cannot buy forgiveness by offering animal sacrifices (Psalm 40:6; 51:16) or even by human sacrifices (Micah 6:6,7). Only the broken and contrite heart receives pardon and reconciliation. But this redeeming power can take the initiative, it can go to the hostile world and take its venom into itself and so precipitate the moment of discernment when eyes are opened and the prisoner of sin and pride is released. Thus Isaiah 53 points to the Sacrifice that is to end all the sacrificial system; it points to the Servant who says, 'Lo, I come to do thy will, O God.' So Message and Messenger become one, the Message clothes itself in flesh and blood, flesh that is broken and blood that is shed for many.

19. (d) *The Recipient.* But the death of the Servant is not the end; it is the means to the end. It makes possible the original goal of creation, the establishment of a new humanity, for the message is addressed to each and every man, wherever and whatever he may be. The vision of that new day when every wrong would be righted, when evil and suffering would be

eliminated, runs through the Old Testament like a golden thread. The hope of that new age of *shalom*, to be ushered in by the Prince of Peace, was never brighter than in Israel's darkest days. The Root of Jesse will lead humanity into that new era of racial harmony when even such bitter enemies as Assyria and Egypt shall worship together with Israel, 'For the Lord of Hosts has blessed them, saying, Blessed be Egypt my people and Assyria the work of my hands; and Israel mine inheritance' (Isaiah 19:23f). Men shall live in full communion with God for 'the earth shall be full of the knowledge of God, as the waters cover the sea' (Isaiah 11:1-10). Every animosity shall die, even the fierce struggle for survival in the natural world where beast preys upon beast shall end in a new harmony where none shall hurt. The Servant, by the travail of his soul, shall change all nature and bring rebellious man back to God.

20. This is the climax of the Old Testament revelation. God reveals in its pages that His whole creative and redemptive activity is to bring men into companionship with Himself. On these foundations the Christian revelation is firmly built. Attempts to cut it away from the Old Testament are as misguided as cutting a tree from its roots and still expecting it to bear fruit. For the Old Testament insists that man is only truly man as he stands before God; he discovers himself in his relation to God. Always man's temptation is to reduce God to his own level and then supplant Him, but in so doing he destroys himself, for God is his life and his salvation. When his full dependence is recognized and accepted in love then the true man emerges. His real nature is hidden and distorted by sin, a term which has no significance at all except to describe the broken relationship with God. In the new humanity sin will be cancelled and forgotten, and man set free to be himself in God. The Messiah, the Anointed, will usher in this glorious Kingdom; so also will the Servant, the despised and rejected one, but the real nature of the Messenger is wrapt in mystery for he also belongs to the hidden life of God. And so eschatology turns to contemplate the 'son of man' whose endless Kingdom replaces all the ephemeral and crumbling empires of men (Daniel 7:13-14). In that Kingdom of righteousness and peace the mission will be completed. The new and perfect law will

be written by God on every man's heart. No more shall any need to be taught to know God, for all shall know Him, from the humblest to the greatest and 'I will be their God and they shall be my people' (Jeremiah 31:33-34). So by the new covenant the full partnership will be established and the purpose of God fulfilled.

CHAPTER THREE

Some New Testament Thoughts on Mission

THE Message of the Old Testament is completed in the New. What the kings and prophets of the Old Dispensation had long sought but never fully found, is expressed in Jesus, the Living Word. No speech, however eloquent or profound can say what a life says. Jesus Himself is the Great 'Apostolos'—He who is sent (Hebrews 3:1). He is Message and Messenger, so perfectly at one with the Sender, that he who sees Jesus sees the Sender. Jesus, the Living Word, fulfils and corrects the partial messages of the past. The writer to the Hebrews puts it succinctly: 'in days gone by God spoke to our fathers in fragmentary and varied ways through the prophets, but now he has spoken to us in the Son' (Hebrews 1:1).

2. All the New Testament is recollection and interpretation of Him. All its explosive thought springs from the Fact of Christ. It is now fashionable to refer to this as the Christ-event, but the phrase is dangerous if by abstraction it distracts attention from the glowing centre of New Testament experience—Jesus Himself. The more we see Him, the more we understand the Message. Belief in the Message is belief in Him, because He is the Faithful and True Witness, the Stamp of God's very Being, the Effulgence of God's Splendour. All the excitement of the New Testament, its thrilling joy, leaps from its delight in Jesus, as in wonder and love it answers the inescapable question, 'Who is He?'

3. The Fourth Gospel, so hastily brushed aside by some radical theologians who do not like its answer to that question, asserts that Jesus cannot be understood except against the background of eternity. His Life and Message break through the limitations of time and space. In Jesus we see God Himself in action. Thus the Prologue deliberately rewrites the opening

verse of the Genesis Creation Story and declares in forthright terms that this life was the creative energy that gave meaning to the universe. 'In the beginning God created' becomes, 'In the beginning was the Word.' The Evangelist is saying that God is now to be understood, His nature and character apprehended by what is seen in and through Jesus. He is Word and He is Life. He comes to give life. The Prologue ends by referring to the hiddenness of God, the impenetrable mystery remains, nevertheless God can be known and wants to be known: 'No one has ever seen God; but God's only Son, he who is nearest to the Father's heart, he has made him known' (John 1:18). In Jesus is disclosed as much of God as man can know in this phase of existence.

4. The Synoptic Gospels, though using different expressions and emphases, bear similar testimony. Round His obscure birth strange stories gather, summarizing the Early Church's conviction that in this man the destiny of Israel is fulfilled and the new unity of heaven and earth is ushered in. In the utter humility of the stable the mercy of God surges through into the world of men. Much of His earthly life is hidden, shrouded in mystery except for a single memory of His boyhood days. As a young man Jesus emerged from obscurity to preach the Gospel of the Kingdom—the new world order with its astonishing welcome of sinners. Faith is its weapon and love its motivation. He preached and lived a Gospel in which love triumphs over legalism, in which goodness is set free to become a positive and creative principle of new relationships based on love, respect, and justice. Jesus fearlessly challenged the rigid religious and theological systems of his day because they no longer helped, but hindered man's true development. He opposed to their exclusive separatism the creative fellowship and health-giving wholeness of the Kingdom, with its war on hunger, disease, ignorance, greed and prejudice. He defended the weak, the sick, the child, the woman, the outcast, and in all this He affirmed that He was doing the will of His Father. He taught His disciples a new prayer, '*Our Father*'. In that relationship lies the charter of the classless society, the repudiation of all division of colour, race, sex, or ability. The Kingdom is not an aristocracy, an oligarchy or a meritocracy of the clever; it is

the Family of God, where everyone counts, especially the weak and helpless, and where none is forgotten or exploited. The Kingdom is the divine society, the Holy Community and it confronts every other social and religious system in judgement. Men enter it violently through the act of faith, that is, through believing Jesus, believing that what He says about God is true, and that He can do what He undertakes to do.

5. Never before had men seen such a life, never before had they heard such a Message. They saw it lived out day by day before their eyes and in it they 'saw his glory, such glory as befits the Father's only Son, full of grace and truth' (John 1:14). It drew all sorts of men and women to Him with compelling power. Round Himself He built a little company and in the brief years of His ministry He opened to them the mystery of the Kingdom. For time was short. Month by month the shadows of rejection gathered around Him. His message was spurned and the institutions He had challenged moved to crush and silence Him.

6. Never have men been loved as Jesus loved men, nor has truth been taught as He taught it. The key lay in His own awareness that He was living in full unbroken communion with the Father who had sent Him into the world. He frankly acknowledged His role of Messenger. 'In very truth I tell you, a servant is not greater than his master, nor a messenger than the one who sent him' (John 13:16). Thought of the Sender completely fills the heart and mind of the Messenger. In this relationship of dependence lies the secret of worship and service—the recognition of the worth of God, delight in His presence and joy in obedience to His will.

7. The New Testament repeats the insights of the Old and reveals even more clearly the darkness of the human tragedy. The Hebrew Story of the Fall does not feature in Jewish theology to anything like the extent it does in traditional Christian thought nor did the Jew develop the idea of Original Sin as did the Christian. Both doctrines are under fire today. Some modern theologians have a very optimistic view of humanity, and are inclined to believe that if everyone was kind we would soon solve every problem and move into a wonderful Utopia. The Bible takes a sterner and more realistic view. It

declares that man is estranged from his Maker and in his self-will and pride drives God out of his thinking. He wants to run his world in his own way. God respects man's right to make his own decisions, even though as a result of his rebellion man only brings ruin on himself. Something malevolent seems to have infected man so that he hurts himself and those he loves. The satisfaction he seeks turns sour. He feels cheated and lost. In spite of his most spectacular technical brilliance, his increasing mastery over nature, he has not mastered himself. The irrational, the savage, the incredibly evil can and does erupt in man. We want peace, but we cannot eliminate war; we are dismayed and helpless before the bestialities of destruction. We know how to produce abundant food, but millions starve. We know there can be social justice only when the disabilities of class and race are removed, but prejudice and discrimination block the way. At every point man is fighting himself and again and again is beaten and defeated by his selfishness and fear. The madness of mass evil which produced the prison camps and gas chambers of twentieth-century Europe confront us with the undeniable evidence of appalling evil which can engulf the most civilized of peoples. The flight into drugs which destroy mind and body witnesses to the failure of man to be himself. The Bible looks this squarely in the face and calls it 'the sin of the world'.

8. Christ's own understanding of mission is summarized in His parable of the Vineyard in Mark 12:1-9. In this story Jesus used the share-cropping system of His day to illustrate the purpose and meaning of mission. A man prepares at trouble and cost a vineyard, not for himself alone but for others. So also God creates the universe for men. The landlord enters into a partnership relation with his tenants who pledge themselves to share the profits. The universe is a field for partnership between man and God. The tenants refuse to deliver his share, they drive off his servants, ill-treat and even slay them. They want to exclude him from any part in their planning or control. So men have maltreated every servant, every prophet of God who would remind them that they are not the owners of the world. 'He had now only one left to send, his own dear son.' The word 'send' is constantly repeated in this story. The

tenants say, 'This is the heir, let us kill him and the vineyard will be ours' God can be forgotten. He is powerless. We can continue to run things our way.' So they kill the Son. Jesus knew that delivering the Message would cost him His life, and that God would ask this of Him.

9. Mission, though presenting an invitation which must be either accepted or rejected, cannot help but initiate judgement should the invitation be refused. But it is not motivated by judgement. 'It was not to judge the world that God sent his Son into the world, but that the world through him might be saved' (John 3:17). Those who believe pass from death to life, but those who refuse the invitation judge and condemn themselves to alienation from God which is the death of lovelessness. Jesus says that His works of mercy are part of mission and testify to the God who sent Him. Had men appreciated them they would have seen the Father who sent Him. 'You never heard his voice or saw his form.' This is the tragedy. Men do not hear or see even though they think they do. Jesus is Himself the light of the world, exposing its humanocentric darkness, but His message falls on stony ground. 'His word has found no home in you, for you do not believe him whom he sent' (John 5:38f). They reject the Message and the Messenger because they are blind.

10. No more tender and illuminating exposition of mission is to be found than in John chapter 9—the healing of the man born blind. In John's mystical and richly symbolic Gospel only seven miracles are recounted—and he never calls them miracles; they are *signs* pointing beyond themselves to the Message. The story begins with a blind beggar, a man who has never seen the light of day, who knows nothing of colour or the wonders of light and shade. He gropes his way through a dark world in which he lives by touch—a blind beggar in a world of plenty. This is also a picture of the human race. Whatever doctrine of Original Sin we hold, the fact is that man is blind to what life ought to be; he has never seen its glories and he lives like a beggar, not as a son at home in the universe. The disciples see the beggar and at once ask Jesus, 'Who sinned, this man or his parents, that he was born blind?' They are Jews and to them all pain and deprivation must be a punish-

ment for sin. Somebody must have transgressed enormously to warrant such suffering. Was it this man himself? The idea of 'Karma' was beginning to flow in from the Far East. Had this man sinned grievously in some previous existence, and was this the due reward of those misdeeds? Or, as the Rabbis taught, was this poor man's unfortunate condition the result of the sin of his parents? We have learned that there are forms of venereal disease which can produce blindness in one's children and the sin of the parent can be visited upon succeeding generations.

11. The disciples were caught in the trap of contemporary theology. The Jews almost alone of all people declared that there could be only One God. They denounced and despised the polytheism of the Gentiles. But monotheism creates its own problems. Where one believes in two or more gods, then evil can be accounted for by ascribing it to the malevolence or anger of one or other of the deities. Persian dualism postulated two Divine beings, one Good and the other Evil, and interpreted life as the struggle between these two forces. But the Jew insisted that there was only one God and so he had to account for the intrusion of evil into the universe. How did it ever get started? Who created and motivated the serpent in the Genesis story? The problem became even more acute with the triumph of the moral ideal. God, said the Jew, was not capricious, nor indifferent; He was just. He had made a good universe. He was all powerful as well as righteous, so nothing in this universe could happen without His willing it so. In presenting the Law to Israel He had promised that He would bless and reward all obedience; and that He would punish all disobedience. Hence the argument was conclusive; if there was pain and suffering it could only come as a punishment for sin, either the sufferer's own wrongdoing or somebody else's. This reasoning produced a fatalistic attitude towards affliction. The sufferer was being punished and should be left to bear his punishment. To mitigate it might be to interfere with the justice of God. No righteous person is punished, only the wicked. The theological system was neat and logical. But it was wrong, for God does not work that way.

12. Jesus dismissed both speculations. The disciples saw only a fascinating subject for discussion; Jesus saw the blind man in

his 'existential' situation. 'It was not that this man or his parents sinned; he was born blind that God's power might be displayed in curing him.' Jesus said God is really seen at work when this man's eyes are opened. The real question is, 'What were they going to do for the blind man?' Their answer was, 'nothing', except talk about him. It never occurred to them that he was listening to what they were saying about him, or to be concerned if he were. So Jesus talked about light, the light this man had never seen, and the more terrible moral darkness of his own disciples. As long as Jesus is in the world, He is the light of the world, and so 'while the daylight lasts, we must carry on the work of him that sent me.' That work is the opening of blind eyes. So He spat on the ground, kneading the dust into a paste and smoothed it over the man's red-rimmed eyes. The touch of those fingers, the cool protecting paste, soothing the inflammation and shielding the sightless eyes from the flies, this miracle of kindness and understanding was the beginning of the sign. In its sympathy and compassion God was speaking through the voice of the man who said, 'Go to Siloam and wash'.

13. Now, says the Evangelist, the word Siloam means *Sent*. This is mission. The healing Word of Power is spoken. In answering faith the blind man rose and tapped his way through the narrow streets to the Pool. He plunged his face into the waters and when he lifted his head he could see. He saw colour and light and the faces of men and women for the first time. The excited crowds who recognized him gathered round while he repeated his story, 'The man called Jesus did it.'

14. But this deed was done on the Sabbath. And God had said, 'Six days shall you labour and do all your work. The Sabbath is for rest and worship.' Current theology taught that Israel's hope lay in obeying God's will—the Law; only so would God redeem her from her bondage to Rome. How could this man who dared to infringe God's law possibly be a good man? There were six days when He could heal, why do it today? Another day of darkness would not matter all that much to the blind beggar. The Pharisees insisted that the healed man should agree with them that the one who had cured him must be a sinner. But the man refused to follow their

argument. He disputed their logic and dared to answer back when they tried to browbeat him. He returned to the charge, 'If that man had not come from God he could have done nothing.' Angrily they demanded, 'Who are you to give us lessons!' and they excommunicated him. It was a terrible punishment for he could never again enter a synagogue or the Temple: no orthodox Jew would receive him into his home. The man in a few short hours of sight had become an outcast, a fearful price to pay for seeing. His eyes were opened indeed. He had seen the faces of his mother and father, filled with fear and withdrawal; he had seen angry and bitter faces filled with hate. In a few short hours of sight he had escaped from one world of deprivation to another and more terrible one.

15. Then follows one of the most lovely verses of Scripture: 'Jesus heard that they had expelled him. When He had found him . . .' Jesus went looking for the man that nobody else wanted to see, the Good Shepherd searching for His lost and bewildered sheep. When He did find him, He asked, 'Have you faith in the Son of Man?' The title is important. In all its rich meaning it meant chiefly, the Proper Man, the Man of God, Man as he ought to be in full partnership with God. For Jesus is Himself the fulfilment of the new humanity it is the purpose of mission to create. He is the head of the new race—the Second Adam—in whose life of love and obedience, every talent is used, and whose whole integrated personality beats in constant communion with God. Jesus is the measure of the fulness that is to be enjoyed; He is the Firstborn of many brethren. For in Christ God identifies Himself with men, so that men can share the life of God.

16. 'Have you faith in him, the Son of Man?' The question seems strange until we remember what this man was thinking in his sighted loneliness. He had seen men—bigoted, angry men, who would not admit that their ideas of God might be wrong, fanatical men who were sure that Jesus was a sinner. But he had also met a Man, the man called Jesus, who could have done nothing unless God were with Him. So he replied, 'Tell me who he is, so that I can put my faith in him.' Jesus says, 'You have seen him!' This physically was not so, for the man was

blind when Jesus first spoke to him. But the blind man had seen more of Jesus than the Pharisees with their open eyes. Jesus gives sight to the sightless, but His act of mercy merely blinds those who will not see. This is mission: it is the opening of blind eyes and the condemnation of those who will not recognize the mercy of God when they see it. Mission is both mercy and judgement. The work of God is seen in meeting the human need, but the theologians and the disciples were trapped in their theological preconceptions and because they were blind they were inhuman.

17. Mission is seeing Jesus, and this is what the blind man succeeded in doing and what the Pharisees failed to do. When a man begins to see Jesus, he begins to see the Father (John 14:9). Already this man had discovered what a price has to be paid for seeing the truth. In a few hours he has been made a stranger where he looked for welcome. In the great Intercessory Prayer of John 17, Jesus prays earnestly that His disciples may be strengthened to stand the same test. 'I have delivered thy word to them, and the world hates them because they are strangers in the world.' That is the effect of mission. It begins in God's love of the world, but it encounters the hate and malice of the world. The Gospel makes us aliens in the world because we belong now to a new redeemed community. This is the paradox that some modern views of mission fail to appreciate. It is not only a matter of feeding the hungry, healing the sick. It is meeting the rancour and bitterness of religious people, the pride and selfishness of the world, the sea of evil that rages in every heart, the blindness that fails to see its own alienation from God.

18. Sin in Scripture is not merely some breach of the regulations, it is alienation from God, the refusal to admit God into one's inner life. God's desire to dwell in us is not an invasion of our privacy, rather it is the provision of the only atmosphere in which one can properly breathe. Without God we violate our own nature. We inflict injury on ourselves and others. The sinlessness of Jesus does not make Him inhuman or superhuman. Because He was the one Man who did not sin He was fully human with a humanity men had never seen before. His coming always presents the option—accept or reject. There

is no middle course and only one end to this way of mission—the Cross.

19. The Fourth Gospel brings this out with a simple intensity. When the Greeks said to Philip, 'Sir, we would like to see Jesus,' the Lord's immediate response is, 'The hour is come for the Son of Man to be glorified' (John 12:23). The supreme manifestation of the mission was to be revealed. The spirit of Jesus was plunged into turmoil for this was the signal that warned Him that the last act had begun. Jesus spelled it out, 'A grain of wheat remains a solitary grain unless it falls into the ground and dies; but if it dies it bears a rich harvest. The man who loves himself is lost.' No man has fully seen Jesus till he has seen the Cross. And no man can be His servant who will not take up the Cross and follow Him. Christ's own awful agony of soul concludes with his proclamation of final victory for the Message. 'And I shall draw all men to myself when I am lifted up from the earth'—the terrible euphemism for the raising of the Cross. The glorification of the Son of Man is the manifestation of the love of God that calls to man from Calvary.

20. The point is repeated again at another turn of the spiral of interpretation. John's account of the Last Supper gives the incident of the Washing of the Disciples' Feet. The chapter begins with sonorous phrases, recalling the Prelude, and taking us deeply into the Lord's own consciousness of mission. He was overwhelmingly aware that the Father had sent Him and that everything depended on Him. In this supreme moment He got up, stripped and tied a towel around Himself. He stood almost naked and performed a slave's task. He washed the feet of His men. Deliberately Jesus made a last effort to stamp the meaning of mission indelibly upon their hearts and minds. The stripping down to serve was a dramatic representation of His incarnation. He had stripped, laid aside His glory, and taken upon Himself the form and character of a servant, 'For the divine nature was his from the first, yet he did not think to snatch at equality with God, but made himself nothing, assuming the nature of a slave' (Philippians 2:6f).

21. Jesus is the Servant. The role depicted in the Servant Songs is accepted not as a limitation but as complete fulfilment and as such it is bequeathed to His disciples. It is the complete

inversion of the lust of domination that drives the world. Real authority, true mastery of life, is the prerogative of those who are ready to serve others. 'For even the Son of Man did not come to be served, but to serve' (Mark 10:42-45), and Jesus completes the thought by adding, 'and to surrender his life as a ransom for many,' for the Servant must become the Suffering Servant if mankind is to be rescued from slavery to sin. Luke places this or a similar discussion into his account of the Last Supper. Shortly after Jesus had broken the bread with the ominous words 'This is my body', the disciples began to quarrel about who was the greatest and most important among them. Jesus concluded His reprimand with the paradox that while he who sits at the table is the greater, He Himself was the servant waiting on them. 'Yet here I am among you like a servant' (Luke 22: 27). He is both Lord and Servant. He is Lord because He is Servant. The revolutionary ethics of the Kingdom with its new scale of values inverts the 'status' ethics of the kingdoms of this world.

22. Christ's stripping of Himself was not only a re-presentation of the Incarnation, it was a rehearsal for Calvary. Tomorrow He will be stripped once more; He will be flogged and crucified. This is the appalling but central mystery of the mission that a life of unbroken communion with God, a life which fully and completely expressed the will of God, should be allowed to die in shame and agony. The idea was completely incomprehensible to His disciples and to everyone else. How could God so desert one who so faithfully served and obeyed Him? Is not the Cross the final defeat of God, the last rejection of the great Invitation?

23. God did not take Him down from the Cross, nor deliver Him from the mockery of sadistic crowds. He died, for this is the Way of the Servant, despised and rejected of men. The defeat of God is the moment of God's victory, for the Cross in its stark horror reveals God, the love that is the mainspring of redemption. Those who see Jesus on the Cross see that mysterious figure of redemption and reconciliation which has haunted men from the beginning of religion, the sacrificial innocent, the Lamb of God, the victim slain from the foundation of the world. For as in the Upper Room Jesus took a basin of water

and washed the soiled feet of His disciples, including Judas, so on the Friday, as He died, men pierced His side and from the wound flowed a little gush of water and blood which to the eyes of faith was the long-promised fountain for sin and all uncleanness (Zechariah 13:1). Such at least was the later thought of the disciple who stood with the Blessed Mother at the foot of the Cross and watched Him die.

24. God did not take Him down from the Cross where men had nailed Him, but God did something infinitely greater—He raised Him from the dead. Had Christ been rescued from Calvary, the nails withdrawn and Jesus uplifted by angel hands, that would have been the end of mission. Magical triumph for Christ, but final defeat for man! Jesus would have lived on, while men died, the generations passing into the nothingness of Death while He remained ever glorious behind. That is not the Gospel. There is no message of reconciliation in such a victory. He died as men die. He was buried as we are buried. But He rose from the dead and we shall rise because of Him. For in His sufferings and death Jesus maintained His unity with humanity, but He also maintained His unbroken unity with God, refusing, despite the agony, to withdraw that love from those who crucified Him. So the Cross became not God's defeat but the triumph of Divine love over the sin of man.

25. Jesus is Life. To believe Him and to live in dependence on Him by faith is to share in His triumph over death. This awful conflict between the Life and the heartbreaking tragedy of death is presented in the incident of Lazarus: 'I am the resurrection and I am life' (John 11:25). The Message refuses to accept death as a cul-de-sac where life ends in tears and fading memories. That is how 'man-without-God' thinks of it. But death cannot destroy the new life that flows in the believer, and to the commanding Word even death must submit and give back its prey. So death becomes a gate, because the Messenger has opened it. Because he lives, we shall live also (John 14:19).

26. This is the glory, the end of the Way, the triumph of life over death, as over sin. The death of Jesus is the guarantee of His integrity and of His refusal to mute or minimize the

Message. God will not coerce men, nor compel them to accept the Invitation, but the Cross shows the Invitation can never be silenced. It speaks its eternal 'Come', for on the Cross God is in Christ reconciling and drawing all men to Himself. The Way of the Cross is the Way of Truth and Life and all the various theories of atonement are but attempts to understand more clearly what God has done.

27. If Christ be not risen from the dead, then let there be no doubt about it, the last word remains with the idiocy of evil and senseless brutality; the universe is indifferent and death buries all things. The Resurrection of Jesus is the cornerstone of Christianity. God vindicates the Life of Love. The Word still lives, free now to be present everywhere and at all times. It was this Living Word who appeared among His bewildered and frightened disciples on that first Easter Sunday evening, the doors being shut and barred. He showed them His hands and His feet. Twice He blessed them with His Peace, and then said, 'As the Father sent me, so I send you' (John 20:21).

CHAPTER FOUR

Mission in the Apostolic Church

ALL the four Gospels affirm that Jesus transmitted His mission to His disciples. They differ in their setting of the occasion and in the precise expression of it, but such blurring of detail and agreement in principle is telling evidence that in the memory of the Apostolic Church there was no doubt whatever that the Commission was indeed given by the risen Lord. According to the Appendix of Mark He appeared to the Eleven while they were at the table, apparently in Jerusalem, and commanded, 'Go forth to every part of the world, and proclaim the Good News to the whole Creation' (Mark 16:15). Matthew transfers the incident to a mountain top in Galilee (Matthew 28:16-20). Karl Barth suggested that the Eleven means the Twelve, for had Judas proved loyal he would have been there, and the Twelve symbolized Israel in all its tribes. The Commission, he argues, is therefore given to the New Israel, the Church, the People of God. Jesus proclaimed that all authority in heaven and on earth had been committed to Him and by virtue of this power and right He commanded the Eleven to 'Go forth, therefore, and make all nations my disciples.' They were to baptize men everywhere and to teach them all that Christ Himself had taught. He concluded with the assurance, 'I am with you all the days, right to the end of the age.' The Commission, therefore, is to occupy His disciples all through the period from the Resurrection to the Day of the Lord.

2. Luke also affirms that the Commission was given to the Eleven and says it took place in Jerusalem at the end of the first Easter Day. Jesus first reproached the disciples for their doubt, then expounded the Scriptures to them showing how His death and resurrection had been foretold, and how the Scrip-

tures also required 'that in his name repentance bringing the forgiveness of sins is to be proclaimed to all nations. Begin from Jerusalem: it is you who are the witnesses to all this. And mark this, I am sending upon you my Father's promised gift; so stay here in this city until you are armed with the power from above' (Luke 24:47-49). In Luke's presentation Jesus emphasizes the universal mission of the Old Covenant which He now transferred to them. The Gospel is a message of reconciliation, for it is by repentance and forgiveness that the new relationship with God is established. But the disciples were not yet ready to go forth; they needed a new dynamic, the gift God had promised by which the New Age would be inaugurated.

3. The Lucan account is completed in the Acts of the Apostles. On one of the Forty Days, the disciples, still dazed by the joy of talking to Him again and dazzled by the power that had conquered death, asked Jesus if He was about to establish the Messianic Kingdom. He replied, repeating what He had said in earlier talks about the End, 'It is not for you to know about dates or times, which the Father has set within his own control' (cf Matthew 24:36). During His earthly life Jesus Himself had not known nor were the disciples to know now, for the results of such information would be most harmful. The disciples must learn the discipline of watching and waiting assured that the End will come at the right time in God's wisdom and love. What they needed was not the knowledge of the date of the End, which could paralyse effort, but the power to fulfil the mission. And so Jesus continued, 'but you will receive power when the Holy Spirit comes upon you; and you will bear witness for me in Jerusalem, and all over Judea and Samaria, and away to the ends of the earth' (Acts 1:7f).

4. Thus there are three elements in the Dominical Commission. First, it is universal—the disciples are to carry the Gospel to the ends of the earth and make disciples of all nations, so completing the arrested mission of the Old Israel. Secondly mission will occupy them to the End of the Age. 'This Gospel of the Kingdom will be proclaimed throughout the earth as a testimony to all nations, and then the end will come' (Matthew 24:14). The preaching of the Gospel is one of the 'signs', a guarantee that the Word will accomplish all that God has

spoken and that the disruptive energies of the Gospel will continue to act till in God's own time He speaks the Word that creates the new heaven and earth, as He spoke on the First Day of Creation. And, thirdly, the mission begins to move with the outpouring of the Holy Spirit, for until He comes the disciples remain weak and ineffective, their understanding of the Gospel too tentative to be forceful and arresting. With the Pentecostal experience they become 'powered' men capable and concise, able to articulate their faith and to impart it with compelling conviction. The gift of the Spirit is another sign of the certain coming of the End, which is the New Beginning, for He fills men with the creative and liberating energy which is the indubitable sign of the Day of the Lord, when all people will be 'Spirit filled' (Acts 2:17). The Pentecostal outpouring was an 'earnest' of the Day, a guarantee that the Spirit was already at work in the redeemed community.

5. The Fourth Gospel also connects the Commission with the Gift of the Spirit combining the Commissioning and Pentecostal experience into two consecutive acts of the Lord in Jerusalem late on the first Easter Day. Jesus first said, 'As the Father sent me, so send I you.' He then breathed on them, saying 'Receive the Holy Spirit!' (John 20:21f.) In this presentation the disciples were placed into direct relationship with the sending Father. But they were not to go in their own strength or in their own spirit. Jesus exhaled; and the act gave visual expression to the bestowal of the Spirit, which is both the Breath of God and the Spirit of Jesus. In this Spirit they would be able to pronounce forgiveness and reconciliation with God. Thomas was not present on this occasion and demanded tactile evidence of the resurrection before he would believe. A week later Jesus granted his request whereupon Thomas made the ultimate declaration, calling Jesus 'My Lord and my God!' (John 20:28). Jesus replies that physical touching was not necessary for effective faith. Those who can recognize Him for what He is are truly blessed. The fact that Thomas was absent at the Commission did not exclude him but means that all who can believe in Jesus are included in the apostolate. The gift of the Spirit is for all.

6. The apostolic Church testifies abundantly that the work

of the Holy Spirit is essential to the operation of effective mission. The language of the New Testament about the Spirit is pragmatic rather than theological. No attempt is made to systematize the experience or to theorize about the nature of the Third Person, rather it is the unity of God that is expressed. By looking into One the other Two are to be discerned. Each includes the Others in a mystery for which there are no words, but to which the Christian experience must bear witness. The heightened creativity, the new dynamism, the gracious sweetness, simplicity, and courage of the believer are unmistakable evidence of the indwelling Spirit received in faith. When Paul lay blinded by his traumatic conversion-experience the humble disciple Ananias came saying he was 'sent' by Jesus so that he might recover his sight 'and be filled with the Holy Spirit' (Acts 9:17). To Paul it was the guarantee that the New Age had begun to dawn. The struggle with the kingdom of darkness would rage with increasing intensity as the Gospel was proclaimed, but the gift of the Spirit was now an 'earnest' of the triumph to come. 'It is God also who has set his seal upon us, and as a pledge of what is to come has given us the Spirit to dwell in our hearts' (2 Corinthians 1:22). Indeed if a man does not possess the Spirit of Christ, he is no Christian (Romans 8:9,11). Since it was the Spirit that raised Jesus, the indwelling Spirit is the guarantee that He will also raise us from the dead. Mission is not complete until the Spirit is given (Acts 19:2).

7. The full range and nature of mission was not immediately apparent even to the Apostles. Just as they had struggled to understand the teaching of Jesus, so they had to learn by painful controversy what mission really meant. Twenty years after Pentecost they were passionately divided over the question raised by Paul's successful 'mission' to the Gentiles. The controversy made them examine several hitherto uncriticized assumptions, and to reject some preconceptions. The climax was reached at what has been called the First Council of Jerusalem (*c*.50) recorded in Acts 15 and Galations 2. Whatever the discrepancies between the two accounts, the main issue was plain: Was mission to be confined to the Palestinian model in which the first disciples had been reared or were the

innovations of Paul to be authorized? The Palestinian Church, cradled in Judaism, expected Gentile believers to behave like converts to Judaism, and in particular to adopt the national marks of Israel—circumcision and the food taboos. But Paul, once as ardent a Jew as any of them, had seen to his amazement the Spirit bestowed on uncircumcised Gentiles, the sure seal of God's acceptance. Faith in Christ was enough.

8. The Judaizers could not imagine that God, who, so they believed, had Himself prescribed the marks of His chosen people, could ever discard them as unnecessary. Moreover, if the Gentile convert really wanted to be like Jesus, he would willingly and proudly accept them, since Jesus was Himself a circumcised Jew. They saw that Paul's proposals would lead to a head-on collision with the Jewish people and to the rejection of the Christian community by the household of Israel. It is to the glory of the primitive Church that Paul's arguments prevailed, the decision could so easily have gone the other way. Yet the future did not lie with the Judaizers but with the alien masses Paul was bringing into membership. Had the traditionalists won the Church would have remained a small Jewish sect, like the Essenes or the Dead Sea Community. The Council established the principle that the Gospel could be preached to the Gentiles free from the heavy load of Jewish ritual observances, and that all who believed and were baptized were thereby members of the New Israel and were equally the People of God with those of Jewish descent.

9. Thus out of the controversy came a new understanding of mission. The Gospel could now be proclaimed to all, free from the cultural and national overtones of the Palestinian Church. These were seen to be secondary, non-essential elements, tolerable enough for Jewish Christians in the homeland, but to the Gentiles a stumbling block that the Holy Spirit had removed. Liberated from these restrictions the new Church was free to become a multi-racial, supra-national fellowship. If this barrier between Jew and Gentile could go down in Christ, then every other wall of partition could also be overthrown. 'Gentiles and Jews, he has made the two one, and in his own body of flesh and blood has broken down the enmity which stood like a dividing wall between them, for he cancelled the

law with its rules and regulations, so as to create out of the two a single new humanity in himself' (Ephesians 2:14f). This vision of a new humanity in which all the old differences were reconciled captivated Paul. 'Baptized into union with him you have all put on Christ as a garment. There is no such thing as Jew and Greek, slave and freeman, male and female, for you are all one person in Christ. But if you then belong to Christ you are the issue of Abraham and so heirs by promise' (Galatians 3:27-29)—heirs of the mission and of all the blessings of the restored humanity. Paul's new teaching did not distort the Galilean Gospel, as some have suggested. The discovery that Christ breaks down barriers and gathers in the Gentiles set the Church free to be itself. It was to satisfy the needs of this New Community that the four Gospels were compiled. Paul continued to write and think from the rich background of his rabbinic training, but at every point he felt the pressure of Christ, enlarging, redirecting, and correcting his ideas.

10. A corollary to the principle of de-culturalization was the affirmation that mission requires for its full impact one Church with a universally recognized membership into which all believers regardless of race, rank or sex are admitted by baptism. Without such universality mission must always fall far short of its promise and belie its own proclamation of full reconciliation between man and God, and man and man. The Council of Jerusalem kept the infant Church together when it could have split into separated fragments each bitterly critical of the other. Churches in Europe and Palestine cared for each other and sent gifts to each other in times of stress. The Christian was welcome in any Church without bar or limitation. A universal Church required a universally recognized ministry and this too began to emerge. The tragedy of Christendom today is that the original unity has been lost; a Christian travelling abroad will not necessarily be welcomed everywhere; he may be excluded or only partially accepted by other Christian communions. We are so accustomed to the present fragmentation of the Church that we regard this scandalous contradiction as the norm and we are blind to its gross falsification of the Gospel. But we have much to learn from the spirit of the debate and the solutions found at Jerusalem by

which they kept circumcised and uncircumcised together in the One Church.

11. Though Paul considered the Gentiles to be his particular concern, he could not forget his own people. His heart ached for them. But he saw even in their rejection of Christ the wonderful way in which God uses the tragedies and disappointments of history. Their refusal to listen had sent him to the Gentiles; their loss was the gain of the nations. By the same principle the evangelization of the Gentiles would lead eventually to Israel's acceptance of Jesus Christ, for God could not forget His ancient people. His purpose of blessing the entire human race would then be achieved (Romans 11:25-36). Moreover, just as the Jewish rejection of Jesus had brought the Gospel of Reconciliation to the Gentile world, so Jewish acceptance would bring an even greater blessing to the new humanity, 'nothing less than life from the dead' (Romans 11:15). In the divine strategy of mission every apparent set-back leads to some new development and enriches the whole, for God is not defeated by man's blindness and ill-will. The persecution of the Church at Jerusalem scattered its members through Judea and Samaria, but did not silence them; on the contrary they preached wherever they went. Persecution, instead of crushing them, drove them to fulfil the Lord's programme—to take the Gospel from Jerusalem to Judea and Samaria (Acts 8:1,4). The planning of mission is more than efficient committee work; it is also waiting on God and being sensitive and obedient to the promptings of the Holy Spirit (Acts 16:6f). The Way of mission, as always, leads to the Cross, and on through death to resurrection.

CHAPTER FIVE

Early Lessons in Mission

IN the first century the Gospel was carried far and wide with amazing energy and speed. The spectacular success has been attributed to many causes—the ease of travel on the Roman roads, the almost universal use of Greek, and the spiritual hunger of the age. But, in fact, very little is known of the persons who were responsible for this advance, the methods they used or the precise contents of the Gospel they preached. We know of Paul's work both from his own letters and from Acts, but we have scarcely any information about the activities of the other Apostles. We have the names of a few outstanding bishops like Ignatius, Bishop of Antioch, who was martyred in 110 and of Polycarp (69-155), Bishop of Smyrna. But we do not know how the Gospel first came to Rome. Paul found believers there. The missionary movement is deeply hidden in the obscurities of history with only little light from contemporary documents.

2. But what does emerge, often from hostile sources, is the picture of an active, caring Church in nearly every great city. The establishment of such urban churches had been Paul's deliberate policy and it was abundantly justified for at that time the Empire was organized into urban units, each town controlling the life of the surrounding countryside. Each church, presided over by its bishop, vigorously preached Christ, maintained worship, trained its young people and new converts in the faith and organized its very considerable relief work. Harnack listed at least ten forms of such social service, from the burial of the dead (and not only Christian dead) to the maintenance of widows and orphans. The Emperor Julian remarked that it was scandalous that the Galileans cared not only for their own poor, but for the pagan poor as well, while the pagan

world did nothing for its own.[1] Such intensive social caring was an essential part of the Gospel. It was good news for the poor; it promised help not only in a future life but now in the miseries of this world. Luke's practical, economic version of the Beatitudes struck a chord of need. 'How blest are you who are poor; the kingdom of God is yours. How blest are you who now go hungry; your hunger shall be satisfied' (Luke 6:20f). This is what happened in the 'ecclesia'. They pooled their resources, they fed the hungry, clothed the naked. They cared and there were plenty to care for.

3. Our modern appreciation of history as the record of the whole human family through its many phases of social and cultural changes, directs attention to the life of the common people, as well as to the doings of outstanding leaders. But information about the social background of the working classes has been until quite recent times very scanty and nearly always incidental, for it did not occur to ancient historians that anyone could possibly be interested in such matters. Much research is waiting to be done on this subject, but what evidence we have suggests that Christianity spoke to deeply felt needs, especially among the depressed masses—slaves and the lower working classes of freed and free men. It told the slave that in Christ he was as good as his master, or as bad, since both were sinners, who by faith could become sons of God and therefore brothers to one another. Though the Church did not challenge the institution of slavery—how could it when most people thought it was the only, and therefore divinely authorized, form of civilization?—it began to eat at the roots of the system by giving to the slave an inner dignity, a sense of being someone who mattered to God. The Church's concern for the widow, the orphan, the sick and incurable, the prisoner, the traveller, the exile, brought a compassion into the callous harshness of everyday life. Its new morality was the ethic of the Family of God. Men belong to each other; they must carry each other's burdens; a man must love his neighbour as himself; there is hope now and heaven hereafter; all things are ours in Christ—this was indeed Good News to those who sat in darkness and in the shadow of death.

[1]See Stephen Neill, *A History of Christian Missions* (Pelican, 1964), p. 42.

4. A study of the history of religions suggests that no new religion captures the masses unless it fills some vacuum of unsatisfied longing and provides outlets for pent-up feelings of denial and frustration. The Early Church through its doctrine of the Holy Spirit assured every believer that he had a gift which it was his duty and privilege to use for the building up of the Church (1 Corinthians 12). The repressed and silent masses learned to speak in the Church and their joy in their discovery of their talents impelled them to tell their friends and neighbours of the relief they had found. The Gospel brought relief, comfort, hope and purpose to the neglected, the underprivileged and despised, many of whom had never previously had any opportunity to exercise their latent gifts of leadership and persuasion. The profession of faith was a symbolic assertion of the value of the common man. By proclaiming himself a Christian he claimed his princely place as a son of God in a world that treated him as a chattel of slight account. Enormous reservoirs of human energy were thus released into missionary channels. Even Celsus (*c.*178) in his attack on the Faith bears unwitting testimony to the fact that the poor spoke to the poor and the faith was spread by contemptible men among the worthless and ignorant, among idiots, slaves, rough characters, poor women, youths and children. Thousands of humble men and women gossipped their new-found faith at work and at leisure, in the market or on the road. Mission was very much a lay movement, the activity of the People of God, and this is another principle we are painfully relearning today.

5. Though the vast majority of the members of the Early Church were poor and uneducated, its leadership was literate and included a small but growing number of outstanding thinkers and writers who were in no way inferior, either in number or quality, to the best that the pagan Empire could produce. But to the pagan world the most obvious feature of the new religion was its welcome for and appeal to the poor and ignorant. This had been the main characteristic of the mission to the Gentiles from Paul onwards (1 Corinthians 1:26-28). When the authorities linked this interest with the notorious refusal of the Christians to share in the ceremonies of the State religion and with their open avowal that they looked for the

coming of a King who would supersede Caesar, it is not surprising that they suspected their loyalty. Just because they were drawn from every race the Christians could not claim that their faith was a national religion. The authorities refused recognition on the grounds that they were not a nation like the Jews practising the faith of their fathers, but had shamelessly forsaken their own ancestral cults for this new multi-racial religion. Yet, in spite of official hostility, the occasional local persecutions, though often severe, entirely failed to halt the Christian advance. They served only to bring the new faith into public notice and to arouse interest in its message.

6. Between 250 and 300 as Hugh Trevor-Roper has shown[1] the Empire in the West was torn by political anarchy while the economic system was collapsing. Shortage of gold, the depopulation caused by the ravages of plague and the breakdown of local government in the towns under crippling taxation combined to shift the balance of power from the decaying cities to the countryside. Alone of all the contending faiths Christianity appealed to the peasant. Because of its evangelistic energy and its highly organized charitable relief it found ready acceptance especially among those agricultural workers who resented the arrogance of the old pagan aristocracy of the towns. Christianity became a rural as well as a town religion and this gave it an impregnable base during the persecution and the upheavals of the time. It was on this base of rural self-sufficiency that the new form of European society—feudalism—was built and it was because Western monasticism adopted as its model the agricultural cell that the monks were so successful in converting and civilizing the barbarian tribes both inside and beyond the frontiers of the Empire.

7. No statistics are available by which the expansion of the Faith can be measured, but Bishop Neill[2] hazards the guess that by the end of the third century there may have been some five million Christians out of a total Empire population of fifty millions and this figure does not include the large Christian communities beyond the frontiers. Osrhoene and Armenia

[1]Hugh Trevor-Roper, *The Rise of Christian Europe* (Thames and Hudson, 1965) p. 66.

[2]*Op. cit.*, p. 44.

were Christian kingdoms. Christianity was still an explosive power busily engaged in its world mission, showing a cohesion and purposefulness which bound its members together into a super-community. Nothing else in the Empire had such power. Indeed as the pressure of the barbarian tribes built up against the European frontiers and the effort to contain them drained away the strength of the Empire, as the office of Emperor became the prize of rival generals or of the highest bidder, the Church began to emerge as the one stable element in a disintegrating society. It needed only a brilliant general to realize that he had more to gain by recognizing the Church than by trying to destroy it. We have insufficient evidence to impugn the sincerity or the motives of Constantine. What concerns us is that by the Edict of Milan in 313 Christianity ceased to be an illicit faith. Within a few years it was evident that Constantine intended to transfer to the Church the support and position previously enjoyed by the State religion. In effect Christianity soon became the official religion of the Empire.

8. During the first three centuries of persecution the Church had worked out its theology of Church-State relations. Following the principles laid down by Paul (Romans 13:1-7), the Christians recognized the State as a necessary organ essential for the welfare and protection of the community, and as such of divine appointment. The Christian therefore paid his taxes, supported law and order, served the State in all offices open to him and prayed for the Emperor and his representatives. But he refused to worship the State gods or the person of the Emperor and he abstained from such sports and customs as offended his conscience. Because soldiers were required to participate in certain pagan ceremonials, few Christians entered the legions until such requirements were relaxed. The Christian, knowing himself to belong to a suspect minority, walked circumspectly and, as far as he could, avoided giving offence which could precipitate persecution and cost the lives of his friends.

9. With the Edict of Milan the situation changed completely. Overnight the Church secured enormous prestige and influence. The middle and upper classes found it no longer a disability, but politic to join and, because of their superior education and

training, quickly began to occupy important positions in the new and rapidly expanding organization. Crowds swarmed into the Church and Neill thinks that by the end of the fourth century the number of Christians had quadrupled, constituting some forty per cent of the population of the Empire. State resources that had previously supported the pagan temples and priesthoods now began to flow into the Church. It was made a corporation entitled to receive legacies. The clergy were also exempted from the office of decurion which carried heavy liabilities for the taxes of the district. To escape the burdensome role many men of curial rank took holy orders, causing Constantine to forbid any man of this station from joining the clergy. The number of priests was limited by law and it was specifically directed that they should be drawn from the poor. This drastic measure stopped the abuse, but it also prevented men of wealth and good education from bringing their experience and gifts into the priesthood of the Church. The result of this legislation was to produce an undistinguished leadership which, with a few exceptions, followed the imperial policy. Though the Church grew rapidly in numbers and wealth, success brought in wordly values and methods. The Church knew how to cope with the State in times of persecution; it had little understanding of how to cope with it in times of recognition, nor has it yet solved this problem which remains one of the most complex and intractable questions of Christian mission today.

10. The political division of the Empire during the fourth century profoundly influenced the shape and content of the Christian Mission. In the East, Constantinople which had been deliberately built to be the imperial and Christian capital of the world, became the magnificent centre of a huge theocratic state in which the Church was almost entirely subordinate to the Emperor, the Christian Prince who ruled the Church as he ruled the State. It was a despotism of the old oriental type. Under its patronage the Church grew wealthy and quietly absorbed and preserved the rich heritage of Greek culture. But the rigidity of the system stifled political and intellectual freedom. It endured for a thousand years, maintaining learning and civilization when the West had sunk into an impoverished

and backward semi-barbarianism. Under such conditions religion, especially in the monasteries, tended to flow into the channels of an other-wordly mysticism with little interest in mission.

11. The non-Greek speaking people of the remoter provinces felt little kinship with the imperial government, to them a foreign and oppressive yoke. Their suppressed aspirations found expression in their adoption of heretical forms of Christianity in opposition to the orthodoxy of Constantinople. The great controversies about the Person of Christ that racked the Church during the fourth and fifth centuries were not resolved and large numbers of Christians broke away or were expelled from the Catholic Church. Apart altogether from the theological issues involved, the fact that these forms of Christianity were different from the official faith seems to have commended them to subject or alien peoples, enabling them to express national distinctions which they wished to emphasize. Monophysites in Syria, Armenia, and Egypt called the Orthodox 'Melchites', that is 'Royalists', and showed thereby that part of their hostility was due to a resentment of Caesaropapism. Similarly the Goths when they became Christian chose Arianism as did other barbarian tribes in eastern Europe. Precisely the same phenomenon is to be observed in Islam where sectarian forms were later preferred by such people as the Persians and the Ottoman Turks to mark their difference from their subject peoples. The same social factor still operates today. In part it may account for the strength of Presbyterianism in Scotland. Successful mass mission appeals to deep needs, and offers avenues of self-expression and identity denied or hindered hitherto, and among such longings social or national aspiration are often determinative. Mission addresses itself to the whole range of human need and the spectrum is much wider than the specifically 'spiritual' feelings to which evangelists usually speak. But such response also carries the peril that only part of the Faith is accepted, that part which meets those needs. There is also the real risk that the Church may be used to further dubious social and political ends and its message may become distorted in the process.

12. Beyond the frontiers the imperial recognition of Christ-

ianity had disastrous effects. Persia, that ancient enemy of the Greeks, had for centuries fought off the aggression of Rome. In the eyes of the Persian ruling class, who were Zoroastrians, Christianity was now seen as the domestic religion of the detested Roman and they came to regard their own considerable Christian minorities as a possible fifth column of doubtful loyalty and subjected them to a prolonged and relentless persecution as severe as anything experienced by the Church in the West. The Western Church survived its ordeals because it was able eventually to penetrate into the centres of power and of policy-making; in the East the Church was crushed because it failed to influence government. The long history of the Church teaches us that a Christian community can survive persecutions if its roots are deep enough in the life of the people and if it can recover fast enough to seize the initiative of advance, and if it is wise enough to establish a political order which protects it from violence. But history also shows that Christian communities can be practically exterminated if the persecution goes on long enough and if the roots have not penetrated deeply into the psyche of the community. Unless Christianity satisfies the deep hungers of a people they can swiftly change their faith, as the rise of Islam illustrates. The whole of North Africa, once a chain of thriving Christian provinces, became almost completely Muslim within a century. Effective mission must penetrate deeply into society, it must not only exert a powerful influence on government, it must hold the common people, and these too are lessons of mission that the twentieth century Western Church is painfully relearning.

13. Osrhoene, in northern Mesopotamia, claimed to be the first kingdom to become Christian. Tradition says its king Abgar wrote to Jesus inviting Him to Edessa, the capital. Certainly Armenia became Christian on the conversion of its king Tiridates by Gregory the Illuminator (240-332). The governing class were compelled to follow his example, the old religion was suppressed and the people pressurized into accepting the new faith, the first known case of the conversion of a nation at the direction of the monarch. The New Testament was quickly translated into the language of the people, an alphabet being invented for the purpose. This established an

identity of religion, language, and race which enabled the faith to take such deep root in the culture of the people that it endured through hundreds of years of conquest, persecution and repression. The faith became almost the only expression of national identity left to the people. The same process of racial identification took place in Ethiopia. In the West the first of the barbarian kingdoms to become Christian was France. Clovis, king of the Franks, was baptized in 496 with his army. Legend says his soldiers held their sword arms out of the water so as to preserve their warrior ethic. Thus the precedents were set for what later became a major principle of mission *Cuius regio, eius religio*—the religion of the king is the religion of the kingdom—which operated so dramatically at the Reformation. It was but a short step from this dangerous doctrine to the disastrous conclusion of mission by conquest. The Church thought it had christianized the barbarians, but the inflow of masses of illiterate warriors, with little understanding of the faith, meant all too often the de-christianization of mission. The military orders that converted north-eastern Europe were land-hungry warriors who justified their drive to the East as a holy war in much the same way as the armies of Islam had surged into the provinces of the Eastern Empire.

14. As the Western Empire disintegrated and new warlike barbarian kingdoms were established amid the ransacked provinces, the Church alone survived as the one truly European institution. It is an over-simplification of a complex and lengthy process to ascribe the collapse of the Empire to barbarian invasion. For centuries the weakening Empire had filled the shrinking legions with barbarian recruits, and allowed barbarian tribes to settle in depopulated regions. The Empire fell apart because of its own inherent contradictions and social imbalance. St Augustine (354-430) in his *City of God* stoutly maintained that the Church alone represented all that was best and worth preserving of the ancient glories of Rome and that the evils of the day were directly attributable not to the new faith but to the sinful pride, selfishness and cruelty of old Rome, the City of Man. The barbarians realized that they lived amid the ruins of a mighty past, rich and skilled beyond their understanding, and they saw in the Church with its clergy

and the devoted men and women in its religious orders the sole heir and custodian of the greatness that was Rome.

15. The christianization of the tribes is a marvellous story of missionary courage and compassion and could never have been undertaken except by the disciplined men and women of the monastic orders—full-time religious professionals impelled by great love to bring the new and vigorous peoples of the northern forests and plains into the fold of Christ. Western monasticism, as it was forged by St Benedict (*c*.480-550), developed the technique of the Christian cell, the small community that fused the life of work and prayer into a new unity. The cells were deliberately planted in strategic positions, generally in some wild country which the monks proceeded to tame. The monasteries were centres of instruction, not only in the faith, but in all the arts, and especially in agricultural skills. The Church thus became the teacher of the new Europe, and the only teacher. In a few generations the Church civilized the pagan tribes and helped to transform the warrior hordes under their war-chiefs into the feudal states of the Middle Ages. It emerged rich and powerful. Education became a clerical monopoly and it is not surprising that in such a society the Church assumed that this status of the world's instructor belonged to it by divine right, and that it alone could pronounce on the truth of any statement or argument. The role of the teacher is a perilous one, especially in adult education, for the teacher is tempted to regard his scholars as overgrown children, and himself as the final unquestioned authority on everything.

16. Because the conversion of the newcomers was the work of clergy and monks it came to be taken for granted that mission work was the responsibility of full-time professionals and no longer the concern of the ordinary Christian layman. Gradually there arose a widening gulf between those in holy orders and the common man. It was the duty of the clergy to teach, and of the layman to listen. The Church through its hierarchy issued instruction, the layman obeyed. The liturgy of the Church constantly harped on this theme and the architecture of the Church emphasized the distinction between clergy and people, separating the sanctuary from the nave by a great screen. As this tendency developed the Church came to

think of itself primarily as a hierarchy and priesthood, the shepherds who looked after the flock, the sheep of Christ. Arrogant and false ideas of superiority inverted the Servant role into one of mastery and lordship. But the greatest loss was the devaluation and muzzling of the laity. Mission ceased to be the responsibility of every Christian and the missionary activity of the Church was catastrophically curtailed.

17. The appearance and rapid spread of Islam was due to many causes, but not least to the failure of the Church to understand and prosecute its mission. The Egyptian Church, though it identified itself with the common people of the land and in its Coptic and Monophysite form represented Egyptian nationalism, failed to interest itself in the Arabian tribes beyond the Red Sea. No sustained effort was made to reach them. The Egyptian Church itself was torn by factions while the violent anti-intellectualism and fierce intolerance of the hordes of ignorant monks presented a sorry and repellent picture of the faith. Though at first attracted by some forms of Christianity, Mohammed (*c*.570-629) finally rejected the divinity of Christ and adopted a rigorous monotheism. He became the fiery leader of a great explosive movement which altered the map and culture of half the world. He spoke to the suppressed longings of the Arab peoples, giving them for the first time a sense of brotherhood, unity, and sublime destiny. He gave them a simple, severely practical religion, restoring the immediacy of the relationship between a man and his God. In the Koran he gave them a Book that moulded their thought and elevated their language into a sacred tongue. He harnessed their warlike energies into the service of the 'holy war' by which the world was to be won for the new faith. Both the Persian Empire and the eastern provinces of the Roman Empire soon fell to the Muslim conquerors. Jerusalem was captured in 638, Syria in 640, then Egypt; Persia fell in 650. One after another the great Christian provinces of North Africa succumbed to Muslim armies which then crossed into Europe and captured most of Spain by 715.

18. Because of their tolerance the new Muslim countries quickly absorbed the culture of the old Byzantine world and gave it a new vigour. Greek scientific works were translated

into Arabic; philosophy, long scorned in the West, was avidly studied. Adventurous Muslim sailors explored the sea routes to India and the East. Wherever they went they took their faith with them, for Islam, like the Early Church, was essentially a lay movement. Wherever they settled they married freely into the local population, eating local foods and adopting local customs, as long as these fitted into the few simple requirements of Muslim observance. They practised the brotherhood they preached and by this means, as well as by military conquest, they carried the Crescent to the Far East. This career of conquest inflicted terrible loss of life, and there was much barbarity, but no more than that inflicted by the warring tribes of northern Europe on each other. Within a few generations the masses turned from Christianity and adopted the new faith; a new rich civilization began to flourish in centres like Baghdad and Egypt, far more sophisticated and intellectually alive than anything to be found in the backward West.

19. Many reasons have been put forward to account for this collapse of the rich Christian provinces before the Muslim invader, but two must be noted. First the political system of the Empire—the remote control of the government in Constantinople, the powerful self-continuing bureaucracy which ran the State, did little to commend it to the common people who groaned under crushing taxation. The Muslim victory merely substituted a new overlord for the old, and one who on the whole was less class-conscious and more tolerant towards the poor. Secondly Muslim preachers presented their faith as a fulfilment and completion of Christianity. Through Mohammed God was correcting abuses and misunderstandings by a new and more recent revelation. To peoples bewildered by the interminable arguments about the divine and human nature of Christ the new faith held the attraction of utter simplicity. Islam in its primitive form was indeed a tolerant fath and Christian Churches continued in the captured eastern provinces for a long time. But they had lost their control of the government and of the new aristocracy of landowners. Though the Arabs used Christian doctors and clerks in their own bureaucracy, conversion was all one way; the old Christian Churches gave up the attempt to win their overlords, while their own

young people, seeking social acceptance and advance, adopted the new faith. Nevertheless Christian communities lasted on in Mesopotamia, Persia, and Central Asia. Marco Polo found Christian Churches in the main cities all the way along the land route to China in the late thirteenth century. The Christians nearly succeeded in converting the Mongols. But this fierce people eventually decided to become Muslim, as were most of their subject peoples, and it was the Mongols who under Tamberlaine practically exterminated their Christian communities in A.D. 1395.

20. The unbroken succession of Muslim victories filled the West with dread of this apparently irresistible opponent, so obviously their superior in culture and skill. The encroaching tide of Islam cut the West off from the old trade routes to the East and seemed about to overwhelm the whole of Europe. The semi-christianized barbarians reacted as could be expected —they fought force with force as they defended their homelands. The Arab conquest of Jerusalem had sent a shudder through Europe and constituted a constant reminder that unbelievers held the holy places. But when the Church itself proclaimed a Holy War and called on the chivalry of Christian Europe to liberate the Holy Land from the infidel the basic idea of mission was twisted and perverted. The response was immediate, not only because of religious zeal, but because of the rich rewards of domains and serfs promised to thousands of impoverished knights. In religious fervour and strong self-interest the flower of European knighthood flung itself against Islam in wave after wave from 1099 to 1291 when the Crusaders were driven from Acre. An exception to this general belief in mission by the sword was the attempt by Francis of Assisi to preach Christ persuasively to the unbeliever. In 1219 he was received by the Sultan of Egypt who heard him with respect. Later, Raymond Lull, 'the Enlightened Doctor' (1235-1315) spent himself in ceaseless efforts to win the Muslim by his preaching.

21. Relations between Muslim and Christian have never recovered from the shock of the Crusades and colour even today the reaction of the Muslim to Christian Mission. In the eyes of Islam Christianity is the domestic religion of an aggressive, un-

scrupulous Europe, bent solely on world domination. To become a Christian is to desert to the enemy and to betray one's own people. Under the blows of the Crusades Islam itself became intolerant and bigoted; a rigid and fanatical fundamentalism replaced the old Islamic tolerance. It gripped the Muslim world and petrified its development for centuries. The memory of the Crusades still lives in the Muslim mind and constitutes an almost impenetrable wall to Christian mission.

22. Perhaps no less disastrous was the breach with the Orthodox Church. The treacherous and utterly unjustified sack of Constantinople by the Fourth Crusade in 1204 left the Eastern Empire so weak that it could no longer hope to drive back the Muslim armies. It managed to stave off defeat until 1453 when it fell to the Ottoman Turks, but considerable responsibility for its collapse rests on the Western Church which organized the Crusades. As the Turkish forces pressed on into the Balkans and up the Danube the Western Church lost touch with the Eastern branch of Christendom. Both Churches became isolated and the very idea of mission to the world was abandoned.

23. One other great failure of the Christian mission must be mentioned, the failure to win the Jews. In the first two centuries Jews had at times instigated Roman persecution of the Christians and after the recognition of Christianity by Constantine the temptation to settle old scores was not always resisted. In the Christians' eyes the Jews collectively and for all time were deemed responsible for the crucifixion of Jesus and so they became the objects of popular hatred and abuse. Legal disabilities were imposed on them, and even such great Christians as Chrystostom, Ambrose, and Cyril of Alexandria persecuted them. Popes like the great Gregory tried to protect them but such dreadful outbursts as the general massacre of the Jews in Spain in 1391 have left indelible scars. Intermittent persecution, pogrom and social ostracism have created an almost insuperable barrier between Jew and Christian. Anti-Semitism still lives on in some European communities. The Nazi attempt to exterminate the Jews is only the latest and most terrible exhibition of this ancient evil. Paul's dream of the conversion of Israel will remain unfulfilled until the Church dissipates the

legacy of hatred she has herself created by her sad mistreatment of her Lord's own people. The Christian mission today is confronted with the calamitous results of these two historic failures —failure to present Christ in the Spirit of Christ to the Jew and the Arab.

24. Yet, with all its grievous faults, inherent contradictions and gross misunderstandings, the Western Church on the eve of the Reformation had begun to recover its sense of missionary obligation. It drew this from three sources. First, the ideal of a unified multi-racial and supernational body—the *corpus Christianum* so vigorously expounded by Innocent III (1160-1216), though challenged by many, remained deeply embedded in Catholic thought. The Pope, claiming to be Peter's successor, claimed also to have inherited the Empire from Constantine. Though the alleged Donation was subsequently proved to be a forgery, the idea behind it rested on the solid evidence that when the Empire collapsed the Church alone was able to carry the load of civilization. The new European peoples frankly and freely acknowledged their debt to the Church. They knew no real rival to the Pope whose claim to universal authority seemed to embody the Christian hope that in time the whole world would become the Kingdom of God and of his Christ; so who more fitting than the Vicar of Christ to exercise that growing lordship? Secondly, the Catholic kings regarded themselves as the Pope's agents in this respect; it was their duty to support the Christian claim to world dominion by ensuring that all their own subjects, and any others they could command by conquest, should also be Christians in communion with Rome. Thirdly, the Pope had at his disposal the religious orders, the trained agents of mission who, free from family ties, could be sent anywhere and given any commission. It was a splendid dream, and though within a few years the unity of the Western Church was shattered it has remained the powerful motive and method of Roman Catholic mission.

CHAPTER SIX

The Rediscovery of Mission

IN the fifteenth century a new spirit of self confidence and adventure stirred in Western Europe, especially among the Spaniards and Portuguese. They expelled the Moorish armies and pursued them across the Straits of Gibraltar into North Africa. Wherever they took military and political control they also established new dioceses. The voyages of Diaz, who rounded the Cape in 1487, and of Columbus, who reached America in 1492, opened new lands for conquest and exploitation. Priests accompanied all these expeditions and from the first the missionary obligation was clear. When Alexander VI in 1493 and '94 divided the New World between Spain and Portugal he categorically enjoined both monarchs to convert the indigenous peoples. So began the great Catholic Mission to Africa, Asia, and the Americas. From the religious houses of Europe came a ceaseless stream of devoted men and women who gave themselves to the task, often at great cost to themselves, and not infrequently in conflict with the colonial authorities. Over the next five hundred years millions were added by their efforts to the Roman Catholic Church giving it the numerical superiority over all denominations it still maintains.

2. No similar missionary impulse stirred within Protestantism. Latourette attributed the lack of concern to the fact that the Protestant states were everywhere fighting for survival against Catholic armies, that their energies were devoted to the reconstruction of the State Church and of the life of the nation and that they were isolated from non-Christian lands.[1] But isolation certainly did not last very long and both the English

[1]K. S. Latourette, *A History of the Expansion of Christianity* (7 vols.) (London; 1937-45).

and the Dutch were soon establishing colonies and provinces in North America, South Africa, India and the East Indies where they showed no inclination to convert the native peoples. William R. Hogg[1] gets nearer the real cause. He points out that the Protestant repudiation of the Papacy and its claim to world sovereignty removed the main motive of mission as the sixteenth century understood it. Similarly the Protestant abolition of the religious orders eliminated the chief source of trained missionary personnel and there was as yet no substitute. Thirdly both Catholics and Protestants were afraid of freelance lay evangelism, such as that fostered by the Anabaptists whom both sides savagely repressed. So in Protestant lands there was no concern for mission overseas.

3. Neither Luther nor Calvin nor any of the other Reformers realized the missionary implications of their own theology. Luther believed that the Great Commission ceased with the Apostles to whom it was given and felt no responsibility beyond preaching the message to the people at home. It took Protestantism nearly two hundred years to discover its missionary obligation and the impulse, when it arrived, came not from the official Lutheran or Calvinist Churches, but from the despised and at times persecuted minorities which produced the Pietist movement.

4. Today the word 'Pietism' is frequently used in a pejorative sense to mean 'the cultivation of depth of religious feeling or structures of religious practice, especially as distinct from intellectual belief or the Christian penetration of culture'.[2] Currently it means an excessive religious other-worldly individualism intent on its own salvation and quite indifferent to social issues. It is sincerely to be hoped that a more reasonable assessment of Pietism will soon be attempted to correct this one-sided picture, for there is no doubt that the Great Awakenings of the Eighteenth Century in Europe, North America and Britain drew their inspiration from Pietism.

5. The roots of Pietism run back deep into the life of the

[1]William R. Hogg, 'The Rise of Protestant Mission Concern' in *The Theology of Christian Mission*, ed. G. H. Anderson, (S.C.M., 1961).

[2]*Report on World Mission* presented to the General Council of the United Church of Canada 1966, p. 303.

Western Church and tap three main sources of spiritual renewal. First is a passionate devotion to Christ of the type that must declare its love and seek to bring others into the same experience. This personal devotion to Jesus, generating its own distinctive form of Christian mysticism, manifested itself in men like Bernard of Clairvaux (1091-1153). Delight in Jesus was the constant theme of his hymns. But his was not the devotion of the solitary remote from the world; it drove him to a preaching mission which renewed not only the monastic orders, but the whole cultural tone of Europe. Choice spirits in every age have followed this road. No critic will ever do justice to Pietism who ignores this Christo-centric element. The hymns of the movements are essentially love lyrics. Love of Christ was the powerful motive of mission.

6. Secondly, Pietism is riveted to the Scriptures, finding in them not only the Rule of Faith by which all doctrines are to be measured, but the very ground of that transforming encounter with the Spirit of God who makes all things new. This approach to the Bible is quite different from that of either the polemic theologian seeking proof-texts, or of the Biblical critic concerned with literary questions. It is a much more humble approach that examines itself in the light of the revelation of God mediated by the Scriptures. It dares to judge society both by the prophetic insights of the Old Testament and by the standards of the Kingdom revealed in the New. Peter Waldo (1179-1218) translated the Bible into the language of his people at Lyons, France, and, out of his new understanding of the Gospel founded a lay preaching order which he sent out two by two to preach repentance. The Waldensians were fearfully persecuted, as were the Lollards, the followers of John Wycliffe (1320-1386) who also translated the Bible into his native tongue and similarly organized lay-preachers. Wycliffe's ideas profoundly influenced John Huss (1369-1415) the Czech Reformer, who was especially moved by Wycliffe's criticism of the feudal system and the harsh structure of medieval society. All of these men and their followers, such as Jean de Labadie who so impressed Philip Jacob Spener (1635-1705), the father of German Pietism, taught that the Bible could be properly understood only under the immediate inspiration of the Holy

Spirit. He was the Great Interpreter. They taught that every believer could have the experience of the two disciples on the way to Emmaus whose hearts burned within them as the Lord opened to them the Scriptures. They believed that the Scriptures offered a meeting place for those self-authenticating moments of enlightenment when the Word becomes 'heart-felt', to use Charles Wesley's description of the experience, when the whole personality feels itself moved and convinced by God's truth.

When quiet in my house I sit,
Thy Book be my companion still,
My joy Thy sayings to repeat,
Talk o'er the records of Thy will,
And search the oracles divine,
Till every heartfelt word be mine. M.H.B. 310

7. The third element in Pietism is its curious blend of inspirationalism and discipline within a group of believers. Separated, these two elements can produce extreme sectarianism, but held together they release a fertile and renewing energy. Many examples of this occurred throughout the later Middle Ages, most notably in the movement known as the Brethren of Common Life, who met in small groups for prayer and study and set up schools in which the best learning of the day was brought into the service of Christian discipleship. These groups grappled with the new ideas of the Renaissance and sought to reform the Church from within. Luther as a boy attended one of these schools at Magdeburg. Implicit in their approach was the conviction that the Spirit of Truth could and would dwell in the heart of the humblest believer, that He bestowed His gifts, especially the gift of inner peace, that He constantly strove to perfect the heart in which He deigned to dwell, and that, therefore, the pursuit of wholeness was also the pursuit of holiness. They developed aids and guides to this new form of spiritual culture, which was called the *devotio moderna*, modern piety. It is believed that Thomas à Kempis's *Imitation of Christ* came out of one of these fraternal groups. The search for holiness inspired several books, such as Johann Gerhard's (1582-1637) *Holy Reflections for Stimulating True Piety* and his *School of Piety*, as did the *Pia Desideria* of Johann Quistorp.[1]

[1]See Paulus Scharpff, *History of Evangelism* (Eerdmans. Engel. 1966).

Spener, a few years later used the same title for his own famous work, in which he pleaded not only for an intensive study of Scripture, but that the laity might fully express their own spiritual priesthood. He maintained that Christianity is primarily a way of life, not merely an intellectual system, that love is its fulfilment, and that therefore love should control all religious controversy and initiate social concern for those in distress. In Pietist circles the laity began to recover their sense of responsibility for participation and mission.

8. Official Protestantism had become stilted and formal, suspicious of enthusiasm and strongly inclined under the influence of the Enlightenment to a frankly rationalist approach to faith, but, underneath, a very different current was gathering force. When under the leadership first of Spener and then of Franke, his successor at the University of Halle, the principles of Pietism were enunciated, there was an immediate response, not only in German Lutheranism and Calvinism but also in England and in North America. Franke's Pietism had a lively social conscience. He established several charitable and social relief works, and launched modern missionary enterprise when in 1706 he sent two missionaries to India at the request of Frederick IV of Denmark, who had himself been influenced by the movement. Zinzendorf, inspired by Franke, passed on his new missionary zeal to the Moravian Brethren who reorganized their Church into missionary units, whole families migrating with the purpose of proclaiming Christ to those who had not yet heard the Name.

9. The revitalization of German religion under the stimulus of Pietism was repeated in the Thirteen Colonies of America and erupted in the Great Awakening of 1737 under the leadership of Jonathan Edwards (1703-1758) and George Whitefield (1714-1770). Both preachers tried to restrain the excessive emotionalism and hysteria that soon appeared in the revival meetings. Edwards also stressed the pietist principle that only the converted person, and one who showed proof of his conversion, was really saved. The distinction which makes conversion 'the test of saving faith' had been clearly articulated by Johannes Arndt (1555-1621) when he declared that his aim was 'to lead believers from a dead to a fruitful faith in Christ'.

Franke, too, after his own shattering conversion had referred ever afterwards to the difference between 'saved' and 'sin-saved'. Emphasis on the conversion experience has remained one of the features of evangelism ever since, especially within the 'holiness' groups.

10. In England the Great Awakening produced not only Methodism but the powerful evangelical wing of the Church of England and affected the older Nonconformist Churches, re-kindling their evangelical concern. Wesley's debt to the Pietists and to their forerunners is obvious at every point. The hymns of Charles Wesley, like the hymns of Paul Gerhardt (1607-1676), are full of the first person, the 'I' and 'Me' of personal experience, as they sing of the heart inflamed with the love of Jesus. Methodism also developed the system of intimate fellowship groups—the 'class meeting', *ecclesiolae in ecclesia*, the little Church within the Church—wherein the work of perfect love, the specific proof of the sanctifying life-giving Spirit, could be encouraged. Christian perfection was the object of evangelism and conversion the vital first step, but no more than a step on the long road. Methodism used the Scriptures de-votionally; the hymns of Wesley contain quotations from the Authorized Version in almost every line. And Methodism brought Christian social concern to the centre of its activity in a flood of educational and charitable undertakings.

11. The Evangelical Revival by the end of the eighteenth century had prepared a great body of Christian opinion that responded magnificently when the obligation to take the Gospel overseas was understood. Though the Society for the Promotion of Christian Knowledge had been founded in 1699 and the Society for the Propagation of the Gospel in Foreign Parts in 1701, these remained largely a service to British personnel in the colonies, and the effort to reach the native population was comparatively small. But when accounts of the successful efforts of American evangelists to convert the Indian tribes reached England, they stimulated intense interest and inspired William Carey (1761-1834), the Strict Baptist cobbler, to per-suade his small denomination to form in 1792 the Particular Baptist Society for the Propagation of the Gospel Among the Heathen. By 1820 all the major British denominations had

established missionary societies and were soon followed by the Churches of Northern Europe. So began the great century of Protestant Mission. By 1914 the number of missionaries was over 22,000, half of them women. By far the greatest proportion of them were maintained by British and American denominations.

12. The staggering success of both Catholic and Protestant missions throughout the nineteenth century came to be regarded by Christians of all denominations as plain evidence of the inevitable success of faithful preaching. The response of the Western Churches to carry the Gospel to the ends of the earth was a truly magnificent outgoing of concern and generosity. The zeal, devotion, and sheer genius of the missionaries is beyond praise. But they rode on the crest of a wave which is now receding. They came with all the prestige and power of Western technology to agrarian peoples whose way of life had not changed for centuries. Though sometimes the missionary pioneered new territory, most went in behind enterprising commercial interests and all were protected by colonial governments. To their credit the missionaries not infrequently withstood the authorities on behalf of exploited native peoples, but in general they assumed, often unconsciously, the status of a dominant people and the superiority of their alien culture. With the collapse of colonialism and the rise of newly independent nations in the East and in Africa, the nineteenth century now seems strangely remote and unreal. From 1910 onwards missionaries themselves realized that the world had entered a new era, that old methods and concepts needed to be changed. The call for ecumenical thought and action came, not from the old centres of European and American Christendom but from the mission field and from the new indigenous Churches that the century of the Protestant Mission had created. By the 1960s however, the older denominations were finding it difficult to maintain their numbers in the field, while an increasing number of missionaries were being sent out by the various Faith Missions mostly of fundamentalist persuasion. We have entered a new phase of mission, but what shape and content it will have remains as perplexing a problem to the overseas missionary as it does to the Church at home.

CHAPTER SEVEN

Traditional Evangelism

FOR millions of Protestants the Evangelical Faith, which was proclaimed in the Great Awakenings and inspired the missionary enterprise of the nineteenth century, is still normative. They regard it as 'the faith which was once and for all delivered to the saints' (Jude v.3), and are disturbed by the attacks to which it is now subjected. But the demand for a new theology of mission comes not only from the radical wing which has developed since the Second World War, but from many who see so plainly that we live in a very different age, one in which the assumptions of the Evangelical presentation of the Faith are sincerely questioned.

2. Methodism, a child of the Evangelical Revival, finds herself at the very centre of this controversy. Under the genius of John Wesley (1703-1791), Methodism took to itself all the great insights of Pietism, fusing them into a new synthesis which combined the positive affirmations of Christian orthodoxy with the power-releasing experience of personal commitment. But by inclination and training Methodists have been more concerned with the 'how' of communication than with the contents of the Message, and this has given occasion for the ungenerous comment that Methodism is long on experience but short on theology. Throughout the nineteenth century the pragmatic approach reaped rich returns.

3. There are historic reasons for this pragmatism. In the eighteenth century Methodism found itself possessed of a simple and most effective theology of salvation. This word, like 'evangelism', has been grievously devalued, and for much the same cause. For early Methodists it described the glorious news of God's redeeming purpose to make all things new in Christ. Salvation included the overthrow of the dominion of

sin, evil, and death, and the ushering in of the new age, embracing a new heaven and earth, and the reconciliation of all things. Above all, salvation meant the Work of Christ who has conquered sin and death and by his death on the Cross has atoned for all. Jesus was the Saviour of the world and Methodist devotion, enshrined in the hymns of Charles Wesley (1707-88), was a burning love of that Saviour, with its attention focused on Calvary.

4. For the Wesleys the living way to God had been opened in Christ, whose death and passion had dealt with sin. What the crucifix is to the Catholic, so the mental image of the crucified was to the early Methodist. His gaze was riveted on the 'wounds of Jesus'. By faith he saw those wounds in the glorious risen body, for ever pleading before the throne for sinful man.

Entered the holy place above,
Covered with meritorious scars,
The tokens of His dying love
Our great High-priest in glory bears;
He pleads His passion on the tree,
He shows Himself to God for me.

M.H.B. 232

Or again,

Come then, and to my soul reveal
The heights and depths of grace,
The wounds which all my sorrows heal,
That dear disfigured face.

M.H.B. 172

5. The Methodist theology of salvation rested on three familiar axioms—(i) All men can be saved, (ii) All men can know that they are saved, and (iii) All men can be saved to the utmost. In thus affirming the universal sweep of redemption, God's 'undistinguishing regard', the Wesleys repudiated the hard and extreme Calvinism of their day, returning to the Arminian and Catholic position. The cruder statements of the doctrine of 'election' appeared to consign the greater proportion of mankind to perdition. The Wesleys rejected this 'horrible decree' and insisted that since Christ died for all, any man could repent and believe. 'For all' became the Methodist war-cry.

The real point at issue, obscured in the fury of the controversy was the mystery of the freedom of the human will. Could a man repent unless God gave him the strength and insight to do so? The question is still open, both sides saw important aspects of truth, but the Wesleys were undoubtedly right that no deductions from this issue should be allowed to limit the offer of Christ to all mankind. They passionately affirmed that no one is excluded from the mercy of God which reaches out to all. They despaired of no man.

6. The Methodist revival produced tens of thousands of converts whose 'experience' was so uniform and regular as to suggest a definite sequence of stages through which the awakening soul passed. Since each phase also seemed to be clearly defined in Scripture there emerged an evangelical theology which claimed to be Biblically sound and which was constantly confirmed in experience. Preachers and 'class leaders', familiar with the Plan of Salvation, knew what to expect and how to help and guide inquirers.

7. The Plan, 'God's wonderful design', was usually described as consisting of seven stages, though sometimes some of these are grouped together, or sub-divided still further. In broad outline they are: (i) Conviction of Sin; (ii) Repentance; (iii) Faith; (iv) Forgiveness; (v) Reconciliation; (vi) Assurance; (vii) Sanctification. The evidence for such a path is impressive. Scores of the greatest saints of all ages and places have traversed this road. Paul, Augustine, Luther, Fox, Bunyan, Wesley—the mere enumeration appears sufficient guarantee. Their confessions, autobiographies and journals eloquently testify to their experience and have become normative for millions who in a lesser degree have known the same spiritual crisis and relief. Nor was there anything mechanical about this process; it only became formal and rigid when expounded within an abstract systematic theology. The early Methodists thought of it as growth, the direct action of the Holy Spirit in the work of grace and love.

8. The first effect of the proclamation of the Gospel is to prick the slumbering soul, rouse conscience, and awaken the soul to its alienation from God and its sinful condition. This is what Scripture says Jesus did. Mark summarizes his Galilean

ministry as the summons to 'repent and believe the Gospel' (Mark 1:15). This was the burden of apostolic preaching: 'Repent then and turn to God so that your sins may be wiped out' (Acts 3:19). Realization of guilt in the sight of God induces a state of intense wretchedness and the misery increases the more the soul becomes aware of its condition. It is lashed and tormented by the whip of fear, remorse and shame. It struggles to rid itself of its sin, but discovers to its horror that it is a helpless slave to its own evil habits, fettered by chains of its own making. It falls back defeated again and again until despair seizes it. The classic description of this state is Paul's 'The good which I want to do, I fail to do; but what I do is the wrong which is against my will. . . . Miserable creature that I am, who is there to rescue me out of this body doomed to death?' (Romans 7:19,24). Bunyan's account in *Pilgrim's Progress* of the soul bent under its enormous burden in the City of Destruction faithfully reflects the same experience.

9. The creation of this state of self-condemnation was the first requirement of successful evangelism. The Methodist preachers exposed the nature of sin, its insidious attack, its numbing of the conscience, its enslavement of the will. They expounded the beauty and justice of divine Law and the inevitable penalties that must follow the slightest infringement. The whole presentation led inexorably to the verdict of 'guilty', acknowledged by the hearer, and then to the pronouncement of the sentence of eternal punishment. 'For sin pays a wage and the wage is death' (Romans 6:23). Wesley had himself laid down the prescription:

> '*I think the right method of preaching is this. At our first beginning to preach at any place, after a general declaration of the love of God to sinners, and His willingness that they should be saved, to preach the Law, in the strongest, the closest, the most searching manner possible. After more and more persons are convinced of sin, we may mix more and more of the Gospel, in order to beget faith, to raise into spiritual life those whom the law hath slain.*'

In days when nearly all Christendom believed in a three-tier universe, with an almost material heaven to reward the good, and a dreadful hell for the wicked, vividly conceived in terms of the medieval torture chamber, sheer physical fear of never-ending agony added its terror to bitter remorse. Eighteenth-century rationalism was limited to a very small circle of educated people; the illiterate masses possessed and were possessed by a rich folk-lore of demons and fiends. The sinner 'under conviction' knew that he was on his way to hell and that nothing he could do could avert that final disaster. Scripture was emphatic; there was no escape for the unrepentant unbeliever. 'And they will go away to eternal punishment' (Matthew 25:46). The abnormal misery and anxiety such fear can generate is very obvious in Luther's description of his agonies during this phase.

10. While preaching was the chief instrument of evangelism it was not the only one. A chance remark overheard in passing, the reading of a passage, especially of Scripture, the singing of a hymn, or the sight of a child's face, anything could be used by the Spirit to awaken a dormant soul and precipitate this awful experience. The phase itself could last just a few terrifying minutes, or months, or even years, depending on the character and history of the person concerned and on the presence and skill of those helping him through his crisis. The aim of the wise evangelist was to initiate this condition, to make sure that it was genuine and went deep enough, and then to end it as quickly as possible by pointing to the Saviour.

11. 'Conviction of Sin' led to regret and remorse, the lash of conscience drove the soul to realize how it had offended God and injured other people. Sorrow over sin, the intense feeling of shame, produced a passionate longing to undo the past and to make amends. The proud heart was humbled; its hardness was melted. The Wesley hymns movingly describe the broken and contrite heart so accurately depicted in Psalm 51. It was for this moment when the penitent soul cried out for help that the Evangelist had been waiting. Now he disclosed the Gracious Invitation of a Pardoning God. There was need for haste and firmness, for danger lay in the soul's concluding that it was not fit to come to God and of continuing its own hopeless efforts. The Message of Jesus was for sinners, not for the righteous (Matthew 9:13). As Joseph Hart sang:

If you tarry till you're better,
You will never come at all. . . .
All the fitness He requireth
Is to feel your need of Him. M.H.B. 324

12. Repentance is the critical moment of inner decision, it is the deliberate and fully conscious determination to reverse the direction of one's life. It is the moment of truth. We see not only what we are, but what we ought to be, and we 'turn round' and prepare to go home. Repentance is the change of mind, but it is not in itself sufficient to effect release. The will is enslaved, and needs a power other than its own. Unaided it is constantly defeated. The evangelist, alive to this condition, declared God's mercy, His willingness to restore the penitent, and to give the power needed. He points to the promises of God contained in Scripture. He affirms that God will keep His promises. 'Only believe,' he pleads, 'Stop struggling; you cannot save yourself, but God can and will save you. Just believe it. Believe that God wants to and will forgive you.'

13. Faith is the human response to the Gospel offer of salvation, it is throwing oneself on God, relying on Him to supply the strength to resist temptation and to turn from evil. Not effort, but trust is the key. Again and again in the Gospel story healing comes in response to faith. Paul's own experience of the Gentile response had shown that faith alone was essential. Salvation is unattainable by human effort. Faith enables us to appropriate God's forgiveness and it imparts the living energy to the will by which we can live freely and naturally as sons of God. 'Scripture has declared the whole world to be prisoners in subjection to sin, so that faith in Jesus Christ may be the ground on which the promised blessing is given, and given to those who have such faith' (Galatians 3:22).

14. The rediscovery of the significance of 'saving faith' by the Reformers at a time when it had been obscured and repressed by later accretions and distortions unleashed immense spiritual forces in Western Europe. It made whole sections of Scripture, especially the Pauline Epistles, immediate, vital, and superbly relevant. Problems still remained and dangerous simplifications only heightened controversy. It had to be made plain that we do not save ourselves by our faith. It is by grace

—God's free, undeserved love—that we are saved. 'For it is by his grace you are saved, through trusting him; it is not your own doing. It is God's gift, not a reward for work done' (Ephesians 2:8). From beginning to end salvation is the work of God, yet it does not annihilate personal responsibility, nor limit the possibility of response to a select few. God gives His saving grace to all who sincerely ask Him for it. Saving faith is itself the gift of God, for the whole act of redemption from beginning to end is the work of God. All man has to do is to believe, God will then reckon him as 'justified', that is, accept him as if he were completely righteous:

Believe in Him that died for thee,
And, sure as He hath died,
Thy debt is paid, thy soul is free,
And thou art justified. M.H.B. 372

15. The believing soul receives the grace of forgiveness. Release from the burden of sin floods the soul with indescribable joy as it exults in its new relationship to God in Christ. The relief brings with it an overwhelming sense of gratitude to God and this is centred in Christ whose death on the Cross was the critical act of redemption. Evangelical theology thought of the Work of Christ in penal and substitutionary terms. Christ took our due punishment upon Himself; when we were justly condemned and under the sentence of death, He took our place and died for us. He paid the price we could not pay. This saving act of love and obedience in all its wonder of self-sacrifice is symbolized by the 'blood' of Christ. This phrase, so repellent to modern ears, spoke vividly to the eighteenth-century evangelical. The Wesleys constantly speak of 'feeling the blood applied'—a reference to the cover of the blood of the Passover Lamb, sprinkled on the doors to protect Israel from the Destroyer (Exodus 12:12f), and to the 'blood of sprinkling' by which Israel was joined in covenant to God (Exodus 24:8). The hymns make it clear that 'feeling' the blood described the 'warming of the heart', 'the rapturous height of the holy delight', the ecstasy and joy of reconciliation:

My Jesus to know,
And feel His blood flow,
'Tis life everlasting, 'tis heaven below. M.H.B. 406

16. Though Wesley himself preached for intellectual conviction the salvation experience was often accompanied by intense emotion. Outbursts of hysteria were not uncommon; people 'under conviction' often burst into tears or groaned audibly. Such outbursts became a regular feature of the 'camp meetings' and 'rallies' of the revivalist preacher and techniques for inducing these states were sometimes practised either consciously or unconsciously by the professional evangelist. In time the convention was established that only those who had gone through such an emotional crisis were truly converted. Emotional excesses helped to bring the whole revivalist movement into disrepute and to discourage evangelical effort. But the recognition of the place of feeling in religious experience was important. The Gospel has to do with the Love of God and love is primarily felt. Emotion needs to be controlled and directed by rational thought, not eliminated. The doctrine of Assurance sought to keep emotion flowing steadily and to harness it so that it stimulated growth. Assurance is not self-assurance—far from it. It is experienced only when we are most conscious of our weakness. It is not boasting in our grasp of God, but rather the knowledge that we are held by Him. It is the 'witness within'. Because the early Methodist had known and felt this marvellous experience of God's tenderness and welcoming mercy, and this inner witness inviting to further and deeper communion, his 'dancing' heart longed to proclaim to others the story of redeeming love. Gratitude and joy drove him to mission.

17. In the practical work of soul-winning, the evangelist was not really satisfied until the penitent had reached this moment of release, which was often described as 'coming through'. When it happened the believer was 'converted'. The professional evangelist believes that he is called by God and equipped by the Holy Spirit for this special work (Ephesians 4:11). Frequently evangelists take the view that they have a roaming commission; they bring people to the moment of conversion; after that the Church takes over the responsibility of nurturing the new-born souls. Many churches have little idea what to do with them and make slight allowance for their immaturity. It is not surprising that the mortality rate among these 'babes in

Christ' is very high. The miracle is rather that so many of them are able to stay the course, and this is often more a testimony to the reality and depth of their conversion than to the caring of the Church.

18. But 'conversion' is not the goal; it marks the beginning. It is a moment of rebirth, and the new life and subsequent growth need careful attention. The Wesleys had learned from the continental Pietists that such oversight was best provided in small, intimate groups, in which a caring ministry, matched to each individual's personal need and situation, could be exercised. In the class meetings the members spoke openly of the condition of their souls, the temptations they had to fight; they confessed their failures, were rebuked, instructed and guided. In the class they prayed and found forgiveness and encouragement. The aim was to 'build each other up' and together seek that holiness without which no man shall see God. They became spiritual warriors who set before themselves the high aim of Christian perfection. They longed to be free from sin, to be cleansed inwardly, to be renewed in Christ so that their heart was a perfect copy of His. A complete section of the Methodist hymnbook was devoted to this subject. This was the glorious hope and it was to be attained, not by 'works', but by faith. Each day had to be lived by faith, each moment had to be offered to God.

19. It was in the class meetings that the goal was set—nothing less than God, nothing less than the final annihilation of sin, the creation of a new heart, perfectly righteous, perfectly holy in unbroken communion with God. Entire Sanctification, Perfect Holiness, Christian Perfection, were but different names for the 'prize'. Hence the battle cry: 'All men can be saved to the utmost.' Much controversy raged round this theme. John did not agree with Charles's sweeping generalization; he suspected that some of those who most stoutly claimed perfection were least convincing. But he hesitated more to deny the power of God to achieve its perfect way in the willing soul. Perfection therefore remained the glorious goal whether achieved in this life or not. The experience of such divine love convinced the early Methodists that there could be no limit to what God wanted to do and would do in the believing soul.

Redemption could not rest until its work was done and this meant the elimination of sin, root and branch, not only in the individual, but in all the universe, when the longed-for 'new creation' was finished.

20. Such sanctifying grace is the Work of the Holy Spirit, though His also are the first responses of the still unbelieving heart. But in the moment of conversion the renewing Spirit liberates locked-up talents and imparts new gifts all of which are to be used, not for self-glorification, but for the building up of the Church. After conversion the Christian life should be a growing intimacy with God, a purging out of the 'old man' and a putting on of the new. The earnest Christian prayed regularly for the gift of the Spirit, not just the charismatic gifts, but for the indwelling of the Spirit of Jesus.

21. This then was the early Methodist theology and practice of Mission: it is still the theology and practice of conservative evangelicals throughout the Protestant world, and its broad principles would be endorsed by the Catholic who also speaks about the Plan of Salvation. It is Scripture-based; it has worked and it still works in many parts of the world. Yet it makes singularly little appeal in the West today, and is vigorously attacked as inadequate and outmoded by liberals and radicals of every shade.

PART TWO

Secular Society

CHAPTER EIGHT

The Bible Says?

NEITHER Paul nor Wesley could travel any faster than a horse or sailing-ship could carry them. Both lived in a fairly static agrarian society based on small country towns and geared to the agricultural year. It is not at all surprising that Wesley, in common with most men of his age, had little understanding of the character of the industrial revolution that began in his lifetime. Much more remarkable was his apparent indifference to the intellectual ferment of the day and his failure to appreciate its significance. He was too deeply possessed by the certainties of his faith to view with anything but suspicion the doubts, speculations and philosophical theories discussed in the *salons* of the educated. His tremendous energies were channelled into the creation and organization of his tightly knit and disciplined religious societies and he had time for little else. Not that he conceived the goal of faith too narrowly; on the contrary he insisted that true holiness required a redeemed society, but he thought of his Methodism as something like a religious order within the life of the Church of England. His instinct was to concentrate effort and interest only on those exercises which would make the Methodist a more efficient spiritual warrior, a true soldier of Christ, fully trained and armed for the fight. Wesley's distrust of philosophy and his fear of democracy and social revolution led him to exclude from the great library of books he published for his people all political, social, and philosophical works, a restriction which was strongly enforced after his death and which gave to early nineteenth-century Methodism an almost anti-intellectual character.

2. The evidence for this has been collected and forcibly presented by Dr E. P. Thompson[1] whose detailed study

[1]E. P. Thompson, *The Making of the English Working Class* (Pelican 1968).

criticizes Methodism most severely. His careful analysis is a necessary corrective to the unsubstantiated generalizations of Methodism's impact on the worker which have been so uncritically absorbed into Methodist mythology. Thompson has no sympathy with Methodism and little understanding of what it is about or of its place in the evolution of religion in the West, but his evidence and the conclusions he draws from the facts must be studied by future Methodist historians. Methodism is in some need of a sound history based on adequate social research. But this censure applies to much Church history, and it is only recently that the techniques required for such research have been developed.

3. Methodism was not alone in its isolation from the intellectual and social revolution that was transforming European culture and society. All the major denominations in Britain remained untouched by the controversies that raged on the Continent, particularly in Germany around the questions of Biblical criticism. Indeed, it was not until 1860 when a group of Anglican scholars, out of the sheer pressures of intellectual honesty, courageously published their *Essays and Reviews*, that the storm broke and the British Churches were plunged into furious debate about the authorship, date, composition and reliability of the Scriptures, and the nature of inspiration.

4. The upheaval was all the more devastating because it coincided with the even fiercer controversy that followed the appearance of Charles Darwin's *Origin of Species* in 1859. The seismic shock administered to popular Christian thought by this epoch-making study can scarcely be over-estimated. From the time of Tertullian (*c.*160-*c.*220) orthodox Christian thought in the West had built its whole edifice of salvation theology on the Genesis narrative of the Creation and Fall. The new challenge to the historicity of these 'stories' could not be evaded and caused immense consternation. Darwin himself did not attack religion; he thought of evolution as the method adopted by the Creator to bring into existence ever more beautiful forms. In point of fact, the most virulent attacks on Darwin's theory came at first not from theologians but from his fellow scientists. Nor did Darwin originate the theory of development; it had long

been maturing in Western thought and had been elaborated by Hegel (1770-1831) into his great speculative system of philosophy which had captivated European thought and supplied Marx with his 'dialectic' principles. Darwin himself carefully described his theory as *The Origin of Species by means of Natural Selection, or the Preservation of Favoured Races in the Struggle of Life.* But in popular understanding the theory was thought to imply the evolution of man from animal ancestry, and to substitute chance for the Christian concepts of Creation and Providence.

5. The Evangelicals were not slow to see that the new theory struck mortal blows against the dogmas of the verbal inspiration and literal accuracy of the Bible. If this bulwark fell then the whole majestic scheme of salvation was also threatened, since it rested on the conviction that man was a fallen creature who had rebelled against his Maker, forfeited his innocent estate, and stood a guilty sinner under the condemnation of God's law. The Evangelicals realized that if the Bible stories were discredited the whole Christian position as they understood it was undermined, since the Work of Christ was to restore man to his lost estate by undoing the havoc wrought by man's first disobedience, and this Christ had achieved by His sacrificial death. The vehemence with which they attacked the advocates of evolution and of Biblical criticism, whom they bracketed together as enemies of the faith, springs from this apprehension.

6. But though the new ideas aroused alarm in Church circles, they were warmly welcomed by the growing number who for various reasons were critical of, or hostile to, traditional Christianity. The theory of natural selection chimed in with the unbridled commercial competition of an age dominated by utilitarian economics. Marx and Engels found in it a confirmation of their theories of the class struggle, while rationalists like Bradlaugh used it in their contemptuous attack on religion. T. H. Huxley, in his lecture on 'Evolution and Ethics' (1893) denied that the cosmic process afforded any support for a belief in a benevolent creator, or any basis for man's ethical ideals. Herbert Spencer (1820-1903) expressed the optimism so characteristic of the Victorian spirit and so implicit in the popular understanding of evolution in the idea of 'the survival of the fittest' which, given enough time, would lead inevitably to

the perfecting of the human race within its environment, when evil and immorality would disappear. Many other leaders of Victorian thought found themselves unable to accept the Church and the faith it proclaimed. Alec R. Vidler in his book *The Church in an Age of Reason* cites Thomas Froude, Francis Newman, John Morley, Matthew Arnold, Leslie Stephen, T. H. Green, George Meredith, and the list is far from complete. A distinguished roll of poets and other makers of opinion could be added. It is a common mistake of churchmen to think of the Victorian Age as a century of religious faith. The fact is that during the century the drift from faith accelerated, and the leadership of thought in Britain passed from the Churches to the new generation of writers and scientists outside the Church.

7. With the gift of hindsight it is easy for us to condemn the Church for ever allowing itself to be caught in so false a position, compelled to defend the indefensible. But such a judgement fails to reckon with the fact that for many centuries the theory of verbal inspiration satisfied reasonable men. Nor does it recognize the weight of inertia developed by a religious system which, once established, can be modified only after tremendous effort, for it tends to persist, treasured as sacrosanct long after the social and cultural conditions that gave it birth have disappeared. One can wonder how different the course of Western civilization might have been if the plea of Galileo (1564-1642) had been heeded. He knew that his ideas conflicted with the traditional understanding of Biblical cosmology, but he could not close his eyes to the evidence revealed by his telescope. In a letter to the Grand Duchess Christina of Tuscany, he wrote in 1615, 'I think that in discussing problems of nature we ought not to start with texts of Scripture, but with practical experiments and convincing demonstrations. For from the Divine Word both Scripture and Nature alike proceed.'[1] Galileo was right in distinguishing between the Word of God and the Bible. But the Church, both Protestant and Catholic, was too deeply committed to the rigid concept of Biblical inerrancy, and by identifying the Bible with the Word

[1]Quoted by J. Bronowski and Bruce Mazlish, *The Western Intellectual Tradition* (Pelican 1963), p. 153. I have ventured to modernize the English translation, I hope accurately.

of God had fallen into a dangerous confusion. It claimed that the Bible had been dictated by God word for word, and was therefore literally true. Whatever conflicts or cannot be reconciled with what the Bible says is therefore manifestly false and must be rejected by all faithful Christians. Galileo was urging that all truth is of God and must be recognized as truth, and that any apparent conflict with Scripture must and could be resolved by further patient and humble study. But the Church was not yet ready for such a new evaluation of the Bible.

8. This conviction that natural and revealed truth complemented each other was shared by nearly all the scholars who advocated and followed the new scientific methods. Certainly it was the belief of Francis Bacon (1561-1626) whose *Advancement of Learning* and *Novum Organum* so clearly defined the new methods of inductive logic. But in the aftermath of the Renaissance and after the emotional shock of the Reformation, an unyielding scholasticism gripped both Catholic and Protestant official theology. Both reacted by retreating into literalism. Anything or anyone who seemed to attack the infallibility of the Scriptures was regarded as a threat to the authority of the Church and the truth of the Christian faith. That was why Rome after some hesitation silenced Galileo and why Luther dismissed Copernicus as a fool.

9. The battle really began with the great mathematicians who were inventing the new tools by which the secrets of the mechanics of the universe were unlocked. They thought they were supporting, not attacking the Bible. Descartes (1595-1650) earnestly believed that he was discovering new defences for the faith. He made doubt the basis of his system, affirming that nothing should be accepted as true until it had been mathematically demonstrated. He thought that mathematics was in fact the divine logic which would in the end justify and elucidate every claim of faith. His insistence on the use of doubt marked a significant shift into the secular age for it reversed the principle that had governed Christian thought for a thousand years during which doubt had been regarded as disloyalty, a malignant and cancerous evil to be resisted by all faithful men and to be eliminated at whatever cost from society. Yet now, in the new thinking, the good scholar was told he must question

everything, take nothing on unexamined authority and test everything for himself to see if it really was what ancient lore said it was. And as nearly every fresh discovery flatly contradicted those ancient authorities the slow erosion of authority began. The earth was round, not flat; it moved round the sun, not the sun round it. Again and again ancient authority was exposed as superstition. Men learned to wield doubt like a weapon, until today it has become as much a characteristic of the Western mind as belief in the supernatural was previously. And today the question is, How does one mission in an age of doubt?

10. The new interest in numbers led the mathematicians to try and construct a chronology of world history on the dates and information supplied by the Biblical records. By placing the passages in sequence some deduced that the world was created in 4004 B.C., the Flood occurred in 2348 B.C., and the Call of Abraham in 1921 B.C. Using his own system Bossuet, the brilliant bishop who so influenced Louis XIV, calculated that Noah sent out the dove on February 18th 2305 B.C. But it soon became apparent that the texts were inconsistent. Some of the brightest minds of the seventeenth century like G. W. Leibniz (1646-1716), the discoverer of the infinitesimal calculus, and Isaac Newton (1642-1717) devoted years which could have been better spent to the futile attempt to reconcile Scriptural numerical discrepancies. The different chronologies advanced by the scholars only emphasized the contradiction in Scripture and served to shake the confidence of the intelligent reader in the authority and reliability of the Bible.

11. Other discrepancies were noted. Free-thinkers sought out every difficulty and ridiculed every miracle. They asked who were the pre-Adamite men that Cain thought might slay him and from what family came his wife. Biblical literalism was attacked persistently by Pierre Bayle (1647-1706) whose *Historical and Critical Dictionary*, popularizing the new sciences, had enormous influence on the intellectual life of Europe. This method of attack was imitated by the French Encyclopaedists of the eighteenth century, whose articles seized every opportunity of exposing these inconsistencies and of denouncing the Bible as not only unreliable history, but of dubious morality.

12. It was obvious to a few Christian scholars that as long as the Faith was wedded to this theory of the verbal inspiration and inerrancy of the Scriptures it would be helpless against such attack. Appeals to State authority and to the political arm to silence opposition only brought the institutional Church into further disrepute. What was needed was a new approach to the Bible and a different evaluation of inspiration. One of the first to attempt this was the Oratorian Richard Simon (1638-1712) who applied the principles of literary criticism to the manuscripts of the Bible, in the same way as they were applied to other ancient texts. To equip himself for the task he learned Hebrew from a Jewish rabbi. In his great *Historical Criticisms of the Old and of the New Testaments* he drew attention to the duplicate and not always consistent accounts in the narratives. He argued that Moses could not possibly have written the Pentateuch in its present form and maintained that the editing of Scripture, for which he found abundant evidence, also bore testimony to the inspiration of the Holy Spirit. Because he wished to speak to ordinary men and women he wrote in French, since Latin, in which it was customary for such serious studies to be written, limited readership to the cultured few who could be expected to exercise discretion. He was expelled from his Order for his trouble, but his books were very widely studied and other scholars built on his foundations, especially in Germany. The more immediate effect, was to give ammunition to those bent on ridiculing Christianity. It was, however, the work of the English Deists that sowed the seed of later German Biblical criticism. Thomas Woolston (1670-1733) assailed the credibility of the sacred narrative and his *Discourses on the Miracles of our Saviour* (published between 1727 and 1729) attacked the literal interpretation as intellectually offensive and suggested that they must be properly understood as allegories and parables of spiritual truth. These ideas greatly influenced Reimarus and Lessing, and through them the main schools of Biblical studies in Germany, but they made scarcely any impression on English orthodoxy.

13. One of the first Englishmen to advocate the new approach to the Bible was Samuel Taylor Coleridge (1771-1834). He had studied in Germany and saw that the new

criticism put the questions of authority and inspiration into a different setting. He argued that if the Bible was studied with an open mind, it had a power of its own to evoke penitence and faith, and a man's faith should rest, not upon an appeal to the authority of infallible texts, but upon that work of grace in the heart which a sincere and humble reading of the Scriptures could induce. But in this, as in much else, Coleridge was a prophet before his time. The orthodoxy of his day held tenaciously to literalism—God had written every line, the writers were merely God's scribes. The Churches of Britain were therefore quite unprepared for the shock of *Essays and Reviews*. This collection of essays not only commended the critical approach to the Scriptures, it ventured to criticize the penal theory of the atonement which, as popularly expounded, maintained that the bodily sufferings of Jesus on the Cross was the price by which our salvation was bought from God. It ventured to suggest instead that salvation came through sharing the spirit of the Saviour. The contention of the writers was that Christianity could no longer stand apart from all the streams of new knowledge, defending the literal interpretation of the Bible against a mounting tide of evidence that rendered such a view untenable. The time had come for a new approach not only to the Bible, but to the theological systems erected on such literalism.

14. At the heart of the issue lay the question of inspiration. Alan Richardson[1] has pointed out that the idea derives much more from pagan Greek than from Hebrew sources, and refers to the possession of a sibyl or prophet by some divine power, compelling them to speak under the direct control of the divinity. Somewhat similar ideas were adopted in Rabbinical thought and were shared by the New Testament writers who regarded every word of the Old Testament as the powerful and creative Word of God, which having been once uttered must fulfil itself. It was this attitude that caused them to note that what Jesus said and did 'full-filled' the Scripture, and even almost to suggest that He did it so that the Scriptures could be fulfilled, as if the Scriptures exercised some sort of compulsion upon Him. Inspiration as the New Testament writers under-

[1]See *The Cambridge History of the Bible*, ed. S. L. Greenslade, 1963.

stood it is affirmed in 2 Peter 1:21, 'For it was not through any human whim that men prophesied of old; men they were, but, impelled by the Holy Spirit, they spoke the words of God' (N.E.B.). Because of this, 'no one can interpret any prophecy of Scripture by himself.' It was first given by the Spirit and can only be rightly interpreted by the Spirit. The same view is advanced in 2 Timothy 3:16 R.V. marg. 'Every scripture is inspired by God', adding that the purpose is to lead men to salvation by faith in Christ.

15. Such texts as these, and the fact that Jesus Himself seems to have shared this general view, have been sufficient warrant for the dogma that the Bible was inspired by God, and must therefore be infallible, for God cannot lie or deceive. If Jesus, who by definition was the Second Person of the Trinity, Very God of Very God, endorsed the Mosaic authorship of the Pentateuch, and the Davidic authorship of the Psalms, then such must be the fact, for He knew all things and would not affirm something He knew to be false. The word of Jesus has always been a powerful argument for the Evangelical. But as the pressure of Biblical criticism grew, revealing discrepancies and contradictions within the text, as the detailed study of the actual manuscripts (lower criticism) revealed the existence of alternate readings and some obvious corruptions in the received text, as the higher criticism examined questions of date, authorship, and composition, the old idea of writers taking down the message as dictated by the Holy Spirit or through some form of automatic writing became increasingly difficult to hold. The theory conflicted with Christian experience, for God never reduces man to a cypher, but fulfils him. The Holy Spirit does not possess a man so as to displace his own personality. The Scriptures themselves contained the evidence that they were written by men who reflected many of the ideas, assumptions, and values of their own age, yet who were challenging some of those ideas in the light and power of their own tremendous experience of God. It was conceded that they used poetry, drama, myth, and song as vehicles of truth and that to take such expressions literally was to violate the intention of the writer. It was also recognized that some attempts to explain away difficulties were too naïve, and arose merely

because of the reluctance to admit that Biblical myth was not to be taken as scientific fact or as historical happening. For instance, the suggestion that the six days of creation really meant six stages in the evolution of the universe convinced few who had any knowledge of cosmology. The true value of the Creation stories began to emerge when they were compared with the creation myths of ancient Egypt and Babylon and when their superb protest against the ultimate meaninglessness of cyclical time was recognized. They were not and never should have been taken for scientific texts. They were profound religious compositions.

16. But many Evangelicals could not stomach any such concessions to the new knowledge. They realized that once the verbal inspiration of the Bible was abandoned, much else, which they were not prepared to relinquish, went down beside it. It is not at all surprising therefore that many Evangelicals reacted to the challenge by insisting on the verbal accuracy of Scripture. Such are the Fundamentalists, who are to be found in nearly all denominations, as well as in those Churches which affirm the 'five fundamentals' in their basis of membership. These fundamentals were defined at a Conference at Niagara in 1895 as (i) the inerrancy of the Bible; (ii) the deity of Jesus; (iii) the Virgin Birth; (iv) the substitutionary theory of the Atonement; and (v) the Bodily Resurrection and the Bodily Second Coming of Jesus. They saw very clearly that if Scripture was no longer to be taken as the actual word of God, then each of the other affirmations was open to very serious question. But many other Evangelicals could not close their eyes to the evidence of Biblical scholarship and they turned to a new and modified theory of inspiration.

17. This new conception emphasized the inspiration of the writers, not the verbal inspiration of what they wrote. These men were inspired, as every servant of God is inspired, by the Spirit disclosing to him new insights into truth about God and man. By hard thought and prayer the man wrestles with the new truth until it grips him; it becomes the key that unlocks many doors, unifies various experiences and opens up a whole new world of possibilities. He is still a child of his age, many assumptions are still unrecognized and unchallenged, but what

he has seen drives him to re-evaluate human relations and compels him to convey his message for he is unable to forbear. In this sense, it was held, the Bible is the work of inspired men who wrote because they were 'full of the Holy Spirit' and could not do otherwise without denying the truth that possessed them.

18. Such an idea of inspiration is certainly more acceptable to the modern mind than that of verbal inspiration which reduced the writer to an automaton. The phenomenon of men driven by an inner compulsion to communicate a 'truth' they have experienced is common enough in human history. Every great religious and political idealist manifests these characteristics to some degree. The theory removed many awkward difficulties. Whatever was contradictory or inaccurate in Scripture was the result of the human element, the inevitable consequence of filtering the truth through human channels. It could not help but take up some of the shape of the minds through which it passed, and these minds were conditioned by the world in which they lived. But some accommodation or failure of consistency in no way invalidated the truth of Scripture, which remained the message imparted by the Spirit of Truth to the man willing to receive it, who placed himself joyfully at the Spirit's disposal, no matter what the cost to him personally, and who thus became the voice of God to his age and to all times.

19. The 'conservative' Evangelicals, as they have sometimes been called, find the modified theory of 'inspired' writers sufficient to enable them to maintain their claim that the Bible is the Word of God, absolutely authoritative and the supreme rule of faith and practice. They believe that inspiration is analagous to incarnation; it is both fully human and fully divine, so that it is God's witness to Himself and man's witness to God. 'It is, therefore, wholly trustworthy and free from error in all that it teaches. The Bible's authority is the authority of God-given truth and of the God of truth himself, who gives it and who addresses the Church constantly through it.'[1] This view rejects the automatic-writing theory of verbal inspiration,

[1]For an admirable summary of the various views of the Nature and Interpretation of the Bible, see paras. 56-60, *Anglican Methodist Unity*, 1968, p. 21.

yet it tries to retain the full claims to inerrancy for the truth.

20. The craving for some such authority is very natural; man knows he is weak and easily confused, he needs a safe guide through the intricacies and uncertainties of life. 'Thy word is a lamp unto my feet' exactly expresses what he often wants. To have readily available such a guide lifts an enormous load of responsibility from the ordinary man who knows his own limitations. This may, in part, account for the appeal of fundamentalism to two main classes—highly intelligent people who need an authoritarian basis for their faith, and poorly educated people untrained in critical method. This is not written in any condescending sense, but as a sincere appreciation of the need some folk have for an assurance outside themselves of what ought to be believed. Many doctors and soldiers, experts in their own field, skilled practitioners in following recognized authority, turn to fundamentalism for their way to faith, and there are stages in the development of nations when the masses respond to a faith that recognizes their spiritual needs, gives them opportunities of self expression, and points them to an ultimate authority to which they have direct access if only they can read. Indeed, it is sometimes argued forcibly that because we so obviously need such a guide, it would be unthinkable that God would have left us without one; the Bible is His gift to men, the open revelation of His mind and purpose, plainly spelled out for all to read. And when it is acknowledged, as it must be, and as the pages of the Bible Societies' reports abundantly testify, that many thousands have been led to saving faith by simply reading the Book in solitude, surely it cannot be denied that there is a power and majesty in the Scriptures which no other book quite shares. Millions can testify to the arresting and transforming power of its words and affirm that in its pages God has spoken to them. Chinese Communists, however, are claiming much the same effect for the works of Mao.

21. But further Biblical study has exposed even this revised theory of inspiration to increasing strain. The pictures of inspired men sitting down to write the books of the Bible is now seen to be an over-simplification of the intricate processes by which the various books came to their present state. As long as

criticism was focused on the Old Testament it did not too greatly disturb the Church and there was a willingness towards the end of the nineteenth and the beginning of the twentieth century to recognize as generally acceptable the current theory that the Pentateuch was derived from four main sources, edited and woven together. This was not felt to threaten the main structures of Christian doctrine. Such findings could be incorporated into a modern or liberal approach. Even the recognition that the Synoptic Gospels might include material from original Aramaic sources did not invalidate their historicity or accuracy, but merely described the mode of composition. It is in the middle of the twentieth century that Biblical criticism, applied with integrity, has once more raised acutely the whole question of historicity. The Gospels, for instance, once thought of as the work of the four evangelists who sat down and wrote their biographies of Jesus, drawing freely on other sources and eye-witness accounts, are now seen by many scholars to be collections of presentations, each passage produced separately within the life and thought of the Early Church to give direction and guidance to the Church on specific questions and issues. The original words and deeds of Jesus have therefore passed through many minds and are inseparably mixed with interpretation. It is held by these scholars that we cannot be certain that we have the actual words He said on anything; what we have is the recollection of something Jesus said or did as interpreted by His followers when they had to face the crises and questions that crowded on them in the early days. The idea of inspiration, if it is retained at all, must cover the formulation, collection, and editing of these recollections.

22. In Wesley's day few ever doubted the authority of the Bible. Today few, apart from the Christian minority, would accept it. Peter Hamilton[1] thinks that apart from the fundamentalists, most Christians today fall into two categories. First are those who believe that the Bible is intrinsically unreliable because it is the product of an ancient people, the Jews, for whom religion played so dominant a role as to make it impossible for them to understand or record events objectively. They

[1]Peter N. Hamilton, *The Living God in the Modern World* (Hodder and Stoughton, 1967), p. 33f.

were so conditioned by their religious presuppositions that they naturally saw things in terms of miracles and religious symbols, and the more they thought about them the more the religious interpretation overlaid the original event. Hamilton suspects that many more intelligent laymen belong to this group than the clergy imagine. They make these reservations reluctantly for they would much prefer to be assured of the reliability of Scripture, but the evidence against it cannot be evaded. They do not readily disclose their doubts, but in small groups where frank speaking is welcomed the reservations are admitted.

23. Those of the second category recognize all the inconsistencies and contradictions, but nevertheless cling almost desperately to the conviction that the overall picture of what Jesus said and did must be reliable. They cannot trust themselves to the shifting sands of a Biblical criticism which leaves the figure of Jesus so blurred and indistinct as to be no longer the Saviour of the World or the Friend of sinners. There is much justification for their protest, for as Professor R. P. C. Hanson[1] has pointed out, Biblical scholarship has felt free to cut up the Scriptures, ascribe dates and authorships, dismiss passages as editorial glosses in a way that would not be tolerated in the strict disciplines of literary criticisms applied, say, to the text of Plato. The liberties taken by some scholars amount to little more than individual guesswork and it is high time that there was a scientific criticism of Biblical critics. But despite these excesses there is more than enough evidence to question even the modified theory of inspiration.

24. Hamilton then asks why it is so many people feel they must insist on the reliability of the Scriptures and then advances the argument of Dr Leonard Hodgson[2] that they are unconsciously putting the Bible in the place of God. This happens because without being aware of what we are doing we are imposing on God the demand for a particular kind of revelation, an authoritative statement written down in human language. We are insisting that the only kind of revelation worth having,

[1] *Lecture Bible Studies and Reports*, Keele Papers, Methodist Home Mission Department, 1968.

[2] Leonard Hodgson, *For Faith and Freedom* (Blackwell 1957), Vol. II p. 227, quoted by Hamilton.

or that we are willing to receive, is that which provides an easily accessible and ultimate authority within creation. We want an immediate, physically present authority, like a statute book. But this, says Hodgson, must be resisted for it is at root an idolatry! It credits a creature—the book—with what belongs to God alone. He alone is ultimate authority and no book, however inspired, can take His place or exercise that power, though it may point to it.

25. But this raises the ultimate questions which we are facing today. What is the validity of religious experience? How does God speak to men? In what ways are the experiences that produced the Bible different from those by which men encounter God today? Hodgson rejects all idea of mechanical or irresistible inspiration. In every experience there is always what he calls 'the subjective element' which influences our own understanding and interpretation of it. The Biblical writers shared in the outlook of their day, e.g. in the belief of demon possession, the prevailing cosmology etc. Our approach to the Bible must therefore be to ask, 'If truth about God's revelation be such that those men saw it and wrote of it like that, what must it be for us?' German theologians from D. F. Strauss (1809-1874) to Rudolf Bultmann (born 1884) tried to seek the original experience behind the mythological form into which it was inevitably cast by those who first interpreted it. The myth was the one mode by which at that time, and under those conditions, the experience could be apprehended and communicated. The task for this twentieth century, it is said, is to recover as far as we can the significance of the original experience and to express that revelation in terms that make sense to modern man. Because the modern Christian has freed himself from the shackles of Biblical literalism, he is free to undertake such thinking—indeed, he has a duty both to himself and to his world to do so as thoroughly as he can.

CHAPTER NINE

The Struggle for Liberty

FREEDOM to think, to criticize and to publish, freedom to act and to live according to the dictates of one's own conscience, freedom from the domination of the powerful ruling groups in both State and Church, was the battle-cry of the awakening mind of Europe, and no ideal has contributed more to the making of modern secularity in the West. It is almost impossible for twentieth-century democrats to understand how strange and alien the cry for liberty sounded in the ears of those classes and institutions which for many centuries had never for a moment imagined that the existing social and intellectual order could possibly be questioned, let alone altered. The longing for liberty was eloquently expressed by John Locke (1632-1704) who was particularly concerned to secure religious toleration, the freedom of belief and worship. He voiced the new mood of disgust at the brutalities of the Wars of Religion which had destroyed so much of the wealth and culture of Europe. The attempt of princes to force their religion on their own and conquered territories, he declared, violated the very essence of Christianity. The true instrument of faith is love, not the sword. In his *Letters Concerning Toleration* he argued that no soul can ever be captured by force and no one has the right or the power to try to impose his opinions on other people.

2. Toleration, which is the recognition of the rights of others to think and act according to their conscience was a frighteningly new concept. For ages tolerance had been regarded as a sign of weakness and culpable confusion, a serious vice which every wise and strong ruler must reject. To tolerate was to condone error. Since the ruler was responsible for the souls of his subjects, he must not allow error to persist and deviationists

from the truth must be saved, by force if necessary, from the error of their ways. It was on this principle that Louis XIV revoked the Edict of Nantes in 1685 and let loose a fierce and bloody persecution of his Protestant minority, in the conviction that it was his duty to unify France, not only politically, but in faith and culture. Bossuet, Bishop of Meaux, justified the use of force in an appeal to the text *Compelle intrare*, 'compel them to come in', which had been used by Augustine in his controversy with the Donatists.

3. Though Augustine himself deprecated the use of the death penalty in the enforcement of religious uniformity, his disastrous justification of the use of force had become part of the Western understanding of Christianity. The seventeenth-century appeal for toleration meant a complete reversal of traditional attitudes and an admission that the great theologian and his successors had been wrong. Louis's persecution, which he thought of as a purely domestic affair, shocked Protestant Europe. It provoked such an outcry among civilized men that it enabled William of Orange to carry through the Toleration Act of 1690 whereby the principle was established in British law that no one was to be persecuted for his religion, nor was anyone to be converted except by persuasion. But tolerance, granted in the sphere of religion, could not be denied to other human aspirations and the door was opened to the next phase, the struggle for political and social liberty.

4. Tolerance is now part of the birthright of Western man, but it is not shared by all industrialized nations, nor is its continuance to be taken for granted. In most Communist countries there is no political freedom, and liberty of thought and expression is rigidly controlled. The same kind of repression obtains in the para-military dictatorships of Spain, Portugal, and Greece. In these countries the attempt is being made to replace medieval by new forms of authoritarianism. The old Catholic and Orthodox countries are among the least industrialized in Europe, and so are much nearer in feeling to the Middle Ages. But pressure for change is mounting as it is realized that authoritarian control has acted as a heavy brake on the evolution of these societies. Communism, with its crude and blatant atheism, rejecting all religion, ought to be the most

secular of all political ideals. It fails to be so just because it imprisons its people in a mental strait-jacket and attempts to coerce thought. Perhaps that is why in European Communist lands a greater proportion of the people still go to Church than in the Christian West. It may represent the common man's protest against the attempt to mould him to the approved pattern.

5. Western secular man is the heir to the freedom won in the struggle for toleration. It is now recognized that tolerance is not a vice, but a great virtue and that it more truly expresses the spirit of Christ than the efforts of the Church to impose religious uniformity. At its base lies a deep respect for human integrity, for the right of a man to think for himself. Life certainly becomes more complicated when everything can be argued. It is far simpler to impose discipline and to do other people's thinking for them. Thus there is always a temptation to resent the new, the strange, the different, the outrageous, and to revert to oppression in the name of decency and respectability. It is trite to repeat that the price of liberty is eternal vigilance; rather the real price is the effort to maintain the debate, to learn to live constructively with the conflict of ideas. The Christian doctrine of man as it is now being developed, puts its whole weight behind tolerance and freedom. It may well be that later generations will realize that both Christianity and Western secularity can exist only where those insights into the worth of the individual and his right to be himself are preserved. Secularity may be freedom from arrogant religious control, but not necessarily from the Christian interpretation of life. It may not recognize that its own claims to freedom of thought and action rest upon a view of man which is essentially Christian, nor that its own survival is bound up with the spread of those ideals. If they be allowed to die, then secularity may fall a prey to new dictatorships, always waiting in the offing to seize the prizes of power, to stifle liberty and to impose their own controls.

6. Christians of the Evangelical tradition sometimes write as if the Evangelical Revival were by far the most important happening of the eighteenth century, but the Enlightenment, or *Aufklärung*, as the Germans called it, had a profound effect

upon the West and the secular mind of today still bears many of its characteristic marks. The movement attracted many able scholars. In strong reaction to the claims made by revealed religion, H. S. Reimarus (1694-1768) pleaded for a purely natural religion which he believed could be deduced from contemplation of the open book of nature. Here everything revealed order and law. In such a mechanically perfect universe which at every hand disclosed the provisions of a generous providence there was no need for the supernatural, for miracles and special revelation. G. E. Lessing (1729-81), like Reimarus, followed the English Deists and rejected the historicity of the Bible and suggested that Christianity was a noble myth. In his play *Nathan the Wise* he advocated a pure humanism, describing the proper and mature man as tolerant, kind, and generous. J. D. Herder (1744-1803) was not prepared to dismiss the historicity of Christianity quite so lightly. He had studied under Kant and was well aware of the weakness in the crude rationalism of the Age of Reason. He was more concerned with the positive gains of liberalism. He studied history as a science and was the first scholar to suggest that in the human story there was to be discerned an ascending and developing process, by which the more barbaric elements would be gradually eliminated from human nature. He thus laid the foundations for the evolutionary theories of the nineteenth century. These three thinkers imparted to modern secularity its characteristic optimism. The rejection of the supernatural and of the possibility of divine revelation, the rejection of the authority and historicity of the Scriptures, the rejection of the authoritarian Church, the assertion that man can and will save himself when he understands and controls the universe, the warm and generous humanism, are all features of modern popular secularity. What was the philosophy of an educated *élite* of the eighteenth century became the popular philosophy of the industrial West at the beginning of the twentieth.

7. Perhaps even more determinative in the making of Western secularity was the rise of social criticism and the long struggle for equal political rights. The watchword of the French revolution—Liberty, Equality and Fraternity—accurately identified and placed in order the steps to the ideal society. Man

must first have freedom to think and act. When he gets that he can begin to shape the social order nearer to his heart's desire. The battle was long and it is still far from finished though some notable victories have been won. The third element, Universal Brotherhood, still remains a dream. The possibility of social engineering had been mooted by Socrates and Plato, but throughout the classical period, during the Roman Empire and right through the Middle Ages, almost everyone believed that the existing order was a divine and immutable institution, consisting of a broad pyramid, at the bottom of which were the slaves or serfs, over them the gentry or lesser nobility, over them the real governing class, and at the top the ruler. The social order retained from primitive thought a divine quality of its own, and it was everyone's duty to preserve that social order. This could be done only by each accepting his proper place assigned him by God. To dare to alter this order, to seek to change one's status was an offence against the divine majesty of the State, punishable by death or exile from society.

8. The first criticism came in slave revolts and peasant risings against intolerable oppression and exploitation and these were invariably put down with a savagery that can be explained only by the measure of the horror and fear insurrection inspired. In such repressive action the institutional Church stood firmly behind the ruling classes. Martin Luther's savage call to the princes to put down the peasant revolt of his day is a horrifying document. Only the newer sects, especially those that wanted to place the Bible in the hands of the people, dared to advocate social reform in the name of Christ.

9. All through the eighteenth century the volume of social criticism grew. The writings of Voltaire (1694-1778), the Encyclopaedists whose works appeared between 1751 and 1780, J. J. Rousseau's *Social Contract* (1762), and Thomas Paine's *Rights of Man* (1791) fanned the flames. The reactionary government of France was entirely out of touch with this ferment of thought and it is little wonder that it was on French soil that the first successful revolution of the common man occurred. England escaped this upheaval, not because of the Evangelical Revival, as is often alleged, but because of the English Revolution which had taken place a century before.

Though the working classes received slight consideration, the small country gentleman had secured a voice in government, thus enormously broadening the support on which the government could call.

10. The French Revolution of 1789 had a shock effect on the rest of Europe. The excesses of the Terror convinced every government that this evil thing must be contained and destroyed. The word 'Equality' which was now added to 'Liberty' threatened every vested interest and privilege in both Church and State. The reaction was violent, halting all reform and even the consideration of reform. The astonishing thing is that the contemporary religious awakening which we call the Evangelical Revival seems so utterly remote from this social ferment. It is possible to read Wesley's *Journal* without a hint of the intellectual and social upheaval that was shaking and reshaping Europe. Wesley himself was a High Church Tory with no interest in Biblical criticism and no sympathy with revolutionary concepts. What he did was to tap and release the pent-up feelings and frustrations of many thousands to whom he gave a new sense of identity and worth in the experience of the Love of God. The crowds to whom he spoke were not educated. They did not understand the philosophical controversies of the age, they were people who found little help in the formal religious life of the Churches, but they did find a character-transforming power in the experience of conversion.

11. Wesley had to walk carefully. The mood of the ruling classes was firmly against any appeal to emotionalism. Britain had emerged a Protestant country and the last thing the government wanted was a return to the religious fanaticism of the previous century. Thus Wesley had to show that his preaching did not stir up the rabble and encourage fanaticism, but on the contrary made decent sober citizens out of the most unlikely material. Persecution of the Methodists ceased after the first few years but the Methodist Conference was always at pains to show its loyalty to the Crown and to the government.

12. Neither the Churches nor the governments of Europe had any understanding of the nature of the industrial revolution which was engulfing them. It crept in almost unnoticed. The Churches were all the more insensitive because, following

the Reformation, both Catholic and Protestant alike had become much narrower in their outlook, withdrawing from the worlds of business, science, and the ferment of ideas to concentrate on 'spiritual' and purely 'church' affairs. Many Protestants today still consider the Church should only concern itself with 'religious' matters. The initiative in thought and science passed to the new lay intelligentsia which was generally very critical of the institutional Church and traditional religion.

13. As a result the Churches did not develop any social teaching by which they could have guided the new industrialism. Instead, they accepted without question the economic theory of the day. This was a crude and heartless utilitarianism, in which labour was a commodity to be bought at the cheapest possible price. Wages should be merely enough to keep the worker alive and to procreate his kind. There was no sense of responsibility for the labourer or his family—that was the concern of the parish and the Poor Law. Burke had said, 'The laws of commerce are the laws of nature, and consequently, the laws of God.' The Churches concurred and supported the upper and middle classes in their belief that industry must not be interfered with either by Church or State.

14. The reaction of the Church was intensified by the avowed anti-clericalism of some of the reformers. Robert Owen tried to humanize the mill and treated his workers as partners, and his establishment of the co-operative movement was an imaginative effort to help the poor to help themselves, but his *Denunciation of All Religions* published in 1817, antagonized churchmen of all denominations. Some glaring horrors like slavery, child labour, and excessive hours were denounced by some leading Evangelicals, who on the whole showed themselves more aware of social evils; but by and large the Church remained indifferent and joined with others in condemning as dangerous agitators those workers who dared to protest.

15. Methodists, in their popular mythology, have accepted Lecky's judgement that Methodism saved England from revolution by channelling working-class resentments and aspirations into the life of the Church. This is a gross over-simplification and bears little relation to the facts. Not only had England successfully contained its own revolution in 1689, it

had created conditions for rapid industrialization which brought a new class of able 'captains of industry' into existence who were just as much opposed to revolution as the gentry and the aristocrats. In eighteenth century England there were nothing like the same conditions as in France, as Voltaire vigorously testified. Indeed, while Methodism began as a movement among what the Wesleys called 'the humble poor', by the end of the century it had become a closely knit body of some 90-100,000 members strongly lower-middle class in outlook with a fair sprinkling of successful and wealthy laymen of the *entrepreneur* class of mill and factory owner. Methodism boasted of the number of men who had risen from rags to riches through its discipline of hard work, individual integrity and social respectability.

16. These rich men found in Methodism an opportunity to lead and to exercise responsibility denied to them politically. Some few of them occasionally built large chapels to which they expected their workpeople to come. A few had two galleries; the mill owners and professional people sat in the mahogany pews of the ground floor; the foremen and their families in the first gallery; the workers and servant girls on the narrow forms in the upper gallery. The pew-rent system, generally practised in the early nineteenth century, effectively segregated the poor. So did the strict convention of 'Sunday-best', a clothing requirement which successfully excluded the poor and ill-clad. The destitute had the option of being herded together in embarrassed exhibition in the few rough benches reserved for the poor, or staying away. They stayed away.[1] It is difficult for us today to imagine, let alone appreciate, how class-conscious the early Victorians were. Nineteenth-century social stratification was, in fact, the last manifestation of the feudal classification which had lingered on long after the decay of the system. It still haunts the minds of certain groups. The working-class resentment against this social segregation is one of the main reasons for its alienation from the Church which it identified with the class system.

[1]See K. S. Inglis, *Churches and the Working Classes in Victorian England* (Routledge and Kegan Paul 1963) also E. R. Wickham, *Church and People in an Industrial City* (Lutterworth 1957).

17. The leaders of early Victorian Methodism declared that they were not raised up to care for the poor of the great new towns, but that they were concerned with rural England—an unconscious revelation of their desire to escape from the problems of the spreading industrialism. They were determined to avoid any association with the advocates of political and social reform. The famous Liverpool Minutes of 1820, a passionate call to revival after the first drastic fall in Methodist membership, contained scarcely-veiled warnings to ministers not to become involved in social issues. They kept aloof from the Chartists, as did every other denomination save the Unitarians. Yet today practically every point of the Charter has been granted. The Chartists were not hostile to religion—indeed they opened their meetings with prayer and sang hymns—but the Church showed no sympathy for their aspirations. Instead it proclaimed that poverty was God-ordained, and that men must accept it as part of their appointed lot, for which compensations would be made in the next world if they patiently resigned themselves to God's will. The Tolpuddle Martyrs, so lauded now in Methodist legend as the first trade-union martyrs, were thrown out of membership by the Conference, nor was any collection for their dependents permitted in Methodist Churches. They were supported by the halfpennies of trade-unionists throughout the country.

18. Following the failure of the 1832 Reform Act to extend the franchise to the workers, they became much more self-conscious and began to organize themselves in increasingly effective trade-unions and to press for better wages and conditions and for a new attitude to labour. The first real challenge to the raw abuses of industrial society came not from the Churches but from the atheistic, anti-clerical revolutionaries. In 1841 Engels published his *Condition of the Working Classes in England* which supplied Marx with the facts on which he built his theory of Communism. These ideals made little appeal to the British working man who relied not on violence but on the right to withhold his labour. Strike action is successful when it is complete, and so working-class solidarity became the chief weapon in the struggle and has entered profoundly into working-class psychology.

19. In all this the Church stood apart, uncomprehending and unsympathetic. When it did speak, it was to emphasize that nowhere in Scripture was the doctrine of social equality to be found. The preachers who made this declaration thought they had given the final answer. They did not realize that the workers drew a very different conclusion, namely, that if this was what the Bible said, then it had nothing to say to them. They began to identify the Church with 'Them', the vague term for the bosses, the government, the gentry, the middle classes, and all who oppressed, exploited, or patronized them. The worker was unwilling to endure for a moment longer than he could, the humiliating, condescending treatment he associated with the Church. It is no wonder that the Religious Census of 1851 showed that the bulk of the working class never went to Church.[1] They had not rejected the Church; the Church had rejected them.

20. There were, of course, exceptions to this general indifference of the Western Church in the early nineteenth century. The Primitive Methodists were much more in sympathy with the aspiration of the workers, and many of their local preachers in the Midlands and North led the trade-unions in their struggle for recognition. But their numbers were never very great. By mid century the total membership of the 'Prims' was about 100,000, a tiny fraction of the working population. The idea that Methodism was once the religion of the workers is a fantastic exaggeration.

21. The other significant exception was the short-lived Christian Socialist Movement founded by J. M. Ludlow (1821-1911). He had met both French socialists and social Catholics and had carefully studied the French Revolution of 1848. He had seen how the lowly industrial worker responded to ideals of social justice and was convinced that socialism could be christianized when it would become a world-revolutionary force that would humanize and transform society. Ludlow greatly influenced F. D. Maurice (1805-72) and Charles Kingsley (1819-75) and together they produced *Politics for the People* and *Tracts on Christian Socialism* which tried to expose the

[1]The Census showed that only thirty-six per cent of the population attended Church.

real social sores and to awaken the conscience of the Church. Maurice vigorously attacked the economics of *laissez-faire* and the ruthless exploitation of labour regardless of the human suffering it inflicted. He denied that economic laws were the laws of the universe, and maintained that the law of God was that men were made to live in community and that only through co-operation did they become fully human. He defined socialism as the science of making men partners. He realized that before the workers could win political and social equality they needed education and so he founded the Working Men's College. The Christian Socialist Movement received practically no support and petered out by 1854.

22. Not till late in the century did the Churches of Britain begin to develop a conscience on social issues. The first break was made by the publication in 1883 of *The Bitter Cry of Outcast London*, a tract written by three young Congregationalists led by Andrew Mearns, which was given immense publicity by W. T. Stead. A similar disclosure with some practical suggestions for dealing with the problems was made by William Booth (1829-1912), General of the Salvation Army, in his *In Darkest England and the Way Out*, published in 1890. Booth had left Methodism in 1861 largely because his aggressive evangelism and strong individualism did not easily fit into the Methodist system of the day, but in losing him Methodism lost a powerful leader whose passionate love of the poor it sorely needed.

23. These exposures chimed in with the changing mood and led to the promotion of several efforts by the Churches to approach the lost multitudes. Leading Noncomformists saw that what was required was far beyond the resources of any one denomination to tackle alone. Out of this came the National Council of the Evangelical Free Churches and the *Forward Movement* of which Hugh Price Hughes (1847-1902) was a leading figure. In his *Social Christianity* he challenged as heartless the traditional view that poverty was somehow the result of sin, a kind of punishment for laziness or irresponsibility, and he also repudiated the tradition that Methodism should have no politics, which he said really meant no criticism of the existing order. Most of all he challenged the extreme religious indi-

vidualism of contemporary preaching and theology. 'Jesus Christ', he wrote, 'came into the world to save society as well as to save individuals; indeed, you cannot effectively save the one without saving the other.' It is a strange comment on the lack of historical sense that some radical writers advance these views today as if they had made a new and profound discovery. Out of such thinking came the Methodist Central Halls, a deliberate and imaginative attempt, sponsored by Joseph Rank, to reach the working class by meeting them in a neutral building, since nothing would persuade them to come to Church. For nearly thirty years these halls, staffed by able evangelists and social workers, attracted huge congregations and pioneered many experiments in social welfare, such as John Scott Lidgett's *Bermondsey School for Mothers*, the prototype of all subsequent Maternity and Child Welfare Centres. They fed the hungry and clothed the destitute. Their appeals for money helped to bring the facts of slum conditions to the notice of the nation and prepared the way for the massive national determination to eradicate poverty and slums, disease and ignorance, and to ensure for every child an equal opportunity.

24. Under the leadership of men like William Temple the awakening Churches began to make strenuous efforts to recover the initiative. Increasing attention was given to economic and political questions and to attempts to relate Religion and Life.[1] But the drift from the Churches was already too far advanced to be easily arrested or reversed. The First World War, in which over five million men were killed, shook the Western mind into a realization that humanity could destroy itself and that organized religion was powerless to restrain such madness. Of the churchgoers who returned in 1918 many never went to Church again. They had lost faith in the supernatural, in Providence and God. Equally corrosive were the effects of the Great Depression when millions were unemployed for years. The workers became convinced that no one cared for them in either Church or State. Just as the Church could not keep the nations from war, it could not save men from the economic

[1]See Henry Carter, *The Church and the New Age* (1911) and the Commission Reports of COPEC—*the Conference on Politics, Economics and Citizenship*, 1924 (Hodder and Stoughton).

scrap-heap. No outside power was going to help men; if the world was to be changed, men must change it themselves. The Second World War completed the alienation. The conscription of women, the shift- and Sunday-working, destroyed the old pattern of churchgoing. Christ remained an appealing idealist but Western man was now convinced that he must save himself. He does not need the Church which has become an optional extra for those who like that kind of thing. It is not related to what he wants of life, and this is what he means when he says it is irrelevant. Thus, after centuries of power and prestige, as the teacher of Europe, as the moral authority of the world, the Church today stands athwart the main stream of Europe's life, her laymen have left her in tens of thousands and her house is left unto her somewhat desolate.

25. It is always difficult to document a sub-culture, especially in a class-ridden society like Britain where the dominant group recognizes no culture but its own, and regards all else as a matter of condescending mirth. This supercilious attitude was very evident in Shakepeare's plays where the workers putting on their simple sketches are natural buffoons for the amusement of the sophisticated upper class. It is still thought by the middle class to be excruciatingly funny to imitate the speech of a Londoner, though the language he speaks is spoken by millions and has affected the speech of Australia and New Zealand. Because most working men leave the secondary modern school still only half-educated it is impossible for them easily to articulate all that they feel, but recently there has been a swift and remarkable development of working class art and drama. Nearly all 'folk' and most 'pop' music is of working class origin. Much of it is frankly vulgar and coarse, yet it is shot through with a moving tenderness and tragic beauty. Until the new race of sociologists appeared it has been desperately hard to get any scholar to recognize the existence of this immensely influential working class culture, with its own distinctive morals and values.

26. Among the last to recognize it for what it is has been the Church, and this also has contributed not a little to the widening gulf. Individual ministers and Christian workers are genuinely welcomed when they have shown real interest and

concern, but the gratitude felt has fixed limits. The remark made to one such minister is illuminating, 'I'll do anything for you, except come to Church.' When teachers and doctors threaten to strike, when air pilots impose their will by industrial action, they are adopting the methods of the workers, their sense of social solidarity. Working class culture is spreading upwards through society. It is bringing a new realism into art and drama; it is earthy and its goals are not in a distant heaven, but here on earth. The Church must remember that it began among working men—a Carpenter, a few fishermen, a tax clerk. They too were looking for a new society which would be just and fair to the common man, and they thought they had found it in the company of Jesus.

CHAPTER TEN

The Moral Criticism of Faith

THOSE who take the liberal attitude to the Bible at least free themselves from having to explain away many of the difficulties which those committed to the theory of Biblical infallibility must face. They also escape from the need to accept the traditional Scheme of Salvation, for once the Bible is conceded to be the work of fallible men reflecting many of the attitudes and ideas of their time, doubt can begin to attack the great edifice of systematic evangelical theology which was erected upon those texts. Indeed, such doubts had already been expressed in the early nineteenth century before the storm occasioned by *Essays and Reviews* broke. Several sensitive thinkers were deeply troubled by current formulations of the doctrine of the Atonement and of the eternal punishment of the wicked. They could not reconcile the idea of a loving Father with the God of wrath who demanded appeasement for the offences of the sinner, and who consigned the greater part of mankind, the unbeliever and the unrepentant, to everlasting torment. The sheer inhumanity of these doctrines appalled them. But the texts supporting them were emphatic and unequivocal. Evangelicals cannot avoid this charge as long as they insist on the inerrancy of Scripture without defining precisely what they mean.

2. Similarly, sensitive people shrank from the idea that a loving and righteous God could ever have devised a Plan of Salvation which required a price to be paid in bodily agony by an acceptable and innocent victim before consenting to cancel the penalties and debts of the actual offenders. The fact that innocent people often do have to suffer because of the wicked and thoughtless acts of the guilty was not, of course, denied; it happens often enough for we are social beings and no man

lives to himself alone. But this was not the issue. What was queried was the very possibility of transferring guilt; guilt implies responsibility; if a man is not responsible for what has happened he cannot be held guilty and if there is the slightest doubt of his responsibility the charge fails. An innocent man might suffer the punishment for another's crimes, but he is in no sense guilty, nor would any just judge allow a substitute to be declared guilty and punish him instead for something everyone knew he had never done. But even more unacceptable was the idea, sometimes put forward as an explanation of the Atonement, that the physical and spiritual agonies of the crucified Jesus were required as the only way of appeasing an outraged deity. When Calvary was explained as the payment of a price whereby mankind was ransomed, inevitable questions followed —Who demanded this price, and why was it necessary to extort it?

3. Yet warrant for the Plan of Salvation and for the Substitutionary theory of the Atonement, basic to traditional Evangelical and Catholic theology, is deeply embedded in Scripture. It is even more explicit in the great Pietist and Evangelical hymns—'*In my place condemned he stood*'—and for those who have been reared in this tradition and whose own religious experience has been moulded by it, it is painfully difficult to stand outside and look at it objectively. A new and sympathetic approach was needed, and this has been opened by Dr F. W. Dillistone in his *Christian Understanding of Atonement*[1] in which he shows how the various ideas emerged and developed and how the culture of each succeeding age has affected our understanding of the significance of the death of Christ. All our theories are pictures or parables, none of them exhaustive; all of them subject to distortion if pushed too far. The New Testament contains several such images besides the forensic pictures used so graphically by Paul, and these all serve to complement and correct each other. The substitutionary theory is only one among several pictures: it is a very important one containing essential insights into the mystery of Christ's death and passion, but it needs very carefully balancing by other New Testament principles of salvation.

[1]F. W. Dillistone, *The Christian Understanding of Atonement* (Nesbit, 1968).

4. Dillistone points out that the forensic images used by Paul reflect the Jewish understanding of the Law. The Jew thinks of Law as a covenant relationship which binds God to man and man to man in a holy community. To break covenant was to put at risk the safety of the community, the offender in his selfishness had proved himself unworthy and disloyal. A means had to be found for a reconciliation, for the reception of the offender back into the holy community, for the removal of the curse he had brought upon himself and upon his people. The prophets saw the final solution in the establishment of a New Covenant, a New Law for men whose new hearts would know and keep the Law. At this point Paul also drew upon the imagery of Israel's sacrificial system which sought by another means to reconcile repentant men to God. The Law of sacrifice provided for the offering of specified victims, whose poured-out blood symbolized the death and rebirth of the sinner, making him acceptable in God's sight. It was in this circle of ideas that much of Paul's thinking moved and he interpreted the death of Jesus accordingly. The actual words he used demand careful study, not only for what they say, but for what they do not say. Later generations soon read into his words other ideas which distorted his intention.

5. For when Christianity took root in the Empire it moved into a very different world. The Roman concept of law was concerned with property and property rights, rather than with persons in a covenant relation. Infringement of rights could only be expiated by the payment of fixed penalties. Dillistone attributes the importation of these ideas into Christian theology to the advocacy of Tertullian, the brilliant Roman lawyer. He thought of God as the supreme Patron whose property rights over all creation had been violated by man. The Law demanded the extreme sanction; man was guilty and worthy of death. But in Roman law many penalties could be paid by the family and friends of the offender, if he himself could not pay what was required. So, argued Tertullian triumphantly, Christ died in the place of man. He took our penalties upon Himself. The debt was paid and man went free.

6. Ransom, to use another great New Testament metaphor (Matthew 20:28; Mark 10:45; 1 Timothy 2:6), also emphasizes

the price paid in exchange for someone or something. The basic idea is that the offended one has the unquestioned right to claim full satisfaction, and that good relations with the offender can be restored only when that satisfaction has been made. In the Early Church, some of the Fathers, like Gregory of Nyssa, thought that the ransom was paid to the Devil who had acquired proprietary rights over the souls of men—because of their sin they were in bondage to him—and this debt had to be paid in full before they could justly be released. This interpretation was fairly popular in the Middle Ages, for it seemed to explain redemption in terms of release and salvation and to make the death and suffering of Jesus intelligible—it was the kind of price a devil would demand. But the main stream of Christian thought rejected the idea. The New Testament witness pointed plainly to the fact that Jesus offered Himself to God in full obedience. The traditional position is ably summed up by James Orr: 'there had to be a great ethical reparation rendered to God's broken law of righteousness. It is to God the ransom is paid, not to another. The Son of God, in humanity, renders it for the world.'[1]

7. In feudal days men's minds were dominated by the conception of honour that bound society together in a series of ascending relationships at the summit of which was the sovereign liege lord. Anselm (1033-1109) used the idea to explain how all men were God's vassals and owed Him complete allegiance, yet all had rebelled and broken away from Him. All, therefore, were guilty and deserving of death. But, again, feudal mentality had recognized that if every offender was executed, society could not survive and so a system of compensation for wrongs done had been devised which could be paid either by the offender or his friends on his behalf. The Atonement, therefore, was Christ's intervention on our behalf, His payment in full of the debt we could never pay. The substitutionary theory uses all these penal and compensatory images. It conceives of man as a fallen creature, guilty of rebellion against God, condemned under the Law, under sentence of death which the Righteous Judge of all the earth will pronounce at the Grand Assize, and from which there is no reprieve, save

[1]Hastings' *Dictionary of Christ and the Gospels*, Vol. II, p. 469.

by faith in Jesus Christ. He died in man's stead, having taken his guilt upon Himself and made full restitution to God. The debt had been paid, the sinner can now be accounted righteous and God is reconciled.

8. Both Jew and Roman conceived of law as an absolute, a perfect and transcendent entity to which all men owed allegiance. It was therefore inevitable that Western Europeans should use Roman penal ideas to interpret Paul's forensic passages. The Law stood over all. God Himself, its author, was bound by it, for He could not deny Himself. It was His will, His righteousness. It was this conception of law that gave such dread significance to the Fall: the first man had disobeyed, through him and because of him all men were by nature disobedient, all were fallen, all guilty before the Law, all under the wrath of God and all unable to escape from the awful penalties of their disobedience save by the one way—faith in Christ who had died for them. By believing, the sinner was 'justified', his debts were cancelled and he was accounted as having done no wrong. Some presentations of this doctrine brought it perilously close to a piece of dubious book-keeping —a payment in by someone else that allowed the real offender to go unpunished.

9. This legal interpretation was the main form in which the death of Christ was understood from Tertullian to the late nineteenth century, but as anthropologists began to study the organization and moral behaviour of primitive peoples it was slowly realized that the law is not in fact a universal absolute but is relative to the conditions and values of each society. Law is a social device for the protection of society from the havoc that uncontrolled individual action could inflict. Respect for law is respect both for society and for the individuals comprising it. Law changes as society changes; what is good or tolerable today may have to be prohibited in the new relations of tomorrow. Law cannot be static save in a static community. Codification must be regularly revised. Modern western man is constantly making new laws for his rapidly changing society, but he does not think of law as absolute. He needs law and uses it. He believes that there are principles and values that make for the good of the community and he agrees

that those who break the law must be dealt with. Society has the right and duty to protect itself, but it is not vindictive and is very dubious about old ideas of punishment. Today the whole penal concept is under scrutiny: most civilized countries have abolished the death penalty and the infliction of torment or of pain, which was thought right and proper until the end of the eighteenth century. The value of punishment as a deterrent or as retribution or as vengeance, even as social vengeance, is questioned. The aim of punishment today is to protect society and if possible to rehabilitate the offender, reclaiming him and returning him to society as a law-abiding citizen. Thus, the idea of hell as a place of torment, a prison where offenders are tortured for ever is seen to be part of the furniture of the ancient and medieval mind. True, the preaching of hell-fire has dropped out of the repertoire of most modern evangelists, but silence merely evades the challenge it presents to the credibility of the Gospel.

10. In the nineteenth century debate, the defenders of orthodoxy maintained that if belief in the everlasting damnation of the wicked were abandoned, the mainstay of morality would be removed and nothing would restrain the wickedness of men, but, in fact, the moral climate of today makes it impossible to proclaim such a doctrine in the name of Christ. It is realized that the supporting texts were seeking to convey deep insights into the havoc sin creates on the person and the consequences evil draws upon itself, but side by side with these texts must be put others which stress the love, the mercy, and the wisdom of God. What we have in the New Testament is not a neat, consistent, and systematic theology but a rich collection of insights challenging us to think and to expose ourselves to the approach of the Holy Spirit. We are driven, not to a text for authority for our views, but to the God who speaks in and through the texts, who treats us as adults and who expects us to struggle for the truth, revealing Himself more and more to us in the process.

11. Thus the ancient concepts of law, judgement, penalty, and substitute which served admirably from New Testament times to the nineteenth century to help men to understand the mystery of Atonement do not readily fulfil that role today. On

the contrary modern society through the spread of other great Christian concepts of caring and seeking has developed a very different attitude to law and punishment. To insist, therefore, that salvation can be appropriated only by translating it into these forensic forms is to place heavy obstacles in the path of mission today, indeed, some would think, insurmountable obstacles. But it does not follow, as some radical critics suggest, that these New Testament concepts are wrong and immoral, and that the Faith is therefore incredible. To reason thus is to lose all sense of history. They were the modes, and as far as we can see, the only modes, by which God's saving action in Christ could be appropriated by ordinary men during those long centuries. The pictures of ransom, of penalty, and cancellation through the intervention of one who could and would discharge the obligation, made sense and spoke movingly to them. It places on us the duty of finding other pictures which do speak as effectively to modern man.

12. The forensic views of Atonement are essentially rigid and belong to an age in which social evolution was so slow as to be almost imperceptible. We live in a day of rapid social changes in which nothing is static. We look for change, we study trends, we plan for a different tomorrow. The theory of evolution accepted change and encouraged men to think in terms of development and progress. It also raised immense questions for traditional theology. Among the first attempts to restate the Christian position in the light of evolution were F. R. Tennant's *Origin and Propagation of Sin* (1902) and his *Sources of the Doctrine of the Fall and Original Sin* (1903). He rejected the literal Biblical story of man's immediate and separate creation as perfect, but innocent man, and accepted as irrefutable the theory that man evolved from animal ancestry. He suggested that sin arose, not through a once-and-for-all act of disobedience, but as a gradual process, emerging when the gratification of natural impulses conflicted with the restraints primitive society was compelled to impose for its own survival. Just as a child in the home moves from a non-moral state to moral awareness, and just as conscience slowly develops as parental authority teaches the child to control his impatient desires, so the human race itself acquired conscience and learned that individual freedom must be subject

to the common good of the community. Sin was the failure to choose the higher and better alternative. Deliberate refusal of the best produces a sense of guilt, the offender knows he ought not to have done what he chose to do. God has made and left man free, delegating to him the independence of a true person so that man can choose the good if he wills or he can choose evil. God therefore permits, but He does not originate evil. To prevent the possibility of evil would also prevent the possibility of goodness for both require freedom. Man, if he is to be a responsible person, must be capable of moral choice. This is what it means to be made in the image of God.

13. Fear and anger, envy and jealousy, self-preservation and self-assertion, our physical and sexual hungers are all part of our animal inheritance and in themselves are non-moral, neither good nor bad. Only in responsible man do they become the raw material of morality. Elementary passions and appetites are not in themselves sinful or degrading, but are the sources from which the will derives material for character-building. Tennant distinguishes between sin and evil; sin, he holds, is moral evil, the deliberate choice of a moral being who knows he ought to have done better. If through no fault of his own a man is ignorant of a moral requirement or standard, he is in no sense blameworthy should he fail to meet it. So, for Tennant, there can be no unintentional sin; unconscious sin is a contradiction in terms. He thus identifies sins with accountability. There can be no accountability without responsibility, and without responsibility there can be no guilt.

14. But does this attempt to get at the experience that lies behind the myth of the Fall really do justice to the facts of Christian experience? Many Christians today would not want to hold to the historicity of the Creation and Temptation stories of Genesis 1-3, and Tennant courageously attempted to face up to what a frank acceptance of the evolutionary theory entailed. But his analysis of sin falls short of the apprehension of its nature and seriousness as sensed by the deepest Christian experience. Tennant, like Pelagius, was inclined to think more about sins, specific deeds, rather than of sin as an individual and social condition or disease. He argues that if a good heathen, living up to the highest standards of his religion, became a

Christian, no one would call his previous conduct sinful, and if sin is only accountability then that is so. But sin is not primarily a moral term at all. An offender is one who has committed a crime. Sin is primarily a religious conception, it describes a broken relationship between God and man. The sense of sin develops only as a man sees himself before God. The very nature of God, His otherness, is usually apprehended as an awful holiness which makes a man feel unclean. A man becomes aware of what he really is, and feels the need for forgiveness, not only for what he has done, but for what he is. And the greater the saint, the keener this sense of sin, his longing for forgiveness and reconciliation. But where there is no sense of God the word 'sin' becomes meaningless. Perhaps one of the most significant differences between our age and previous centuries is that modern man does not conceive of himself as a sinner just because there are no God references in the grid of everyday experience. He sees other explanations for antisocial behaviour.

15. But though the new sciences found in the theory of evolution a most useful tool, it was soon seen that it had its limitations and that the buoyant optimism with which it was first hailed needed to be corrected. Evolution described certain processes, but it was going far beyond the evidence to assume that progress was inevitable. Recent advances in astronomy showed systems in process of decay as well as development and an astronomer like Eddington could ask of optimistic new theologians, 'Since when has the teaching that "heaven and earth shall pass away" become ecclesiastically unorthodox?'[1] Indeed, some scientists put forward the view that the universe was running down like a clock. Certainly, as far as this earth was concerned, it appeared certain that the world would eventually perish, either by falling into the sun, or out into the wastes of space. In any case life would cease, and the evolutionary process would end in nothingness. This theory of Entropy, as it was called, has profoundly affected the thinking of western man, who now questions the ultimate value of everything. It produces a despairing scepticism about all Utopias and earthly paradises of either the Communist or any other variety and

[1]Sir Arthur Eddington, *New Pathways of Science*.

leads to Nihilism, or to the gentle ineffectiveness of the flower people. The end of all human endeavour is the Nothingness, the Meaninglessness, of Cosmic Dissolution; there are no ultimate values, only immediate relationships, and these too will pass.

16. An attempt to answer this ultimate pessimism was made by S. A. McDowell in his *Evolution and the Need of Atonement*. He argued that though the universe is running down, every living thing is struggling against this disintegration. Life, by its very nature, cannot remain static, it must either evolve into something better or degenerate. If man has reached the limit of his physical development, his only progress must be ethical, that is, in the production of a higher type of personality. McDowell argues that the whole world development has been and is a unit and tends Godwards. By allying himself with this upward movement man becomes more divine, and each victory creates power for further progress. Sin is throwing the weight of personality against the world process. Man's ideals, which have always called to him, prove that man knows that the stream of life is making towards a goal. When he opposes this upward stream he experiences a sense of guilt. All are under this constraint and no one can cease to progress without injuring himself and the whole community. This thinking leads to the process ideas of Henri Bergson, Pierre Teilhard de Chardin, and Alfred N. Whitehead to which we shall return.

17. On this analysis sin is over-emphasized individualism, a refusal to live a full and balanced community life. Sin is turning from the path of true progress in a wrong direction which ends in a spiritual cul-de-sac, and this is where man finds himself today; the spiritual and moral struggle has ended in failure. But God is not beaten by man's rejection of the higher way. In the Incarnate One God saves man from the consequences of his sin, and sets him going again towards true freedom. Incarnation is not only God identifying Himself with man; it is also man identifying himself with God. The Incarnation and the Atonement together constitute the final vindication of perfect altruism, the total giving of the One for Others. When man, convinced by this revelation of love, dedicates his will to the cause of progress, he is enabled by Christ's death and passion

to renew his growth towards perfect personality and finally to become like God. In this way McDowell tries to relate the Christian experience of salvation to the whole cosmic process and to find purposefulness within the universe.

18. As theologians sought to adjust traditional doctrines to the new facts about the origin of man and the relativity of law there occurred in the science of psychology a revolution as epoch-making as Darwinianism. The discoveries and methods of Siegmund Freud (1856-1939) exposed the inadequacies of the older academic psychology. The radicals of the early nineteenth century, for instance, believed, like Plato, that if only man had more knowledge, he would naturally choose the right and become a more dignified and glorious being. Above all, if he knew himself, he would never demean himself by foolish and inconsiderate action. Freud's methods of psychological investigation led to a complete revaluation of man, revealing a new ocean of being beneath the threshold of the consciousness, a submarine world of instinct and desire, of hates and loves, of suppression and conflict. To Freud, religion was illusion, and belief in God a derivation from the Oedipus complex. 'Perhaps the sense of guilt of mankind as a whole, which is the ultimate source of religion and morality, was acquired in the beginnings of history through the Oedipus complex.' If the idea of God is the projection of an unconscious desire for a Father-figure, if prayer is a form of autosuggestion, if worship is a mild form (usually) of mass hysteria, then religion is just so much useless, perhaps dangerous, mental junk that a wise man will discard as quickly as possible. Moreover, if the techniques of the evangelist can be shown to be an exploitation of the art of mental assault, a form of brainwashing calculated to induce certain emotional states and responses, then religion and all its works becomes suspect.

19. Freud's teaching came like a new religion to a world in revolt against the grey legalism of Protestant ethics, commonly called Victorianism in this country. His exposure of the mechanisms of sex brought immense relief to both the sex-obsessed and the sex-starved. For centuries Christian theology had been afraid of sex, regarding it as something shameful and the real root of all sin. Because in the Myth of the Fall the

primal pair after their sin knew themselves to be naked and were embarrassed by the discovery it was assumed that the Fall itself was in some way a sexual act. In some Catholic circles celibacy and virginity were held to be most pleasing to God, while marriage was justified as preserving men from worse excesses. Tertullian, Ambrose, Augustine and many other theologians tried to bind this restless evil in the flesh, which warred incessantly against the spirit. All sex relations outside marriage were sternly forbidden, but human nature is not easily tamed, and periods of religious domination when attempts were made to restrain sexuality were invariably followed by periods of licence. Just as the Restoration with all its bawdy gaiety followed the Puritan domination, so today our permissive society is in strong reaction to nineteenth-century puritanism. Freudian psychology came just as the tide was turning and gave to the ordinary man what appeared to be a sound scientific justification for his rejection of conventional Christian morality. We can never return to the old devaluation of sex; it must be recognized for what it is, be freely and frankly discussed in the new society created by the emancipation of women. Unfortunately the identification of the Church with fear of sex has given the impression that Christian conventions are old-fashioned, ignorant, and unhealthy. But the fact remains we do not think of will, desire, intention, motive and instinct as did the theologians of previous ages, nor can we ever again use the older definitions of guilt, anxiety, shame and forgiveness. We turn for our pictures from the courtroom of justice to the consulting room of the psychiatrist.

20. Our approach today is not to condemn a man immediately because he has done something wrong, but to ask why he did it, what were the pressures both inside himself and in society around him that turned him in that direction. Our aim is to resolve his conflict, to help him to live with himself, to become more integrated. We do not think of salvation as a kind of transaction between Jesus and God which changes God's attitude to men; we think of salvation as a process which, because it reconciles a man to God, reconciles a man to himself and to the world around him; it takes away the enmity, it breaks down dividing walls, it liberates us from our inturned

self-absorption and defeatism and sets us free to enjoy and build community. The weakness of traditional evangelical theology is that it tended to externalize salvation, reducing it to some incomprehensible payment of debts. The penal theories are concerned with punishment at the very point where modern man senses the need for help. The substitutionary theories again are in danger of externalizing sin, treating it almost like a physical entity which Jesus is said to have carried away when He stood in our place. Such metaphors are alien to the modern mind, and yet they contain elements of truth which the modern man needs to know. Freudian ideas swiftly percolated through Western society and were popularized by the psychological novel and film, but the Church scarcely appreciated the changing climate of thought. Indeed few of its leaders were capable of dealing with it for they lacked psychiatric training. They retreated further into their defensive circle, while western, secular man concluded that the new psychology had undermined and exploded the claims to the validity of religious experience.

CHAPTER ELEVEN

The Liberal Response

THE moral criticism of traditional salvation theology was only one example of the general questioning which has extended to every doctrine of the Christian faith. All through the nineteenth century a great line of Christian scholars tried to meet that challenge. Because they accepted the new approach to the Bible and claimed the liberty to defend the faith in terms which they hoped would be intelligible to modern man they have been called 'liberal' theologians. It has recently been fashionable to speak disparagingly of their efforts, yet, as the rejection of the faith in the West accelerates, we are beginning to see that these men were facing the real questions and were more aware of the true character of the secular revolution than were the orthodox churchmen of their day and some of their modern critics. They may not have discovered the answers but they probed the new concepts, and if we are to arrive at a sound theology of mission today, we cannot afford to disregard their contribution. They knew the world was moving steadily away from institutional religion and that traditional evangelicalism had little understanding of the pressures of the new age. Their aim was to bridge what is now called 'the credibility gap' and so to present Christ that modern men could believe in Him.

2. The first, and in many ways, the greatest of these thinkers was F. D. E. Schleiermacher (1768-1834) whose life covered the tumultuous period of the French Revolution, the Napoleonic wars and the Years of Reaction. As a boy he was reared in the fervent Moravian tradition; later he responded to the warmth of the Romantic Movement, and he studied the philosophies of Spinoza, Leibniz, and Kant. In Prussia he had seen the union of the Lutheran and Reformed Churches, result-

ing in the formation of a rigid institutional State Church. He had witnessed the rejection of Christianity by its educated detractors who declared that religion was suitable only for ignorant peasants and workers. Schleiermacher contended that such misunderstanding was due to the attempt to base religion upon rational proof of the existence of God and so to leave out its most essential element. Religion, he said, derives, not from reasoning, but from dependence upon the Infinite. This feeling and the experience it generates precedes all creeds and definitions—they are attempts to explain the experience. By feeling he did not mean mere emotionalism but the intuitive contact with and apprehension of reality. All religions, Schleiermacher claims, derive from the recognition that God is grasped only when we feel our utter dependence upon Him for our existence. What makes Christianity the greatest of all religions is that in the perfect God-consciousness of Jesus, and in His sacrificial life and death, this feeling of complete dependence received its highest expression. Sin is the repression and denial of our utter dependence on God: it is deficient God-consciousness. Schleiermacher's debt to Pietism is great; his insistence on the validity of religious experience was a much-needed corrective to the rationalism of the Enlightenment. It also speaks a cogent word to the quasi-rationalism of some recent radical theology.

3. Schleiermacher was trying to rescue Jesus from imprisonment within a formal theological system which turned Him into an abstract magical figure through whom salvation could be obtained by a kind of mental acrobatics called 'faith'. Salvation is the revelation and appropriation of man's true relationship to God. He tried to make Christian experience intelligible, not in the legalities of ransom paid, but in joyful acceptance of complete dependence upon the life of God. Another and somewhat different attempt to explain what Jesus did was made by Albrecht Ritschl (1822-89) who was strongly influenced by the new Biblical criticism. He declared that the God of Jesus and of faith has nothing to do with metaphysical ideas of a First Cause or of Absolute Being. In rejecting Hegelianism he fell back on Kant's contention that the Ultimate Mystery of Being can never be known, but he added the important rider

that it could and did reveal itself in action. God in His ultimate nature cannot be comprehended by men, but He can make Himself known to men and He does reveal Himself in history. The difference therefore between science and religion is that the task of science is to establish facts; but religion has to do with judgement on facts—it deals with questions of values and purpose and measures them by the way in which they either help or harm humanity. Thus Jesus is a historic fact, but He is much more. When we believe in Him, we make a value judgement; we approve His way of life. By believing we encounter Jesus in an experience of pardon and reconciliation. Through this common experience of faith Jesus establishes the community of believers to whom He has entrusted His Gospel. It was for the Holy Community, the Church, that He died and in its fold the believer is 'justified'. Justification is not an individualistic qualification: it is a new social relationship within the redeemed community, for God's purpose is to bring all men into the Kingdom through the Church in a salvation which embraces the entire social and cosmic order. At the heart of the salvation experience is encounter with the living Christ. To bring men to Him is the permanent commission of the Church.

4. Ritschl objected to both metaphysical theology and to mysticism because neither was firmly fastened to the historic facts of the life, death, and resurrection of Jesus nor did they drive men to the moral effort needed to build the Redeemed Community. Christianity is first and foremost encounter with the Jesus of history, who is still met in the act of Faith. The same conviction was magnificently expounded in the works of Adolf Harnack (1851-1930), another great figure in this chain of German liberal theologians. He too believed that at the heart of the Gospel lies the historic Jesus, but he held that the Lord's original teaching had been overlaid by later accretions. In their efforts to explain the Gospel to the Greek world, the first missionaries had poured it into the thought-forms of Greek philosophy and religion. Harnack, who had an unrivalled knowledge of early Church history, further suggested that in the Western provinces the local churches began to organize themselves into a highly centralized institutional

Church with its hierarchy, laws and discipline. These two movements, the Grecianization of the Gospel and the institutionalization of the Church, coalesced to produced the Christianity of the Empire which imprisoned the original living faith in formal creeds, which smothered the dynamic Jesus under the speculations of Christology and theories of Atonement, and which shackled the original free Christian communities within the authoritarian and monolithic structures of the Church. Harnack, like Ritschl, believed that the Reformation which set out to set faith free, was only partially successful. Protestantism had soon built its own prison walls around Jesus. In his *What is Christianity?* (1899) he maintained that the original teaching of Jesus, which we must recover if faith is to survive, consisted of the proclamation of the Kingdom of God, the revelation of the Fatherhood of God, the infinite value of every man, and the affirmation of the supremacy of the way of love.

5. In his study of the 'pure' religion of Jesus, Harnack made a distinction between what he regarded as the original contribution of Jesus, namely, the realization that the Kingdom of God is already here (for it is the eternal rule of God in every obedient heart), and the mistaken belief which Jesus shared with His contemporaries that the Kingdom would arrive dramatically in blazing theophany at the end of the age. Thus Harnack dared to assert that in some things Jesus could be and was indeed mistaken, a view which orthodoxy could not accept, for it seemed to deny the divinity of the Lord. How could He be divine if He was not infallible, if He did not know everything? If He did not speak the truth in all things, how can we rely on anything that He said? Harnack's answer was that the truth must always be sifted out, there never is an absolute authoritarian statement of eternal truth. He argued that the claims of the Church to be a divine and infallible institution were seriously misleading for it was primarily a free association of believers. It had lost both the flexibility of the original federal structure and its freedom of thought.

6. The liberal theologians believed they were carrying forward the work of the Reformers. The sixteenth-century 'Protest' had been directed against the distortions and additions

which had accumulated in medieval Christianity. The liberal aim was to recover the original Gospel and the simplicities of the New Testament Church. The Reformers appealed to the primacy and authority of Scripture by which they claimed all later tradition and development must be measured. But in their new evaluation of the Bible they had fallen into the trap of substituting an infallible Book for an infallible Church. The nineteenth-century liberals tried to avoid this snare and to seek the original Gospel within the Book. They had to distinguish between the essential and the secondary elements of the Gospel. Throughout the nineteenth century Protestant theologians insisted that however else we think of God, He is the Father who loves all He has made and to whom all men can turn, sure of a welcome, and that such a loving relationship sets a man free to love all other men, his brothers in the all-encompassing family of God.

7. These new emphases on the Jesus of history were susceptible of over-statement and some presentations like those of the French Protestant Jean Reville (1854-1908) come very near to Unitarianism. He saw Jesus as the greatest of all prophets whose death was an act of supreme self-sacrifice which confirmed the truth of His teaching. The Church was merely the organization through which the moral idealism created by contemplation of Jesus was released into the service of the community, a conclusion that is repeated in some radical thinking today.

8. Church life in Britain remained largely unaffected by German and French liberal theology. Those who preached and taught it were regarded as dangerous innovators by the traditional majority. But at the beginning of the twentieth century the religious calm of these islands was violently agitated by the appearance of the 'New Theology' of R. J. Campbell (1867-1956) who popularized the new thinking in his City Temple sermons and in his book *The New Theology*. Its effect can be estimated from the fact that so acute an observer as Henry Carter could suggest that it may have contributed in no small measure to the distinct change in the religious climate about 1906-7 when church attendance in the major Free Churches began to show a significant fall.[1] Though later

[1] *Op. cit.* Membership returns are given for the years 1901-1911.

Campbell withdrew his work because of the criticism it received, it was nevertheless, as A. R. Vidler points out, a valiant effort to face squarely the ultimate questions of liberalism, questions which though raised by the nineteenth-century liberals, had not been fully answered. Campbell asked himself, 'What is the purpose of the Universe?', 'Why does it exist at all?' He was driven back to the idea of progress, he saw in the concept of evolution, a hope of better things. He was one of the Christian leaders whose social conscience had been awakened by the appalling conditions of the slums and of raw industrial society. He saw in the struggle for social justice the search for the Kingdom of God. He believed that man's supreme weapon was love and that God was to be found only as we shared in the struggle. But Campbell's language was often unguarded and he left himself open to attack. It was a pity for, as Vidler says, he understood the challenge of the age more adequately than his critics and was nearer to the real issues than were the guardians of orthodoxy.

9. Liberal theologians of all shades of opinion were convinced that the Church with its creeds and theological doctrines had misunderstood, distorted, or strayed from the original simple Gospel of the Jesus of history, and they tried to separate out the fresh and original thought of Jesus from the religious and cultural preconceptions which He shared with His age. All agreed that among those assumptions were the eschatological hopes of Israel, but most writers thought this element scarcely influenced the basic teaching of Jesus. Albert Schweitzer (1875-1965) contradicted this view and declared that the Jesus of history firmly believed that the Day of the Lord would come in His lifetime. Only when it failed to materialize did Jesus rethink His role and saw Himself as the sacrificial victim whose death would precipitate the coming of the Kingdom in power and glory. Schweitzer was not only a brilliant theologian but an equally brilliant organist. He also qualified as a medical missionary and went to work in Lambaréné in an act of sustained witness as if determined to show the world that liberal theology had as much dynamic in it for mission as the evangelicalism which had revived the sense of world mission in Protestantism. The example was needed, for traditionalists

often spoke caustically about the lack of evangelical concern in liberalism. But the liberal theologians with their emphasis upon the ethical content of the Gospel were very sensitive to the social implications of Christ's teaching, to the cry for social justice, for education and for the abolition of poverty, disease, and slums. They supplied the ideas behind the Christian struggle for better conditions for the under-privileged. They were largely responsible for the proclamation of the Social Gospel in America and for its counterpart in Britain. They were deeply concerned with the application of the Gospel to society as a whole and were suspicious of evangelicalism on the grounds that it drew men out of the social struggle, rather than inspiring them to devote themselves to the cause of social reform.

10. The weakness of later liberalism was its facile and superficial optimism, its naïve belief in the essential common sense and goodness of human nature, and its conviction that men could create the earthly paradise by adopting the ethics of Jesus, the simple Gospel of love that they had distilled from the New Testament records. This optimism, which was so characteristic of the opening years of the twentieth century, was rudely shattered by the outbreak of the First World War. A black horror gripped Europe as the new barbarism inflicted appalling slaughter and suffering. A Swiss pastor, Karl Barth (1886-1969), gazed in shocked agony asking himself what the Gospel had to say to a civilized world gone insane, seared with frightful evil. He was driven back to the Bible, not as a liberal seeking a Jesus of history who gently proclaimed the brotherhood of man, but as a man listening to the mighty voice of God speaking in judgement on the proud and evil world of men and on the Church which had dared to put human speculations into the place of God. Barth turned to the great figures of Church history, to men like Augustine, Luther, and Calvin who lived in ages of collapse and confusion, and who saw the true nature of God revealed in all his sovereign greatness in the pages of Scripture. He recalled that during the nineteenth century the same note had been sounded by the despised, ignored, and well-nigh forgotten Existentialists and he drew deeply from their experiences of spiritual agony.

11. Of these the most influential was Søren Kierkegaard (1813-55) whose work was scarcely known outside Scandinavia until the turn of the century; yet this neglected genius was the first to recognize the underlying causes of the restlessness so characteristic of our age. Like Nietzsche and Kafka he was super-sensitive and suffered dreadfully from depression, due in his case in no small measure to the guilt-laden atmosphere of his home. He knew that his own complex nature was incurably unhappy and twisted and perhaps this was why he severed his engagement, but these psychological tensions helped him to identify the real pressures in western society. He swept aside as worthless and misleading the philosophy of Hegel because, as understood in Denmark, it reduced reality to a series of abstractions remote from the harsh actualities of existence. Kierkegaard retained only one Hegelian concept—that of the alienation of man. He agreed that man was lost and lonely in a universe that ought to be his home, but was in fact a wilderness. Life was meant to be great and noble but had become a round of petty trivialities; our boasted liberty was a self-deception obscuring the real fact that we were all slaves to stupid conventions and all under bondage to sin. Because of our superficial view of the freedom of the will in which we imagined man was master of his destiny, we had lost the tragic dimension of existence, the discernment of man's pathetic weakness and ingrained sinfulness which makes him torture and destroy himself. True Christianity, he argued, fully recognizes human responsibility but it combines it with the solidarity of humanity in the common experience of sin and salvation. The Existentialist insists that all valid theology must arise from personal experience in a here-and-now, it must relate to life as it is, not try to fit human beings into some formal theological system created by abstractions and generalizations. Kierkegaard demanded that religion should speak a revealing and healing word to sin-sick man as he is, not to man in the abstract or as the theologians think he ought to be.

12. Kierkegaard thought of original sin as a kind of infectious disease which affected all men and the cure was to find the eternal in the here-and-now, to recognize God in the present moment. This can be achieved only through a deeper

knowledge of oneself, the realization that while a man cannot change his past, he can incorporate it into his present being in a continual act of repentance and self-acceptance. Such self-acceptance is not self-complacency, it involves the experience of forgiveness. Because God has accepted us, we are able to accept ourselves. Forgiveness requires an inner honesty and openness and a willingness to be dependent on God, to receive acceptance. The moral struggle is self-defeating and an obstacle to faith which becomes effective when a man in his own experience comes face to face with God. Ethics, by teaching us what we ought to be and do, only makes us aware of our failures, whereas what we need is new life, a rebirth. In his great work *Fear and Trembling*, Kierkegaard studies the story of Abraham's offering of Isaac. Here morality and faith conflict. Is Abraham to obey God and murder his son? Only because he is willing to trust God beyond the evidence of the conflict, is the conflict solved for him by God. In this act he leaps beyond the finite into the infinite, beyond the temporal into the eternal. He returns to the world apparently the same man as before, but he is utterly different for he has endured the tragedy of the world, shared its sorrow and mystery, and knows himself to be at one with all the other common things of life, both great and small. He is the Knight of God, hidden behind the pedestrian figure of the ordinary man that everyone takes for granted. Shabby, genial, and unnoticed, he is the salt of the earth, the true servant and son of the Most High. He goes his quiet unassuming way, bearing the sin of the world and transforming it by his obedience.

13. For Kierkegaard man stood at the focal point of inner torment confronted by insoluble paradoxes, and relief could come only by the leap of faith created by the eternal spectacle of One who had himself stood in that position of ultimate tragedy, betrayal, desolation, and dereliction. But whereas Kierkegaard found his release in living faith in the Crucified, F. W. Nietzsche (1844-1900), starting from much the same premises, took a very different direction. He too agreed that man's predicament is his inability to make sense out of life. He spurned Hegel's idea of God as indefinable Ultimate Being, declaring that God is unthinkable, unimaginable, unplaceable.

The secular mind which has to think and work in a world of law and order cannot conceive of God. We can see men and men's needs, but our modern way of observing leaves no place where God fits in. Hence his famous cry, 'God is dead!' He added, 'We have killed him, you and I. We are his murderers.' Since, then, God does not exist in this kind of world, we must save ourselves and that calls for a different type of man, a man with will and courage to do what has to be done, a superman. The will to power, he claimed, must manifest itself, not in the mob, but in the great man, the supreme leader of mankind ruthlessly pursuing the goal he sets himself regardless of all standards of good or evil. Nietzsche maintained that the main obstacle to such pitiless perfection is Christianity with its ethic of humility and caring, which preserves degenerates and weaklings. These ideas were to find dreadful expression in the Fascist and Nazi movements, both of which sought to build their empires on strength and ruthless determination, overriding any moral considerations in the conviction that the supermen would create the super-race and that the rest of mankind existed only as a servile caste to tend the needs of the *Herrenvolk*. Yet it is from this crazy philosophy which can exist only by denying the Way of Christ and which begins by asserting that God can no longer exist in the modern world, that the radical 'God is dead' theology collected its battle-cry.

14. The Existentialists were trying to understand secular man and his predicament; to Kierkegaard it was tragic; to F. M. Dostoievski (1821-81) it was demonic, a world in which man no matter how he tried, could never find God. Men cannot even co-operate with God. Neither reason, will, nor moral effort will take man to God, for man lies helpless in the disease of sin. Salvation comes as a free gift of God which reaches man when he has reached the limits of his effort and knows he cannot save himself. What comes from God is an infinite compassion for us, and in his great novels Dostoievski's heroes are those who feel and share this compassion. He believed that the Church in institutionalizing itself had distorted the Gospel. The West, he said, was losing Christ and that was why it was disintegrating. Nowadays Christ has to compete with science and the machine and with research data, and

these, as Miller says, are powerful and precise, against Christ's weakness, suffering, and death.[1] Dostoievski and Kierkegaard were trying to show that Christ alone was near to the common man in his embarrassments and personal tragedy and they wanted to point to Jesus when the Church and the theologians were using language and ideas which put Him out of the reach of the common man.

15. Such atheism and doubt shocks and disturbs those who have never allowed themselves to face the challenge of secular society. What they have to grasp is that at its best atheism is a scathing criticism of indequate presentations of our faith. The Church is itself responsible for much of this rejection of faith because we have tried to domesticate God and to fit Him neatly into our schemes. As Samuel H. Miller[2] has said, if God is dead, we killed him, we tried to teach Him our rules, to work in the ways we approved. We did not distinguish between God and our idea of the Church. We identified Him with our morals, our feelings, our beliefs, and we are only just discovering that God is not in them any more, though we go on acting as if He were, behaviour which Kierkegaard called 'twaddle in the Holy of Holies'. We are all guilty of this. The Reformers had moved out loads of superstition and false religiosity, but we have filled the house of faith with more rubbish—our false abstractions, our comforting platitudes and generalities and God is no longer in them; they are empty words, dead symbols, meaningless forms. Pietists who longed for inward knowledge of God and who yearned for deep personal communion have become seekers after sensation who engage in the self manipulation of their emotions. Liberals who sought for a Gospel which could commend itself to secular man and which would stand up to all the attacks of its enemies, ended with a set of harmless platitudes. The Traditionalists with their formal scheme of salvation are left with their questionable formulae. In this sense it is true that God has been killed by His friends. If the idea of God is unintelligible today Christians bear considerable responsibility.

16. The bankruptcy of current theology drove Barth, like a

[1]Samuel H. Miller, *The Dilemma of Modern Belief* (Hodder and Stoughton, 1964).
[2]*Op. cit.*

second Calvin, to a new appreciation of the God of the Bible. He drew deeply on the Reformers' conviction that man is corrupt and quite incapable of thinking straight about God. He rejected liberalism and asserted that all human reason, effort, art, and science are worthless and cannot provide a road to God. Though at one time Barth had hoped that the labour movements of Europe would make war impossible, he now realized that man could not control his demonic nature. The Existentialists had taught him that humanity is imprisoned in its own dark sinfulness. This is also what the Bible says. The Liberals had concluded that the Bible was man's thought about God, but Barth insisted that it was God's thought about man. It is the Word of God. Man by reasoning cannot find God, but in the Bible God speaks and reveals Himself. He speaks in judgement on man's pride and self-will, but this Word which speaks so emphatically in Jesus can be heard only by those who know they are lost and are prepared to cast their pride away. Barth wrote from passionate conviction, thundering out like a prophet of the Old Dispensation that the judgement of the Word hangs over the world and the Church. God, the Creator, is still Absolute Lord and Judge who offers in love the one way of reconciliation in Christ, the Word become flesh. Christ is the living centre of Barth's theology. By faith and by faith alone can the repentant sinner receive the gift of salvation. Only so can his will, perverted by the Fall, be restored and his nature cleansed. Only so can the creature be reconciled to the wholly Other, the transcendent Creator God.

17. Barth's insistence on the Word of God seems to be a full return to Reformation orthodoxy and that is why his system has been called 'neo-orthodoxy'. At times it sounds very much as if he were preaching a thoroughgoing fundamentalism, for here is the doctrine of the Fall, the depravity of man, and the traditional concept of Atonement, all resting on the assertion that the Bible is the Word of God, infallible and beyond all question. Yet Barth and his followers were in no way opposed to Biblical criticism; what he did was to draw a clear distinction between the Bible as a piece of literature to be studied critically like any other ancient manuscript, and the Bible as the Word of God, proclaiming its message by the power of the Holy Spirit.

The two approaches are quite independent; for the first approach one needs the requisite scholarship, but for the second one needs humility and faith. To the humble believer the Bible is the quickening Word of God which speaks, arrests, convicts and becomes a vehicle of saving grace. On this foundation Barth developed his vast dogmatic theology, a dialectical system of paradoxes. His emphasis inspired a generation of Christian preachers, especially among those of the Reformed tradition; but the paradoxes were too contradictory and it was not long before some of the inconsistencies were challenged. Indeed, it may be that Barth's Christ-positivism paved the way for the Death of God theology.

18. Emil Brunner (*b*.1889) was among the first to note the difficulties. He too had rejected the liberal emphasis on the immanence of God and the ideas of Christian mysticism, but he very much questioned Barth's return to Reformation theology based on the Adam stories. He asked how we could retain the theology if we did not accept the historicity of the Fall. He accused Barth of evading this issue. He saw that the whole Miltonic picture of the 'First Man' had been finally and absolutely destroyed for us today. The evidence of natural science and palaeontology on the origins of the human race has made the ecclesiastical doctrine untenable.[1] Brunner offers another explanation. Man, he says, is a duality; there is a contradiction between true man, which is man as God has determined he will be, and actual man; what we are now is a man de-natured by sin, a poor relic of the original God-given nature. By sinning man has lost himself and become unnatural and inhuman. Sin is dehumanization; the Devil is not a person but the inhuman spirit. 'When we talk about the origin of man we are not speaking of a certain man called Adam who lived so many thousand years ago, but of myself and yourself and of everyone else in the world.' According to Brunner wherever human beings are found there too will be found both the Divine Origin of Man and his Fall, the image of God and its destruction. He describes this inner conflict as man in contradiction. Nor does Brunner share Barth's doctrine of election and the limitation of grace. He declares that even

[1]See Emil Brunner, *Man in Revolt*, Eng. trans., 1939.

the unbeliever is still related to God, and is responsible, in the sense that he can still respond to God.

19. Barthian theology was welcomed by many Christians of the West who were wearied of the lack of drive and authority so characteristic of amiable liberalism. Stern times called for stern doctrine and Barth's trumpet call back to the realities of man's weakness and God's greatness spoke, many felt, to the need of the hour. But, as Brunner had shown, the cost was high; it meant evading the real issue which the great nineteenth-century liberals tried to face—namely where, in fact, does the authority of the Bible lie. The Barthian paradox that it was both a human literary compilation and the Divine Revelation, while it contained a startling truth, needed to be explored, and when this was attempted it fell apart. The Barthians, as Vidler perceived, thought they could get inside the minds of the Biblical authors and could expound exactly what the revelation meant not only for the original writers, but for the present age, since the Word was God's Word to all men of all times. This assumed that there was in fact one consistent Biblical world-view which any competent preacher should be able to elucidate and then show its implications for today. But most Christians first feel the challenge of their own time and then turn to Scripture for some Word of God on the issue. The Biblical theology movement found itself using a highly specialized terminology to convey the ideas of the alleged Bible world-view, and this esoteric language widened rather than narrowed the gulf between the preacher and the people he wanted to reach. Meanwhile, the questions with which nineteenth-century liberalism had wrestled had returned in increasing complexity and severity, for the processes of secularization were accelerating.

20. Both the Biblical theologians and the traditionalists began to realize that though they were sure that they had a Gospel to proclaim, fewer people in the West were listening to them. On the contrary tens of thousands were moving out of the Churches, 'voting with their feet'. Churchmen asked themselves, Why? and concluded that there was a breakdown of communication. The chief question was, 'How do we get our message across?', 'How do we use the mass media of today—

radio and television, the drama and film, to present the great Christian truths?' It was assumed that the Church knew precisely what those truths were. There may be different accents and emphases, but the main elements of the traditional Scheme of Creation and Salvation were that man was made for God, man was a fallen creature, God redeemed him by faith in Christ into the Kingdom which is now and which is to come in complete fullness. Strenuous efforts were made to communicate this Gospel. Methodism, for instance, inaugurated the 'Christian Commando Campaigns' which sent teams of ministers and layfolk into factories and mills, canteens and market places to 'offer Christ'.[1] These efforts were often ecumenical and those who joined the teams returned with deeper conviction. Christian witness in the factories continued and laid the foundation of what is now industrial mission with its many full-time and part-time Chaplains. But the impact on the nation was negligible, the drift from faith continued, the Gospel somehow did not strike fire in many hearts. The Commandos sadly concluded that they did not know how to communicate effectively. A puzzled Church began to lose confidence in itself and in the efficacy of its message.

[1]See Colin A. Roberts, *The Christian Commando Campaigns* (Epworth Press, 1945).

CHAPTER TWELVE

The Radical Revolt

THE theological scene quickly changed as Christian scholars began to grapple directly with the problem of the secular rejection of religion. Just as a century ago *Essays and Reviews* had aroused English theologians to the burning issues of the day, so *Soundings* (1962),[1] a collection of essays by a group of Cambridge scholars, indicated the concerns where much more research was needed if Christianity was to become meaningful to many intelligent people who remained quite unconvinced by traditional presentations of the faith. This was followed in 1963 by *Objections to Christian Belief*,[2] a frank examination of the difficulties such people feel. In the same year came *Honest to God*[3] the little explosive book by John Robinson, then Bishop of Woolwich, which popularized the new approach, disclosing the doubts which surround belief, itemizing the main obstacles to faith, and pleading for honesty in admitting our reservations. This work triggered off a widespread and lively debate which still continues inside and outside the Church, especially among those intelligent laymen who were relieved to learn that theology was beginning to tackle the questions that had puzzled them for a long time. Dr Robinson did not originate this new thinking; he brought it together brilliantly and stated it in a way that opened up the main issues for ordinary people without specialist training.

2. Biblical criticism had advanced through Form Criticism to the drastic reappraisal of Rudolf Bultmann (*b.*1884) who, going back to some of the ideas of Strauss, maintained that the

[1] *Soundings*, ed. A. R. Vidler (C.U.P., 1962).

[2] *Objections to Christian Belief*, ed. A. R. Vidler and J. B. Lippencott (Constable, 1963).

[3] John Robinson, *Honest to God* (S.C.M., 1963).

language of the Bible was essentially mythological. Not only did the writers share the preconceptions of their day, which were saturated with myth, they were incapable of describing any historic event in any other form as this was the only way known to them of expressing truth. Thus they accepted the three-tier system of the universe and thought of God as 'up there in heaven' with angels and attendant host, with earth the home of men and of some demons, and with hell the domain of Satan, his fiends and the damned. The task of New Testament study according to Bultmann is to recover the actual historic events and their true significance by the process of demythologizing, i.e. taking the myth out of the narrative. Such a process involves the elimination of all miracle, divine intervention, and every intrusion of the supernatural. The Resurrection stories, especially the allusions to the empty tomb, are typical myths, not historic events, but attempts to express the ultimate, death-destroying significance of the person of Jesus.[1] As a result of such sifting, we are left, says Bultmann, with the compelling person of Jesus, who demanded and still demands from every man a decision as to whether what He lived and died for is not the disclosure of life's ultimate mystery. What His disciples saw could only be expressed in their thought forms as the 'Son' *sent* by the God-up-there-in-heaven with a message of salvation. The actual life of Jesus was thus translated into the supernatural saving action of God.

3. Thus Bultmann reduces the Bible concept of mission to myth. Fritz Buri carried the argument to its logical conclusion—the very idea of God's saving action is a poetic construction which does not fit into ordinary human experience; even the idea that God speaks or sends is a myth, the attribution of a human activity to God. Thus all we have left is the fact that we exist and we can, if we choose, understand our existence as a gift from God. But if the demythologizing of the Bible requires the surrender of God sending His message of reconciliation, it is very difficult to understand how Bultmann, himself an ardent Barthian, can still cling to the concept that the Bible remains the Word of God. The paradox seems unsupportable, for how

[1]See *Kerygma and Myth*, ed. H. W. Bortsch, Vol. I, 1953, Vol. II, 1962, also Rudolph Bultmann, *Jesus Christ and Mythology* (S.C.M., 1960).

can it be right to demythologize the Bible to the extinction of the very concept of a God who speaks and still retain the dogma that the Bible is His Word? For if God does not speak, there is surely no Word.

4. Existentialism, both in its Christian and atheistic forms has had a salutary effect on the thought of Europe, especially in the imaginative fields of drama and poetry, where its characteristic mood of tense sensitivity to the pain, sadness, and frustrations of life has received brilliant expression. Barth's response to this disclosure of the human predicament was too contradictory to sustain the weight he put upon it and his disparagement of reason too drastic. A new approach had to be attempted and this was undertaken by Paul Tillich (1886-1965). He agreed that man cannot reach God by thought, but in strong disagreement with Barth he saw that man could have no contact at all unless he had some ideas about God and that these ideas arise when man contemplates the ultimate questions of the meaning and goal of life. It is because man knows he is finite and must die, and that his world is finite, that he begins to think of infinity, of that which makes the finite universe possible. Thus there is a place, and a necessary place, for 'natural' theology. Tillich believed that when we do face the really ultimate questions we encounter the ground or power of being and this is God. But this is all we can say about God, for any other language is symbolic. Symbols are useful but inadequate in themselves to do more than point in a direction; they all fall short of the reality to which they point. Thus to speak of God as personal, loving, and just is useful and right, but these words do not define God, they are pictures of aspects of Him and He himself transcends them all.

5. *Honest to God* begins with a protest against the idea of God-up-there, supported though it is by so much New Testament language. Then Dr Robinson describes the relief he experienced when he read Tillich's sermon on 'The Depth of Existence'[1] in which Tillich says that the infinite and inexhaustible depth and ground of all being is God. He urges us to think of the depth of life, our ultimate concerns, the things we take seriously. This dimension of depth, which is apparent

[1]Paul Tillich, *The Shaking of the Foundations* (Pelican, 1962).

once we get beyond the superficialities, is what the word 'God' is about. It is understandable that such an emphasis must bring relief to those whose idea of God has been thwarted and distorted by spatial images of a distant heaven. But what Tillich offers is mainly a change of direction. Depth is just as much a spatial image as height. Because the God-up-there has disappeared in the emptiness of outer space, he suggests that He is to be found by turning inwards. 'Depth' is a portmanteau word, with overtones of mystery and meaning that 'height' once carried for the people of the ancient world. It is also associated with a search for meanings in such phrases as 'research in depth', 'depth psychology'. Tillich suggested that the idea of God becomes intelligible when we contemplate the mystery of existence and probe for answers about its possible meaning and purpose. If we feel it has significance then that which imparts that purpose is God.

6. Perhaps no Christian leader of our times has had more effect upon the younger ministers and laymen than Dietrich Bonhoeffer (1906-1945), for he raises the questions which are most acute for them and which directly challenge the traditional evangelical presentation of the Gospel. In his *Letters and Papers from Prison*[1] he maintains that secular man no longer feels he needs God—he has no sense of sin and therefore has no need of salvation. He simply does not feel, as the Church has always supposed he must, a need for a God to whom he can give himself, and so the Church can no longer make its appeal to men on the basis of the experience of salvation, because modern man is incapable of such experience. Bonhoeffer suggests that we have moved into a new phase of Christianity in which God is calling us to live as men who do not need the salvation experience which in any case could be experienced only by a few. He argues that just as Paul freed Christianity from its imprisonment within Judaism, so today it must be liberated from the outworn formulations of orthodoxy. He criticizes Bultmann for not following his own process to its conclusion. Bonhoeffer claims that you cannot separate God from mythological conceptions like miracles and the ascension; you have to demythologize God as well and proclaim Him in a non-religious sense.

[1]Dietrich Bonhoeffer, *Letters and Papers from Prison*, ed. E. Bethage (1953).

7. Bonhoeffer argues that the process of secularization which began in the thirteenth century has led to the establishment of man's autonomy in field after field of knowledge and responsibility. The idea of God is not needed as a working hypothesis in science, art or ethics. But during the last century this autonomy is extending even to religion itself. God is being more and more edged out of life. The world has come of age and now, for better or worse, men must live without the tutelage of God. 'God is teaching us that we must live as men who can get along very well without him.' Bonhoeffer claimed that the only sphere in which religion will operate would be in the private world of those unhappy individuals who feel, or can be induced to feel, a need for the protecting or saving act of a god. This, he says, is not the Gospel, for the Gospel points not to a Saviour God, who comes down from heaven to rescue believers, but to a powerless and suffering God who conquers this world by his weakness. Religious man wants a god of power to whom he can turn for help, but modern man does not need such a god for we have to learn to save ourselves, and that is done by suffering. Therefore the true god, not the god of religion, is the God who allows Himself to be edged out of the universe.

8. Radicals describe secular man's insistence that meaning must be found within and not outside the universe as the loss of transcendence. Just as the idea of a God beyond the skies is now incredible, so even the idea of a God who fills the gaps in knowledge has become inconceivable. We shall no more find God on the new frontiers of our knowledge than in what we have already discovered. We do not need the idea of God as an element in research or as an explanation of what we find. But this realization that God cannot be now used as merely a name for the undiscovered does not mean that God does not exist at all. We have allowed ourselves to be tricked by our 'transcendental theology' which by using spatial images has removed Him from His universe. He must be found, not outside, not in the imagined supernatural of magic, but within the experienced universe. He is the Ground of all Being. As Bonhoeffer says, we must conceive of Him as 'the Beyond in the midst'.

9. Bonhoeffer, and here he is followed by Tillich, asserts that

this really means the abandonment of theism, that is, of the idea of God as transcendent being, the supreme Person, wholly other, distinct from the universe in majestic spiritual isolation. Tillich says that the nineteenth-century atheists were right in regarding such a Being as the enemy of man whom man had to slay in his march to maturity. A transcendent God has become a stumbling-block to ever-increasing numbers who cannot accept this 'projection' of our unconscious minds. This belief which for centuries has been the foundation of orthodoxy must be replaced, by a new conception that does not think in these transcendental terms. Tillich tries to do this with his conception of depth. The Ground of all Being is not *another* being and He is reached, as Kierkegaard said, by 'a deeper immersion in existence'. This is achieved by openness which occurs when we give ourselves in love. We must trust ourselves to the conviction that the universe, reality, total being, is at heart personal, capable of loving and of being loved; we are not postulating *a* separate Being out there who is *a* Person. The Ground of all Being is the love of God in Christ.

10. But, as Robinson remarks, the danger of such statements is that unless we are very careful we end up with the deification of man and theology becomes anthropology and God becomes ethical love. 'God is love' is not quite the same as 'Love is God'. The New Testament does not identify the two. It affirms that God is love and that those who live the life of love, live in the life of God, but at the same time it declares that Love is 'of' God, that is, arises from what He is. The writer of 1 John is not defining human love, he is declaring that when we love we recognize that we are sharing in the divine reality which underlies all existence and that reality was most marvellously revealed in Jesus. The quality of this love and of this attitude to life is so refreshing and so revolutionary that it has come as a revelation to many, a breaking in of new light and meaning which has transformed those who can respond to it in commitment.

11. The understanding of an ultimate personal Being owes much to the thinking of Martin Buber (1878-1965) the Jewish theologian and philosopher, whose little book *I and Thou* distinguishes between our relationship with things, 'I and it',

and our relations with person, *I and Thou.*[1] The 'I' is the centre of consciousness in which all our experiencing is done, but our relationship with things is one of exploitation; we use them, we control them and regard them as subordinate to the 'I', but we cannot treat persons in that way without violating them. Between persons a reciprocal relationship of respect, reverence, and acceptance leads to mutual understanding and enrichment. In such rich relationships we touch the divine mystery, the Thou behind all 'Thous' and all 'its'. The ultimate meaning of existence is to be found in our relationship with ultimate personal Being whom we can never treat as an 'it' but as the Ultimate Thou to be loved and reverenced for His own sake. Attempts to exploit God prove that we have a false idea of God, an idea of our own making, but in this new thinking God is not conceived of as a Person surveying and controlling all things from His 'throne' in heaven. These transcendent images belong to the thought world of pre-Copernican monarchical society to whom the picture of the Divine King was perfectly familiar. Here we are looking at another type of King, one who does not intervene in direct action, miracle, or providence. Such invasion of divine power and authority has no place in the universe as modern man experiences it. As Samuel H. Miller says, 'Our faith now must be in a God not seen directly; a God whose acts are not separable from existence itself; a God in whom we must have faith, not because we have been overwhelmed by direct epiphanies, but because his glory pervades the common structures of things.'[2]

12. A new school of theologians has arisen who have tried to understand what the arrival of urban secular society means for the Church. Harvey Cox[3] whose *Secular City* has had such an influence on many young clergy and ministers, defines secularization as 'the loosening of the world from religious and quasi-religious understandings of itself, the dispelling of all closed world-views, the breaking of all supernatural myths and sacred symbols'. The decision-makers of today in politics, economics, industry, etc., work in a world in which for all practical purposes

[1] Martin Buber, *I and Thou*, 1923, Eng. trans. 1937.

[2] *Op. cit.*, p. 16.

[3] Harvey Cox, *The Secular City*, p. 2.

God does not exist. In this process the Church's old position of power and prestige is being steadily eroded, her congregations are melting away and the status and role of her ministry has become peripheral. But the radicals assert that this shrinkage and humiliation of the Church is nothing to deplore, it is part of God's design to make men accept the responsibilities of their maturity. They have 'come of age' through what Ronald Gregor Smith has called 'the Great Revolution' following the collapse of the medieval synthesis.[1] It is therefore mistaken tactics and a misreading of God's purpose for the Church to seek to save itself, or even to engage in mission in a desperate effort at survival. The Church can never reclaim her old eminence of authority, but must accept her new role in the secular world and that is to follow and to express the way of Christ. These ideas are also advanced by van Peursen and van Leeuwen[2] who both urge that the present age is one of liberation, the result of the Hebrew and Christian tradition working throughout the history of mankind. We are returning to the true Biblical concept that history is the dialogue between God and men. Cox stresses the fact that the Hebrew understands that God has made man free to dominate nature and this is the basis of the scientific and technological approach. Man need not be afraid of abusing its sacred nature for he is its master. We now organize the world on a vast scale, having moved from the tribal and the small country town stages, and are now in the great city or conurbation stage. We must find any meaning in the universe from our own experience and knowledge of it. Society, like nature, has been desacralized. Gone are divine right, the rule of sacred kings and of divine or semi-divine authorities. We are free to engineer society and shape it as we will. Everything is relative, there are no absolute values left. There is no absolute law, no record books, no Grand Assize. God has freed us from the old fears of punishment and left us free to decide for ourselves what is right behaviour.

13. Convinced that the traditional view of God is no longer

[1]Ronald Gregor Smith, *The New Man* (S.C.M., 1956), ch. 2.

[2]Arend Th. van Leeuwen, *Christianity in World History* (Edinburgh House Press, 1964). See also *Faith in a Secular Age* (Fontana).

meaningful, radical thinkers have tried to find support for their views in what they think was the religion of Jesus. John Wren-Lewis, writing as a scientist who is also a Christian, thinks that Jesus himself did not believe in the idea of God as the Supreme Judge who recorded all men's actions and who guaranteed that sooner or later due reward or punishment would be meted out. Wren-Lewis supposes that Christ's original protest was soon forgotten or suppressed as the new faith absorbed current religious ideas so that soon Christian orthodoxy was proclaiming a world 'beyond', complete with heaven and hell and the certainty of final judgement, the very opposite of what Jesus taught. Men have lived with the fear and hope of this imagined 'world to come' always at the back of their minds instead of living openly in the here and now. We cannot enjoy or manage this actual world because of our overheightened guilt-complex due to the absolute moral claims of an imagined world of which we have no direct experience.[1] This distorting fear is an illusion which modern man has abandoned and it is useless for the Church to try to revive it. There is sheer relief in the discovery that we do not have to justify ourselves before some Omnipotent Judge, nor are we under condemnation for failing to fulfil some Divine Purpose. We stand free to mould the world to the shape we choose and we have to work out for ourselves what that shape ought to be. The moral standards are not imposed from on high; we have to fashion them ourselves as we learn what humanity really is and what kind of society can best give it expression. For this reason Wren-Lewis believes that the scientific revolution has occurred because there has been a progressive decay of religious beliefs; it is the effect, not the cause of that decay. Man had to discard those magical and religious strait-jackets in order to establish his right to think. He lumps metaphysical ideas together with religious doctrines as part of the mental junk that had to be removed before man could use the scientific method.

14. Wren-Lewis seeks to justify his radical treatment of both the New Testament and traditional theology by emphasizing that the first Christians were called 'atheists'. He says they lived the life of love as Christ lived it, believing that in such

[1]John Wren-Lewis, *What I Believe* (1966), p. 22.

love they encountered God. They did not believe in the Super-Judge who existed in some other world; they believed in the power of love eventually to transform mankind within the ongoing life of God. Thus early Christianity was a denial of religion and an affirmation of the way of Love. But this view is highly conjectural and ignores much evidence to the contrary. The charge of atheism was brought against Jews and Christians because they would not engage in Caesar-worship. The Christians were even more suspect because they claimed that the rule of Caesar would eventually submit to the power of Christ, the King of kings. They were certainly opposed to the polytheism of Hellenic and Oriental cults, but they went to martyrdom convinced that He who raised Jesus from the dead would likewise raise them, and they were convinced that they had a 'Friend behind the Phenomena'; they believed in the unseen that conditions and survives the seen, and in the eternal that conditions and survives the temporal.

15. In the nineteenth century Christian theologians could rely on the sympathetic support of mainstream philosophy. The predominant metaphysics favoured a type of personal idealism, an explanation of the universe in terms of the evolution of self-conscious personal spirit, fulfilling the increasing purpose of Ultimate Personal Being. But during the mid-twentieth century philosophy turned once more away from metaphysics to the fundamental questions of logic, verification, and the meaning of language. It examined the principles by which the truth or falsehood of scientific language can be established, the empirical tests by which statements can be verified. It then applied these principles to religious language and discovered that religious statements mostly do not admit of such verification, and so do not make sense in the same way as a scientific statement does. They are, therefore, non-sense. It was a dangerous conclusion to draw, because if it meant that religion does not deal with run-of-the-mill scientific facts, facts that can be measured by the senses, it is obviously true. But as the words also mean 'nonsense', that is, ridiculous and untrue, it seemed to deny that religion made any sense at all, and that rational men would have none of it.

16. The challenge of the linguistic philosophers such as A. J.

Ayer[1] could not be ignored, and Christian answers were attempted by Ian T. Ramsay[2] and by R. B. Braithwaite.[3] The latter emphasizes the distinction between scientific and religious language. Because it does not deal with the same kind of facts it needs a different kind of verification. Braithwaite contends that religious language is like moral language; it involves a value of judgement, and the real question is how do we know that these judgements are reliable and sound? How do we ascertain their truth? Moral conviction, he says, discloses how a man intends to act, religious belief also discloses a man's intention and includes the stories that are associated with and influence that intention. So the belief of a Christian is his intention to behave as Jesus behaved, that is, it carries the intention to follow Christ's way of love, and it includes the Jesus-stories in which those principles are enshrined. In this way and in this way only can the validity of Christian belief be tested empirically and verified. If the Christian apologist wants to go beyond this and to talk about God as personal Being, then, says Braithwaite, he must demonstrate in what ways the world would be different if there were no such Being. Only so can he give an empirical proof of the existence of God. But this demand for empirical proof is far too rigid. Much human experience of the good, the beautiful and of the personal, cannot be entirely reduced to intentions which express themselves overtly in behaviour. Religious language, as Ian Ramsay shows, is always straining to express what it knows only too well to be beyond expression; it is concerned with insights, with appreciation of depth and dimension that gives new meaning to the facts of existence. It involves commitment to the newly discerned truth, a shift of personality into new relationships. Such religious experience, like falling in love, turns naturally to the language of poetry and symbol rather than to scientific equations.

17. Nevertheless the trenchant criticism of logical positivism has made theologians aware that they must be cautious how

[1]See A. J. Ayer, *Language, Truth and Logic* (London, 1936).

[2]Ian T. Ramsay, *Religious Language* (S.C.M. 1957)

[3]See *Christian Ethics and Contemporary Philosophy*, ed. by Ian T. Ramsay (S.C.M. 1966).

they both make and interpret religious statements, for modern man is no longer prepared to accept any religious statement merely on authority; he wants to know what it means and how far, if at all, it can be verified. It was to meet this challenge that Paul van Buren wrote *The Secular Meaning of the Gospel.*[1] He frankly admits that the existence of God cannot be empirically demonstrated, and therefore statements about God cannot affect in any way the nature of the actual world in which we live, though they can affect our view of life and the way in which we live. Because of this the words God, Almighty, Father, etc., are either meaningless or misleading, and we ought not to use them. Instead we have to concentrate on the commitment we have made, the new perspective we have on life and its meaning which our faith creates. Thus the empirical test, says van Buren, of loving God is to love one's neighbour. If we do not love our neighbour, we cannot love God. He argues that the commandment to love God really means that we must love our neighbour as Jesus did and the God-reference is in fact eliminated. He believes that the whole Gospel can be expressed without including the idea of God which has become almost unintelligible for secular man.

18. The Resurrection stories seem utterly incredible to the modern mind. Apart from the very considerable discrepancies in the various accounts which cause doubt about their reliability, the event itself defies all human experience. Everyone knows what happens to the cells of the body at death, and the belief that Christ's risen body, still bearing its wound-marks, was capable of appearance and disappearance at will seems sheer myth. Van Buren feels the full force of this rejection of the supernatural but concludes that we have insufficient evidence to say what exactly occurred; that something did happen cannot be doubted. The myths are trying to express the new way in which the disciples saw Jesus and their entry into His freedom to love and to live for others. The Gospel, therefore, is truly proclaimed when a believer testifies that he has gained in Jesus, in His life, death, and what happened at Easter, a new perspective on life which now controls his thought and action; mission is the invitation issued by the believer to others to

[1] S.C.M., 1963.

share that same appreciation of Jesus and to accept His way of love. But as A. J. Wesson and Richard Jones say in a shrewd criticism of van Buren's theology, the attempt to eliminate the God references from the Gospel ignores the New Testament evidence that Christ's freedom to love arose from the fact that the centre of His life was indeed outside Himself and located in God. 'He was the man for God as well as the man for others. There was much more to Jesus than his passionate concern for people.'[1]

19. The empirical theologians are convinced that secular man can no longer conceive the idea of God. This conviction was given arresting and novel expression by Thomas J. J. Altizer whose book *The Gospel of Christian Atheism*[2] gave immense publicity to the 'Death of God' controversy, and marked the high-water mark of the recent radical protest. It is written in the belief that we who are caught in the present crisis of faith and in the current collapse of theology and ecclesiology must transform our Christian heritage and go as far beyond the New Testament concepts as the New Testament writers went beyond the Old. The nineteenth-century atheists had seen that the real enemy to the new humanity was the traditional conception of the Creator, Law-Giver, and Judge. The Good News for today is that this God is dead. Blake, Hegel, Nietzsche, Dostoievski, and Marx, all were attached to the man Jesus; what had to go was the God-out-there, the Watchful-One, the Judge. Faith in such a Being is dying and Christianity can no longer live in its traditional form. Traditional Christianity, says Altizer, has been corrupted by infusions of oriental mysticism which is an attempt to regress to the Primordial Totality by denying the reality of the material world of motion and time. True radical Christianity is a forward movement towards an apocalyptic end. The Creative Word has become incarnate. It is not Spirit which will return again to Primordial Spirit by resurrection. It is committed now to a process of permanent incarnation, it is for ever imprisoned in flesh. Altizer thinks both Paul and John failed to understand what

[1]Richard G. Jones and Anthony J. Wesson, *Mission and the Death of God* (Methodist Home Mission Department, 1968), p. 13.

[2]Westminster Press, Philadelphia, 1966 (English edition, Collins 1967).

had happened and both attempted to force the actual facts into the current metaphysical frame. They wanted Christ to return to the Primordial Spirit. But there is no such return. Blake was right, we must not say Jesus is God, but God is Jesus, and when Jesus died, God died, and there is no resurrection.

20. Altizer says that traditional Christianity has reduced human existence to sin and guilt, confronting a broken humanity with a wholly-other God who demands total submission to His power as judge; and so, in Christianity, religion receives its most repressive form. Only religionless Christianity can save us from this nightmare and the fruitless effort to return to the Primordial One. No religion has so stressed the Fall Myth as Christianity, yet Christianity has misunderstood the myth; its real message is that man can never return to the primordial paradise. The purpose of the Incarnation was not to restore man to a lost paradise, but to bring God to man. Man must live now in truly profane history. There has never been and can never be a fully final revelation. Radical Christianity accepts the totality of the Fall and condemns the religious quest for the unfallen sacred. Christianity accepts the brutal finality of death. Ideas of immortality are unchristian. By identifying Christ with the Eternal Word traditional trinitarian forms of Christianity have eliminated the finality of death. It cannot be real in the presence of eternal Word. There is no regression to an unfallen, unhistorical, unmoving Word. The truly Incarnate Word must die. It is a fallen Word, kenotically emptied. It is real now only in the profane reality of fallen history. Only in the death on the Cross does the Word actually and forever become flesh. Altizer concludes, 'We cannot open ourselves to a new form of faith while remaining bound to a primordial God who has once and for all "revealed His Word". We will never pass through a new Reformation until we liberate ourselves from our Christian past.' He sees the Goal as the complete incarnation of the Word with the totality of humanity and the entire universe, so that history is, in one sense, the body of God.

21. Altizer's Christian atheism provoked a storm of denunciation. It certainly made no attempt to placate traditionalists but fearlessly sought to relate Christianity to its own

reading of the present drift from faith. It shares the general secular revulsion to the supernatural and to the idealist metaphysics on which orthodoxy had rested for centuries. Its adoption of the phrase 'God is dead' shocked the traditionalist to whom such a statement is plain blasphemy. Yet by it he was fastening on the characteristic feature of modern experience, the fact that for secular man the experience of God seems to have evaporated; the category of the supernatural no longer exists for him. He was attempting to explain this as the action of God Himself, who by becoming incarnate, fully identified Himself with man. Altizer was also skilfully using the modern concept of evolution as an explanation of the painful movement, through suffering and death, to the consummation of all things in a new unity of flesh and spirit. These are all pregnant ideas which reflect modern hopes and fears. But closer examination of his thought reveals grave weaknesses. Why should it be reasonable to believe in the existence of a transcendent Creator right up to the Incarnation, but be absurd to think of Him existing now? If the universe can exist without a Creator-Sustainer or Ground of Being now, why did it need one in the beginning? Or if God still continues as Ground of all Being in humanity by incarnation, then has not man without knowing it become divine? Or, again, even if God did enter humanity in the Incarnation, how did He survive the death of Christ on the Cross? Is He incarnate now only in those who follow the way of Christ? If He is incarnate in all mankind, has not Altizer arrived at a form of humanistic pantheism?

CHAPTER THIRTEEN

Process Theology

THE tumultuous torrent of modern theology has been fed from many different sources, and we are keenly aware how inadequate and uneven our treatment has been.[1] The effects of recent psychological and sociological studies deserve much more adequate recognition than we have attempted. There is another source, however, which we suspect may profoundly affect our understanding of mission and our presentation of the Gospel. It flows from that much denigrated discipline, philosophy, from which western man can never really escape. The logical positivists may shy away from metaphysics and the radicals may deride the classical speculations about the nature of God, but man will always come back to the ultimate questions. He lives in a universe, not a chaos; a universe in which his own reason, at least, exists, and he cannot rest until he finds some kind of picture that makes sense of his experience. He asks himself, 'Who am I? Why am I here? What is my relationship to this universe? If a man die, will he live again?' It is currently fashionable to smile condescendingly at anyone who is naïve enough to ask such questions, let alone try to find an answer, but the fashion will pass and, unless we are much mistaken, in a few years the perennial questions will be discussed again and we shall then discover our debt to some of the neglected thinkers of our time.

2. In general reaction to Hegelian idealism, Positivists from August Comte (1798-1857) to A. J. Ayer have rejected metaphysics and the consideration of all ultimate questions and have

[1]For a much fuller treatment see David L. Edwards, *Religion and Change* (Hodder and Stoughton, 1969), which came into my hands as this MS was going to the printer.

tried to limit philosophy to positive, that is, observable facts. They also reject religion, precisely because religion is concerned with these ultimate questions and because it makes statements which cannot be verified as scientific statements can. A quite different road was taken by the Pragmatists who realized that religion was as much a fact of human history and experience as any other fact and that it ought to be studied with equal objectivity and freedom from prejudice. One of the founders of this school was William James (1842-1910) who distinguished between establishing the scientific proof of a belief and the practical outcome of holding it. He was a brilliant psychologist and his *Varieties of Religious Experience* gave the first scientific analysis of various types of religious experience, distinguishing between the 'once-born' and the 'twice-born', that is those who have gone on to a further stage of illumination and integration. His main argument was that if a belief is helpful, it is likely to be true. We therefore have a right to believe in God, because to do so is morally uplifting and ennobling; such faith produces on the whole better character. We cannot go much beyond that, for the validity of our assertions of faith about the nature of God cannot be scientifically established.

3. Interest in religious experience as worthy of intensive study was further developed by Rudolf Otto (1869-1937) who in his *Idea of the Holy* insisted that beneath all the theologizing and paraphernalia of Church organization was the elemental and intuitive awareness of the Holy, the *numinous*, immediately and non-rationally apprehended in encounter with God. Like Schleiermacher he emphasized the centrality of feeling, the intuitive sensitivity to the divine presence which characterizes all religions. Man is capable of such apprehension however much secularity may have blunted and dulled his spirit. Otto has been severely criticized by those psychologists and theologians who deny the existence of any such special 'religious' faculty, but his thought has won a deep response from many Christians whose own experiences of worship, wonder and adoring love seem to be better understood by Otto than by those Christian rationalists for whom Christian experience is either purely subjective or unhealthy. Otto was drawing attention to neglected facts, even though his explanation of

those facts may be inadequate. Both James and Otto reminded an unheeding world that the great religious leaders of all ages who had influenced the lives of millions and shaped the culture of continents were men whose religious experience had been the dynamic centre of all their amazing power and activity, and that their experience to some lesser degree had been shared by tens of thousands in so regular and recognizable a form that it could not be dismissed as illusionary. The facts demanded another explanation.

4. Such an explanation was attempted by the French philosopher, Henri Bergson (1859-1941). Like Otto and Schleiermacher, this Jewish thinker believed that man could never reach ultimate reality by reason alone; the contact was made not through the intellect, but intuitively, in the depths of our being. Bergson contended that we used intuition far more than we realized. It was most evident in our personal responses to people and situations: we used intuition where animals used instinct. All our intellectual activity is secondary and serves the purposes we have intuitively selected. He maintained that all our intellectual categories and concepts have been derived from our mental pictures of objects in the three dimensions of space and in the dimension of measured time and these concepts have no relation to reality at all. The universe in its totality is not a fixed entity spread out in space and ticking away like a cosmic clock. Reality is always developing into something new. The old traditional philosophies were closed systems, they conceived of reality as fundamentally perfect and unchangeable, but instead it is evolutionary and progressive. Hence the title of his great book, *Creative Evolution*,[1] in which he expounded his theory of process. Only in an open system, he claimed, can we escape from determinism. Creative Evolution gives to man, in the exercise of his free will, the power to shape the future. That power, in spite of the dead weight of habit and the past, is always present in the eternal 'now'. As Bergson said, 'The gates of the future lie ever open.' Man has moral liberty and always urging him on to the noble and heroic is the '*élan vital*', the life force itself, manifesting itself in those impulses and promptings which great men know so well.

[1] *L'Evolution Créatrice*, 1907, Eng. trans. 1911.

5. Bergson's ideas greatly influenced another Frenchman, the Jesuit palaeontologist Pierre Teilhard de Chardin (1881-1955). Because of his scientific training he could not ignore the evidences of evolutionary processes which were the subject-matter of his study. He spent many years in China and shared in the discovery of Peking Man in 1929. He saw that to maintain faith man had to reconcile Christian theology with evolutionary philosophy and this he attempted in *The Phenomenon of Man* and *Le Milieu Divin*[1] whose poetic beauty magnificently conveys his sense of awe and wonder at what he has discovered. Teilhard accepted the findings of modern astronomy and geology as scientific truth, revealing the way in which the universe had developed. He sought to give a religious interpretation to these facts and maintained that religion and science could be reconciled if we dared to ask certain elemental questions of the scientist. Assuming that the cosmological theory of the origin of the universe in a cloud of sub-nuclear particles to be correct, and assuming that the first atom was formed by the coming together of those elemental particles, why, asked Teilhard, did they move towards each other? Why did they not move apart, or stay still? This movement towards one another is supremely significant and reveals the nature of reality. To attribute the movement to chance is merely to give a name to our ignorance of what happened. Right from the beginning the higher forms of life were potentially present. The movement was all in one direction—towards closer togetherness, to more elaborate organization, from atom to molecule, from molecule to living cell, from cell to fish, then bird, then animal, then man and next the perfect man in perfect society when this movement of togetherness, which in humans we call love, is fully conscious and completely controls the entire universe. The whole process beginning in the Alpha of unrealized potential moves towards the Omega of fulfilled potential in which everything enjoys the life of God. He is the First and Last, the Beginning and the Ending.

6. Teilhard's sweep of thought is breath-taking; his aim is to work out the destiny of man from the evidence of what man is.

[1] *The Phenomenon of Man*, 1955, Eng. trans. Collins 1955. *Le Milieu Divin*, 1957, Eng. tran. Collins, 1960.

He makes no excuse for beginning with the sub-nuclear particles which are the concern of the modern physicist. But the chemist sees only one aspect, and chemistry moves into biochemistry and biochemistry into biology. Biology leads to anthropology, which is not complete without the insights of psychology and sociology. Culture, economics, politics and international relations are all involved in understanding man, where he has come from, why he is here and where he is going. Teilhard thus brought together the achievements of science and a profound sense of the human aspirations to which they minister and of which they are an expression. He also brought firmly back into the centre of Christian thought the insights of devotional and mystical experience. God revealed Himself through the whole cosmic process and in Christ that redeeming and transforming process is disclosed in full self-giving. Man is a phenomenon like everything else that has emerged in the evolutionary process, but he is something more. He can reflect upon the process and can in measure begin to control it. Reflecting on his successes and failures man also recognizes that he participates in a non-material process and can share in the ultimate purpose, the spiritual destiny of the universe. This merging of the eternal with the temporal is what the Incarnation means, in it supra-history became history. Christ was the measure of how much God loved the world. Progress is not inexorable; it has to be worked for in the agonies of personal choice and moral responsibility. The Cross reveals God Himself totally involved in the struggle, His love triumphing over sin and death. Teilhard dedicates his book to those who have learned to love the world in God's way. To many who have endured the penitential and sometimes arid discipline of radical theology, and who have lived long with the current criticisms of the institutional Church, Teilhard's thought brought hope and renewed courage. In its satisfying insights and glowing purpose they caught a glimpse of a faith deep and broad enough to speak to this age, just when they had begun to wonder if faith itself could possibly survive.

7. Teilhard was a Jesuit, steeped in the devotional tradition of the Spiritual Exercises of Ignatius Loyola, besides being a world-famous scientist. There was another scientist Alfred N.

Whitehead (1861-1947) who earned distinction as a superb mathematician at Cambridge and London, and who at the age of sixty-three moved to Harvard and earned a new reputation in the philosophy of religion. He too sought to reconcile religion with the facts of the evolutionary process, for he too had been influenced by Bergson. In a few years he produced *Science and the Modern World* (1925), *Religion in the Making* (1926), and *Process and Reality* (1929). It is in this last that he outlined his philosophic system. His ideas were coldly received by theologians and ignored by scientists until they were expounded by a small band of scholars, notably Charles Hartshorne, Schubert Ogden, and John Cobb, who carry Whitehead's system a stage further. Their impact on the theological scene is still slight, but much more may be heard of them in the near future, because they do attempt an answer to one of the most difficult problems confronting Christianity today.

8. That question is, 'How can we conceive of God in a way which scientific man can find meaningful?' Whitehead begins his reply by drawing attention to the fact that we experience reality as a succession of changes; the reality of our essential selfhood is not an unchanging entity, rather it is an identity that persists through constant change. We arrive at our idea of persistent selfhood by recollection and by abstraction from the everchanging actuality of our existence. Not only the self, but all things down to sub-nuclear particles share this mysterious characteristic of successive change. Whereas the old classical philosophers conceived of God and things-in-themselves as immutable and impassible, eternally the same, reality is quite different: it is always in process of becoming. It is moving progressively in a purposeful development and 'entities', such as human beings, find their fulfilment and identity through change. Time, therefore, is not an illusion or a limitation, but belongs to the very nature of reality. Everything in the universe is inter-related and behind each event lies all the past there has ever been. Each single event, likewise, is influencing the future which has not yet become reality, but this does not rule out the direct contribution to the future that each entity or person can make by the exercise of his own free will. Each is thus the product of his past and each is making now his own future and

affecting the future of all others. Reality is not a closed determinist system; it is on the contrary the sum total of all that now is moving forward in the totality of changes to the reality of the next successive moment. What holds all entities together and gives unity and actuality is God; He is the ground of the continuing process of reality—'in him we live and move and have our being.' God experiences relation with every part and element of the universe and so He feels all pain as well as all joy, defeat as well as success. He is not the unfeeling Absolute of classical theology.

9. Like Teilhard, Whitehead maintains that the dynamic of this process is the attraction of love. Love is the power that makes for unity and co-operation which leads not only to the fuller development of the potentialities of persons but to the enrichment of society, which in turn further enhances the life of the individual.[1] Love derives its motive from God for it is by love that He holds the universe within the reality of Himself. But the process philosophers are careful to point out that this is not to say that the universe is God: process theology is not pantheism. Neither is it transcendental theism. It is what Hartshorne has called panentheism; God, because He is related to everything, feels everything; but because He too is an entity, and not just the totality of everything, He can influence everything and does so in His love for the world, a love which seeks in every way that love may to bring the loved ones to their highest possible development. He respects, as love always must, the freedom of every entity. The word 'entity' here means not only what we call persons, but every constituent element of the universe at whatever degree of elaboration or freedom it may have attained, and so it could include even those apparently random movements of elemental particles in their successive appearances in what we commonly call wave-motion. God as the ground of being, provides every entity with each moment of its existence.

10. But though God is Himself an Entity, He is not an object among other objects in the universe, and therefore He can

[1]For a valuable introduction to Process Theology see Peter Hamilton, *The Living God and the Modern World* (Hodder and Stoughton, 1967); Charles Harteshorne, *The Divine Reality* (Yale U.P., 1948); J. B. Cobb, *A Christian Natural Theology* (Westminster Press, 1965).

never be experienced as if He were an Object to be encountered. When modern man says he has no experience of God, this does not invalidate the religious experience of past ages, it merely means that modern man does not now identify his experiences in the language and thought-forms of other days. When secular man says that he does not find God in his experiences of the universe, process theology replies that God is the reality that underlies all his experiences, that God is totally aware of all his experience and is affected by it. Religious experience is the discernment of this relationship. It is an opening of eyes to the deeper dimension, the recognition of that Cosmic Love and response to it. If we really understood it, all our experience is religious; even our evil thought which wounds God, is a religious fact. This is the meaning of the Cross for the God of Love wants us to be free. As free men we can turn from Him or as companions join our creativity to His in the onflowing reality in which He is for ever making all things new and bringing them to their full potential.

11. Process theology, as David A. Pailin[1] says, takes seriously the insights of the 'Death of God' school and offers a more adequate solution to the modern understanding of the idea of God. It takes account of the fact that for many millions in modern society religious language has ceased to be of significance and 'talk' about God is empty because of the inherent contradictions of orthodoxy, especially the ideas of God as a transcendental Being controlling the universe from outside. Process theology declares that God is in the universe, that He holds it together and is related to everything. Secular man may not experience God, but process theology tells him that everything he does and thinks is experienced by God. Man may not find God in experiences of consolation and salvation; in that respect we have entered into the experience of dereliction that Christ knew, the experience of the 'Silence' as Martin Buber calls it in his *Eclipse of God*. Process theology affirms that God Himself is at work in the immediate now, shaping the future with us. Our ideas of God are therefore released from the prevailing convention and fashions of our contemporary culture

[1] 'A Christian Possibility of Proclaiming the "Death of God" ', *The Church Quarterly*, Vol. 11, No. 3, Jan. 1969.

and from past images that once were significant. The recognition of God's independence of our cultural pictures sets us free to direct and change our culture in keeping with the new insights that are emerging with every creative thought and impulse. To push man further along this road of partnership and responsibility, God has not withdrawn from the scene as some radicals suggest, but is encouraging every man at every moment through those impulses to act and think in freedom, responsibility and in fellowship with Himself.

12. These ideas are all stimulating and help modern man to a new sense of the religious dimension. There are also some remarkable deficiencies in the system, not least the conclusion that there is no personal survival after death. It is argued that personality relates to the entity as a whole and that when it disintegrates at death there is nothing left to survive, save what is remembered of it by God. In that divine memory only that which is good and of value is remembered. This is a sobering thought and in one sense it could be merely a restatement of the deep Christian conviction that there is no existence for anything except in the mind, will, and purpose of God. But to live on only as a thought in someone else's memory is quite different from living as a self-conscious, self-determining entity, and so Paul's searching criticism cannot be evaded—'If it is for this life only that Christ has given us hope, we of all men are most to be pitied' (1 Corinthians 15:19).

13. Nevertheless, process theology throws light on the way ahead. It asserts that man has every right to feel after a total world-picture that will not only make sense of life as he experiences it, but open a way to God. This is not to say that man by searching can find out God, but it does mean that God is not far from any that do sincerely seek to know Him and that even modern man is not confined to an interpretation of life which renders him incapable of fellowship with God. Perhaps especially in the majestic movement of Teilhard's thought is there to be found that insight which might provide a common ground for Catholic and Protestant in this secular age.

CHAPTER FOURTEEN

The Catholic Contribution to the Debate

THROUGHOUT the first three-quarters of the nineteenth century Roman Catholicism remained rigidly opposed to all attempts to come to terms with the results of Biblical criticism and with the evolutionary concepts of the new sciences. It was not until the pontificate of Leo XIII that there was a sufficient relaxation to allow Roman liberals some freedom of expression. What has been called the Catholic Modernist movement was initiated in France by Louis Duchesne (1843-1922) who dared to apply critical method to Church history, though he avoided applying those methods to the study of the Bible. His pupil Alfred Loisy (1857-1940) was removed from his professorship in 1883 for teaching modernist views. Rome emphasized its traditional position by an encyclical affirming the inerrancy of the Scriptures. Undiscouraged Loisy maintained his views which he brilliantly expounded in his *L'Évangile et L'Église*, his answer to the Protestant liberalism of Harnack and Sabatier. He claimed that historical criticism of the Bible and of Church history did not lead necessarily to the humanist ethics of Protestant liberalism, but could be shown to demonstrate the necessity for the hierarchy, dogma, and cultus of the Roman Church. But while this appeared to be a new and exciting defence of Catholicism, it was achieved by rejecting the dogma of Biblical inerrancy and much of the scholastic theology of traditional Roman orthodoxy.

2. Rome could not accept such a defence and condemned the work, excommunicating Loisy in 1908. But his work influenced many young priests, notably George Tyrrell (1861-1909), an Irish Jesuit. Gradually he rebelled against the traditional view that the truths of Christianity were defined in

a fixed, infallible, and intellectualist system of doctrine and dogma. He became convinced that theology must reflect the living experience of the people of God and that therefore dogmatic forms could and should be modified to express the fresh insights of each new age. But again Catholicism was not ready for such a relaxation of its rigid orthodoxy and in the encyclical *Pascendi* of Pius X, modernism was condemned as heretical and as the work of a group of proud intellectuals who were plotting the overthrow of the Church. Stern steps were taken to eradicate modernism from the Church and by 1910 the movement was apparently finished. Catholicism seemed utterly impervious to the pressures of all the new thought.

3. But, despite the apparent triumph of an unyielding conservatism, Rome could not and did not isolate itself from the developments of modern society. Some of its leading theologians such as Karl Adam (*b*.1876) took up the challenge and did so with refreshing originality. Adam argued that since the Renaissance the West had fallen prey to an arid rationalism which cuts man off from God and from the deep spiritual wells of his being, and so had become a victim of a competitive individualism which separates man from his fellow men.[1] He contended that liberal Protestants had capitulated to these forces and so had lost the dynamic power of true Christianity. By their highly intellectual analysis of the source documents they had lost the essence which Catholicism preserves, namely that there is a supernatural dimension to the Christian life and that man discovers himself and the true unity of mankind only within that life. Man can think about God and arrive at certain philosphical conclusions, but he cannot of himself rise to God. But God can and does graciously reveal Himself to man and this He has done in Christ, the Incarnate Word.

4. Adam claims that we know Christ, not primarily through the Bible, but through the Church, which is His Body. Christ is the Head of the Body and the Pioneer of the new humanity. The Church manifests the new and supernatural life of the holy community. Adam defends the aristocratic and authoritarian structure of the Church on the grounds that it exists by divine

[1]For a concise summary of Roman Catholic thought see John Macquarrie, *Twentieth-Century Religious Thought* (S.C.M., 1963).

appointment to serve the sacred Community, while the whole Body of the Church exists for God and for the whole human race. He summarizes the life of the Christian in the sentence, 'I experience the action of the living God through Christ realizing himself in his Church.'[1] He admits the faults and failures of the Church in the past, but insists that this is what it is meant to be, and what it is when at its best.

5. Few contemporary Catholic theologians have had more influence than Karl Rahner (*b*.1904). He frankly recognizes secular man's experience of the silence and apparent absence of God, so forcibly expounded by Protestant radicals. But, says Rahner, this evaporation of the sense of God and of experience of Him is due to the fact that we have been looking for Him in the wrong places. God is not one observable Object among many, nor one intervening agent among others; He works through the whole process, He is the ground in and through whom the whole universe exists. Modern man must find and know Him in the totality of experience.

6. But perhaps Rahner's most striking contribution is his challenge to the pessimism of modern secular thought both in its atheistic and radical Christian forms, for which death is cessation, the final disintegration in the all-embracing Nothingness. Rahner replies that death is not just a physical phenomenon occurring when the last breath is drawn; it is a human experience affecting the whole man and one through which we are constantly passing as our present slides into the irrecoverable past. We die daily. Rahner says we can either regard death as an invasion of destructive forces which disintegrate us leaving nothing, or we can think of it as the crowning act of life. Because we are sinful creatures, with our attitudes and values perverted, we think of and experience death as utter privation. But, says Rahner, if we were sinless and could appreciate life as it really is, death would be experienced not as irretrievable loss but as the moment of consummation, a passing into fuller and larger life. We do live in a sinful world where men's understanding is darkened, but Christ has come into this world to those who sit in darkness and the shadow of death. He died and experienced the silence of God, He felt the full horror of

[1]Karl Adam, *The Spirit of Catholicism*, quoted by Macquarrie, *op. cit.*

death but went on to the renewal of life in the resurrection. The Christian life is a sharing in this death and resurrection of Jesus and this is above all what Holy Communion offers. In this way the Christian triumphs over death and makes it the supreme act of his faith, hope, and love.

7. Other Catholic theologians like van Balthasar and Erich Przywara have also accepted the challenge of western secularism and exposed some of its weaknesses. The thinking of these scholars has profoundly affected the Roman Church and in no small measure paved the way for the revival initiated by John XXIII in the Second Vatican Council. The range of this new thought and the impressive scholarship behind it is exemplified in *A New Catechism* of the Dutch Catholics, a bold, well-reasoned, and attractively-written explanation and defence of the Christian Faith which must rank as one of the greatest pieces of Christian apologetics that has appeared for some time. It endeavours to restate Catholic doctrine by drawing a distinction between truth as such and the expression of truth. It is only the expression of it with which we deal and this must constantly be adapted to new conditions. The truth itself remains fixed, but not immobile. Just as a mother is the fixed centre of a child's life yet moves freely about her home, so the Gospel is not a rigid system but a living voice. The interpretation of the Gospel is always capable of improvement.[1] The *New Catechism* is a reconciling work, one which with some few reservations, commends itself to many Protestants also, who rejoice to see their common faith so ably expounded.

[1] *A New Catechism, Catholic Faith for Adults* (Burns & Oates/Herder and Herder, 1965), p. 366.

PART THREE

Gospel and Mission Today

CHAPTER FIFTEEN

The Fact of Jesus

WHAT then is Mission in the secular world? Is there still a Gospel to proclaim and if so how is it to be done? Is there sufficient common ground between all these divergent views to enable Christians to unite in any effective programme of Mission? The answer can only be 'Yes', for otherwise we are confessing that Christianity is indeed a spent force, petering out in the squabbles of its intelligentsia and in the disappointment and disillusion of the faithful.

2. What then do Christians hold in common? All would surely agree with P. Carnegie Simpson that at the centre of Christianity is the Fact of Christ.[1] Whatever mythological elements may have entered into the records and their interpretation, it is inconceivable that the massive impact of Christianity on the world could possibly have been made without the man Jesus. Whatever uncertainty attaches to details, such a movement could never have started apart from a man whose life left so indelible an impression on His associates. That Jesus lived there can be no reasonable doubt.

3. Can anything more be said with certainty, besides the bare fact that He existed? What reliance can be placed upon the witness of the Church? As we have seen, theology has been a sustained attempt to understand the fact of Christ. The interpretations may be questioned or rejected today, but it is not enough to dismiss them as inadequate or false; they are to be seen as sincere efforts to understand that central person, to know who He is and to grasp what He has done. They spring directly from, and bear witness to, the overwhelming significance of this man. Admittedly all kinds of vested interests took

[1]See P. Carnegie Simpson, *The Fact of Christ* (Hodder and Stoughton; first pub. 1900). It was reprinted twenty-one times up to 1937.

root in the Church. Through long ages there were strong pressures to depict Christ as the King of kings, but the same Church that tried to dress Christ in the robes of earthly splendour which He himself had spurned, also preserved the memory of the humble man who thought of Himself as the servant of all.

4. For nearly two hundred years the doctrine of an infallible Bible has been attacked as strongly as that of the infallible Church. As we have seen, a major question today is to draw out from the Biblical records a reliable picture of the man. Many Christians can no longer think of Him as the wonder-worker performing miracles in order to demonstrate His own divinity. The secular mind rejects the miraculous and the supernatural. But do such stories of miracles reduce the sacred narrative to fairy tales, to the naïve beliefs of very credulous and superstitious people? A cool reading of the New Testament does not yield that impression. They are not just tales of wonders. As the writer of the Fourth Gospel specifically says, they are 'signs' and, as the Synoptic Gospels insist, Jesus Himself regarded the suggestion to work miracles as a temptation unworthy of both Himself and the God He loved.

5. What then are we to make of these stories, for it is impossible to erase them from the Gospels without spoiling the presentation of the central character? We must conclude that these were the ways in which His contemporaries saw and understood Him. They knew Him as a healer, a charismatic man who again and again cured the sick in body and mind, but they also recorded that He Himself diagnosed the deeper diseases of the personality, the guilt and shame, the selfishness, hate, and pride that poisoned human nature. Which is more difficult, to forgive sin or to heal a paralysed limb, to make the inner man well, or his body well? The figure that emerges from behind the miracles is not a wonder-worker, but a physician of the deep maladies of mankind.

6. When we turn from the healing miracles to the 'supernatural' wonders, like walking on the water, turning water into wine, multiplying the loaves, raising the dead, there is room for a wide diversity of view. Some Christians can take these quite literally. They expect the Son of God to behave like a god. They argue that He does not break natural law, but

rather suspends it, or brings some higher law into operation. But other Christians regard such stories as not only incredible, but an embarrassment, for they remove Jesus from the realm of ordinary humanity and transform Him into a divine hero. Since the object of the Gospel was to help men the aim is defeated if Jesus is not completely one with us. Such miracles remove Him from our class. Yet this is not the view the Bible takes, for it records Jesus as promising that His disciples will do much greater marvels than He had done. Granted that their attitude to the supernatural was very different from ours, that they expected such things to happen in a world of inexplicable happenings, nevertheless they believed that Jesus was introducing them to a new world of power, a world in which they would walk the waters by faith, they would bring the new and better wine of triumphant life to those for whom the old wine had run out. This is not to maintain that the Gospels deliberately allegorized the actual prosaic events into fanciful stories; it is to say rather that the more they thought of Jesus, this is how they saw Him and this is how they formulated and recorded the memories of what He said and did. It was as near as they could get to what they wanted to say, for they were trying to capture in words the inexpressible man whom they had known and loved. Let us also grant that it was natural for them to see things mythopoeically; the detached observation of the scientist was not part of their mental equipment as it is of ours; but the question remains, What did they see that made them use such pictures?

7. The work of the nineteenth- and twentieth-century Biblical critics cannot be ignored. They have not only shown the nature of the problem, they have gone a considerable way to finding the solution. True, they disagree among themselves and the debate is far from finished, but they have established beyond all reasonable doubt that the Gospels as we have them are the end-product of a very considerable process within the Early Church. Just what that process was and how much it has distorted the original events is still a matter of research and debate, but many Christians can no longer accept the Gospels as historic evidence of what Jesus actually said and did. On the other hand they are agreed that through these narratives

emerges the startlingly clear and compelling figure of Jesus of Nazareth.

8. P. Carnegie Simpson is surely on the right track when he maintains that Jesus Himself was content to submit Himself to the judgement of every man. 'Who do you say that I am?' is the recurring question whether spoken directly or unexpressed. His technique, if that is the word, was to mingle freely with men, talk with all who would listen to Him, preach and teach when given the opportunity. He did not try to draw attention to Himself, He had caustic words for those who loved the limelight; He himself taught with the easy grace of humility which puts others at ease and melts barriers of pride and position. But the quality of life He lived, its depths of love and compassion, its concern and its disclosure of God raised the question, Who is this man? No one had ever spoken like this before; no one had ever lived like this before. To be with Him was to rise to a new level of humanity, His level, and to sense that this was how life ought to be lived.

9. All the Gospels testify to this life. For the Fourth Gospel it was the key to the riddle of the universe. Jesus was the Life, the Truth, the Way; but the others bear the same witness. Here was a life lived on a new ethic, one which defied systematization, yet could be reduced to one word—love. Here was a well of sympathy for all, for the lonely, sad, forgotten, and helpless. Here was a courage that could take on Church and State and outface them, transforming the ignominy of crucifixion into a triumph of redeeming love. Here was a man who lived for others in selfless devotion.

10. He was the man for others. Is the last phrase, so popular in radical theology, a sufficient description? Certainly He lived for others, but if anything certain emerges from the demythologized pages of the New Testament it is that He lived for others because He lived for God, He loved His neighbours, and all men were neighbours to Jesus, because He first loved God. In one sense no one can command love; it must be given freely and spontaneously. You cannot love God because you are told to do so, no matter how you try. You love what is lovable, what you wish to draw into yourself, what you admire and prize. You cannot really love an abstraction. There are men

who are more at home with ideas and generalizations than they are with people, and they make poor ministers. They evoke no warmth of response; they are insensitive to need and emotion. The love of Jesus for God was the mainspring of His life. He nourished it in prayer and communion, He strengthened it with daily obedience to His Father's will. For that word, always on His lips in the Aramaic He used—*Abba*—disclosed the relationship as Jesus Himself understood it. The very way He said it, the awe and love, the caress of adoration, stuck in the memory of His disciples and echoed through the Early Church enabling thousands of Greeks and Romans to cry, 'Abba, Father!', claiming for themselves the same relationship with God that Jesus had.

11. The Christian atheism of Altizer, attempting as it does to cope with secular man's inability to experience God, and the insistence that man has come of age and must live as if there were no God, leaves man Fatherless. These teachers are asking us to be followers of Christ without the faith of Christ, to live as Christ lived without the resources and power which Christ derived from His complete dependence on God. It is to ignore the sober fact, attested by many thousands of years of human history, that man cannot live at that level without any infusion of power from somewhere else than his own resources. The proclamation of an ethic of perfection without the power to live up to it only intensifies human misery, and there is no Gospel in it, no good news for defeated man, no rest for the heavy laden. Such humanism is not the Gospel as proclaimed by Jesus and it would never have launched the movement of which He and He alone is the Captain and Pioneer. Few radicals in Britain espouse this extreme position.

12. All the nineteenth- and twentieth-century liberals and radicals agree that the essence of the teaching of Jesus is selfless love. The constant peril of such a summary, however, is to smother the sharp and powerful figure of Jesus under a thick blanket of sentimentality and drooling sweetness. The character that emerges from the demythologized records could be and often was wonderfully kind and tender, especially to the weak and penitent, but He could be and often was hard and unyielding in His exposure of hypocrisy, religious cant, and false

idealism. The way of love which He advocated and lived was a costly road demanding the discipline of every other passion. He was clear-eyed and devastatingly frank with a childlike simplicity. He demanded of His disciples that they should sit down and count the cost of following Him, before committing themselves to His Way. Yet He did not present His Gospel as a way of ascetic discipline and mortification; rather it was a great prize, a marvellous treasure which any man could buy at the bargain price of total commitment; it was liberty, sight, life, health, and peace; it was escape from the prisonhouse of illusion and bondage to those elements in the self which, when they command, produce only misery and suffering. Harnessed to the true end they serve and enhance the life of the disciple.

13. Nor was the ethic of Jesus a search for individual perfection; He proclaimed a Kingdom, a new community which was open to men of all nationalities and colours, a new society based on mutual respect and caring, a society which extended the narrow interest of the family to all humanity. In the Kingdom every man is neighbour and brother, and the children of every other man matter as much as do one's own. Perhaps the world has not recognized how much this teaching of Jesus has penetrated its thought as a result of the great nineteenth- and twentieth-century liberal emphasis. Certainly the Welfare States of Europe with their determination to eliminate poverty, disease, and ignorance, derive their idealism from this vision of world-brotherhood. The graduated taxation systems of Western Europe, providing enormous sums for social and educational services, work on the principle that it is the duty and privilege of those with most wealth to help those with least. The same principle underlies the help that the richer nations of the West are pouring into the under-developed and backward countries of the world, and more and more people hope that within the next few decades the conscience of mankind will ensure that the total resources of the world are organized to meet the needs of the whole human family, as of right, not charity.

14. The ethic of Jesus was not addressed to every particular problem, but stated in vivid story, parable and aphorism. He left the detailed application of the principles of the Family of

Man to His followers. It took them nearly eighteen hundred years to realize that the family ethic could not tolerate the exploitation of weaker races through the institution of slavery; it took another century for them to understand the essential equality of the sexes and to emancipate women from millenia of subjection and roles of political and economic inferiority. It has taken another half-century for Christians to begin to realize that discrimination against men of colour also violates the principles of the brotherhood of man. It seems a far cry from Jesus of Nazareth to the cry for civil rights, but despite the fact that many Christians still refuse to recognize that the human race is one family, the idea is steadily taking hold of the imagination and conscience of the world. Many who would reject the name of Christian with anger, such as the Communist and Humanist, also share these dreams of classless world-brotherhood, and despite their disclaimers, there is much evidence to show the source of their ideals. Indeed, a good case can be made that both Communism and Humanism are Christian heresies, which in their ways have preserved and developed the hope of the Kingdom so often forgotten or etherealized by the institutional Churches. The determination to seek these social goals fires the imagination of tens of thousands of devoted workers outside the Churches. They do not profess the name of Christ, nor call Him 'Lord', but in this respect they are sharing His vision and doing His will. Was it not such as these He had in mind when He distinguished between those who profess to serve Him but are blind and deaf to the need of their fellowmen and those who deny ever knowing Him, but have given themselves for others? (Matthew 25:31f.)

15. Such human interest and concern is a striking feature of this late twentieth century. Were ever such funds raised for charities, or such vast operations for relief of famine, plague, or any other disaster ever mounted in previous years? There is a vast amount of goodwill, and there are devoted people, many of them young and comparatively inexperienced, who are leading the attack against forms of social evil which have been all too long regarded as capable of only gradual remedy. The battle for the homeless, for instance, conducted by *Shelter*, and such organizations, speaks in the name of our common

humanity. The major Christian Churches have realized that they now have no monopoly of compassion and are ready and willing to co-operate with other relief organizations. Christian Aid, which canalizes the benevolence of the British Council of Churches, co-operates with other funds, not specifically Christian, in several projects.

16. For many young people, both inside and outside the Church, social work of this kind, directly related to human need, has a tremendous appeal. They are willing to devote a year or more in service almost anywhere; a steady stream of them are choosing social work of a remedial or educational character for their careers. Many of them have turned away from worship and from institutional religion, but they are passionately concerned to help their fellowmen and to help with more than words. Surely inasmuch as they are sharing the vision of one world, one brotherhood of man, they are sharing the vision of Christ. They may be outside, or only tenuously connected with the Churches, but do they not belong to a great Christian movement which is erupting in our day, one which is not organized or controlled by the Churches and their hierarchies but is nevertheless activated by the Spirit of Jesus, and known to Him? Is this what is meant when some speak of the hidden Church, the Church which grows in secret like yeast in the dough?

17. Social concern of this type is frequently labelled 'do-goodism' by those who think it is a kind of superficial activism which achieves little but rather creates new difficulties. We must discount sneers at 'do-gooders' by those who have never done anybody any good, and we must also blow aside the silly criticism with the devastating platitude that 'do-goodism' is a sight better than 'do-badism' of which we have more than enough. Those who know first-hand the young people who have toiled in the work camps, know their quality and sincerity to be superb. They far outnumber the small groups of delinquents, drug addicts, social misfits, and young criminals whose antics receive such full publicity. They constitute one of the most important features of our present rapidly changing society, and they are acting in the firm secular belief that man can and should change the social order, that he can do much

to save himself if he will make the necessary decisions. They not only believe this, they are doing something about it. They are not all starry-eyed, nor do they believe that the earthly paradise will be achieved with sustained effort; they know how insane men can become when material and ideological passions are raised. They take a more immediate and practical view. To sink a well in India can save lives, so they sink a well; to teach peasants how to grow miracle rice, how to institute elementary sanitation, how to read, can lift people from misery to a far higher economic level. They are therefore content, like Jesus, to go about doing good and they leave the future to the future.

18. Is not this a new form of mission, largely lay, theologically inarticulate, but immensely potent? It is very much this-worldly, not other-worldly. It does not look for future or personal reward; it is a way of life which is its own reward. It makes its own companionship in service. And it measures up to much of what Jesus proclaimed as Gospel. It gets on and does the job in the spirit of the Good Samaritan, the man who saw need and did something about it while the unresponsive religious men went on their way to the temple to proclaim the love of God and the duty to love one's neighbour. It finds the sick and dying Lazarus in the street outside the rich man's house and feeds him. It demands more than crumbs from the rich man's table. It says to the rich West, 'Feed your starving brother', and it begins by sharing what it has at its own disposal. It refuses to lay up all its goods in store and settle back in selfish complacency; it wants to make sure that food flows to starving peoples. It gives more than a cup of cold water, it irrigates deserts. It serves the world. Jesus cured a few lepers and told His disciples that they would do far greater miracles. Modern man now saves tens of thousands of lepers every year, and is determined to eradicate leprosy and every other scourge. The battle is here and now, the scene is this world of men and that moon out there, now also part of man's domain; the aim is fuller and better life, the removal of injustice and deprivation, the enlarging of mind and heart, the search for greater truth and beauty. All this is mission and all this is an essential part of the mission of Jesus. Unfortunately it

has been allowed to hive off from the major activity of the Church so that now the Social Gospel appears to be entirely separable from, or at least subordinate to, the main business of the Church, which is to worship God.

19. Liberal theology led directly to the Social Gospel. Its easy optimism which brought it into such discredit when the two World Wars disclosed how irrational man can be, has been corrected. The radical revolt has brought back the Social Gospel into the forefront of Christian Mission. In this particular phase of changing society the excessive individualism of traditional evangelism makes scant appeal, because it is socially defective; it stands condemned in the eyes of men because it forgot that Jesus came to establish a new order of society and that the Christian ought to be in the very vanguard of reform, fearlessly exposing whatever may limit or blight the lives of men, no matter what powerful interests may be disturbed or embarrassed in the process. Jesus has escaped the bars of a theology that would restrict Him to personal spiritual communion without social content or which dresses Him in the robes and pomp of an imperial Caesar or medieval monarch. When Jesus said, 'My Kingdom is not of this world' He meant it was no earthly monarchy, that He did not want adulation, glory, and honour. He did not mean that it was other-worldly, with no interest in what wicked men do or how they organize their cultural, political, and economic life. That is the error that the Church has too often made. Jesus corrects this by insisting that the Kingdom is amongst us, that men and women are entering into it, and that His people must live according to its principles, producing new stresses and strains in the clash of ideal with rough reality. The Gospel of His Way will challenge each succeeding age; the Christian of today must live in that Way here and now, in the private and social situation in which he actually exists. In this world he must live and die and his faith must relate him directly to it, not take him out of it. It must help him to conquer the world, not escape from it.

20. But is the call to social and community service the whole Gospel? Is, as some radicals have argued, everything else just religion, the cloying mixture of false reasoning and spurious emotionalism in which the Jesus of history has been buried by

the Church? Is religion really an attempt to use God? We would have to admit that through the long centuries human weakness, ignorance, and the naked lust for power have all too often obscured the Gospel. But whatever criticisms the Church has merited and received from outside, it has never ceased to hear voices within that would not be silenced and whose criticisms were far more scathing and searching. Today the severest critics of the Church are among its own people; indeed some criticism is so one-sided and savage that one detects unbearable tensions in the critics that blind them to other facts that ought to be taken into consideration. Some of them forget that it is the bewildered Church of today that is maintaining the critics and that if the Church disappeared as quickly as they seem to wish, they would have to seek other occupation, for much of the work they are doing would not be done without the support of the despised Church. Can there be religionless Christianity? Must the Church disappear? Are we well into the post-Christian age?

21. Here again we must return to Jesus. Did He live as if God did not exist? Did He preach that man can and must save himself? Only by excising large sections from the pages of the New Testament can such a view be maintained. This was not the impression He gave His disciples, nor was it the response He seems to have deliberately provoked. His question, 'Who do you say that I am?' was intended to make them think out for themselves the implications of what they had seen and heard. This was the evidence He offered the disciples of the Baptist when they came to ask if He really was the Coming One. The answer is that the works of mercy and the message of salvation are the indubitable marks of the Anointed. They fulfil the Messianic role, which is 'to preach good tidings to the meek, to bind up the broken-hearted, to free the prisoner, to proclaim the acceptable year of the Lord' (Isaiah 61:1f). 'Go tell John what you have seen and heard.' Christ's reply did not mean that John was to be released from prison: on the contrary, it was intended to prepare him for his own execution. John was the Forerunner. He went ahead along the road that Jesus would go. As they slew John, so they would slay the Christ. It was no good looking for another kind of deliverer.

There is no other Way for either John or Christ. When the soldiers dragged John to his death, and when the crowds yelled to Pilate, 'Crucify him!' there was little sign of the brotherhood of man. There was every sign of the triumph of hate and fear, of prejudice and sadistic irrationality. No man can follow that Way unless he is prepared to take up his cross daily.

22. Some liberal theologians, so sure that the Gospel of the Kingdom was the joyous message of Jesus, have sought to argue that Jesus came very late in His ministry to the realization that He would be rejected. But this is to make the facts fit the theory. His ethical teaching was never presented in systematic form like the moral philosophy of Socrates, Plato, Aristotle, the Stoics, and the Epicureans. Always His ethics spring from the requirements of His relationship to God. He does not argue about the nature of justice or righteousness; to Him it is a matter of obedience to the Will of the Father, and again, not from any sense of a duty unwillingly or reluctantly fulfilled, but in glad agreement that what the Father seeks, is the welfare of every one of His children. What impressed those who lived near Jesus was His intense awareness of God, His utter and complete identification of Himself with the mind and will of His Father. It was so close as to make identification inevitable. When the Fourth Gospel puts into His mouth the words, 'I and the Father are one' (John 10:30), 'He that has seen me has seen the Father' (John 14:9), it was expressing the conviction that in Jesus men saw as much of the character of God as it was possible for man to see. The Fourth Gospel is emphatic. 'No one has ever seen God; but God's only Son, he who is nearest to the Father's heart, he has made him known' (John 1:18).

23. Is the testimony of the Fourth Gospel to be disregarded? Even if it is a later interpretation of the Fact of Christ, the judgement of those who had spent a lifetime in reflection upon that life, were they not throwing into mythopoetic form that identity with God which Jesus experienced? The Gospel admits that most of those who knew Jesus, who grew up with Him, did not see God in Him; 'The world did not recognize him,' 'his own did not receive him.' But there were those who did—they beheld His glory, and they became the Church which

produced the Gospels and wrote the Epistles. From the beginning Christianity has required an act of faith, a leap beyond the superficial evidence, a commitment to Jesus, a belief that what He said about God was true. The New Testament and the Church are a response to the question Jesus asked, 'What do you think of me?'

24. Jesus was a first-century Jew; He shared many of the preconceptions of His age. If He had not done so He would never have been able to communicate at all. He was ignorant of many things that are commonplace to us. He had never seen a railway train, an aeroplane, or a radio. It is almost impossible for us to imagine the conditions under which He lived, so wide is the cultural gap. But He speaks to our fundamental humanity and His words have an ageless quality. He touches the chords that abide all cultural change and He does so because He speaks from His own experience of God. For while He shared the thought forms of His day, His idea of God was very different from current belief. He had fed Himself on the insights of the prophets and the psalms, He had drawn them together into a new synthesis and in a response of complete acceptance He had identified Himself with the Will of the Father.

25. The relationship was unique. Not even the greatest of Israel's prophets had even approached that inner identity which so fascinated yet bewildered His disciples. In sudden flashes of intuition and inspiration they groped for the truth and were drawn nearer and nearer to the incredible solution. He was so much in God and God was so much in Him, that even to identify Him as Messiah was not sufficient explanation. Nor, when later they recognized Him as the Holy Servant, the mysterious figure of the despised redeemer, had they reached the final conclusion. God was in Christ and this fact demanded exposition. God had become man. How? Stories of semi-divine heroes, the offspring of the union of gods and beautiful women were rife in the Greek and Near Eastern world. But the disciples were Jews to whom polytheism was an abomination and for whom the High and Holy One was so transcendently separate that any thought of physical union was the foulest blasphemy. Yet the Fact of Jesus could not be evaded and as

the Church tried to voice its own experience of Jesus it was driven to impress the stamp of its own pecular Christian consciousness on the mythopoeic forms. It remembered Mary, the Blessed Mother, it recalled strange stories of His birth preserved in the privacy of the family memory. And just as the Jewish nation had taken the Near Eastern Creation and Flood myths and transformed them into great poems of revelation, so the infant Church dared to proclaim the story of the coming of Jesus—*Conceived of the Holy Ghost*; *born of the Virgin Mary*; the Word; God with man: God was in Christ. The Church dared to say that whatever God was so also was the Word; the Word had been made flesh and they had seen His glory.

26. Whether or not a Christian today can take the narratives of the birth of Jesus as faithful accounts of events precisely as they occurred and as they would be reported by an objective journalist of today is surely now a matter of private judgement depending on the need of the individual. What is not optional is the fact that those who knew Jesus best were absolutely convinced that in Him God was present, revealing Himself as completely and fully as human nature would permit. The Birth of Jesus is to the Christian the foundation fact of the Incarnation, the entry of God into humanity. The New Testament says plainly that once one begins to answer the question, 'Who is he?' one cannot confine the answer to what we know of humanity; it includes another reference, a far richer content which demands the affirmation, 'God was in Christ.'

27. Here, then, it would seem there is sufficient agreement between nearly all Christians to enable them to work together in mission and to proclaim a common Gospel. They can witness by word and deed not only to the ethical content of the Gospel with its vision of world brotherhood based on mutual love in the family of God; they can also proclaim that God was in Christ. In this full identity of will and purpose God reveals His real nature. In Jesus God gives Himself completely to man, for the life lived by Jesus is one of unbroken and unspoiled obedience to the Father's will. All the records agree that in Jesus the obedience was complete, because His love for God was so unreserved. The ensuing life of unhindered communion has been called 'sinless' not in any legal sense, but in the

fundamentally religious sense of unclouded love of God. Jesus lived in the light and warmth of that love. From this central relationship the ethic was derived; not the relationship from the ethic.

CHAPTER SIXTEEN

The Search for Faith

THE radical protest and the irritation with which it is occasionally uttered rises out of a strong emotional reaction to the present helplessness of the Church as well as from impatience with traditional theology. In so far as it castigates the Church for its failure to understand the new society and culture into which we are entering the rebuke is only too well merited, and in so far as it reveals how unsatisfactory are many of the traditional theological arguments it is also justified. But when radicals cease to be negative and essay constructive theology they are no more successful than those they criticize. They must learn to accept criticism as well as to give it without being so touchy. Radicals have frequently written disparagingly of religious experience and speak about its 'evaporation' from the secular world. They reject the validity of evangelical experience because they hold it is generated in a hot-house of emotionalism, artificially created by the preaching of the traditionalist plan of salvation. They deny the Fall of Man as an historic event; they dismiss the idea of Divine Law as a dreadful bogy from which secularity has mercifully delivered man; they consider conviction of sin to be an unhealthy preoccupation with failure, exacerbated by the idea of God as Judge and Executioner. They maintain that Western Christianity has been sin-obsessed and that secular man is much more healthy than traditional evangelicals realize, too mentally sound to go through the unhealthy procedure of conversion. Salvation, say the radicals, is concerned with Peace—*shalom*—the happy, contented, and prosperous society of integrated persons too mature to torment themselves and others with the ancient concept of sin. These, of course, are all extreme statements of the radical position, and in total amount to a caricature; but it is no more a caricature than the radical's own picture of traditional evangelism. Is not the task of the Church today to search for the common ground of mission?

2. We begin with the admission that all the words and phrases we use to describe God are pictures and are all inadequate. This at least we have learned from the modern study of religious language. They attempt to describe some aspect of His nature which men have recognized. That all the images are human or drawn from human experience goes without saying, for we have no other words or modes of expression. We must use what language we have. The religious man uses language like a poet, not like a scientist. A scientist describes objectively what he does or sees, almost as if he were himself a disembodied intelligence surveying objective facts from outside. But modern philosophy is also teaching us that God is not an Object among other objects. He is that which makes being possible. 'In him we live and move and have our being.' He is the First and the Last, or, as Tillich said, 'the Ground of All Being'. Such terms really describe not what God is, but what He is not. All are attempts to stop us taking something less than God for God Himself, to escape from the idolatry that always tries to imprison God in a shape of words or forms. This is why Moses and Mohammed refused to permit any image of God; they were all false. But it is also true that without them we are equally defeated. If God is completely incomprehensible because He is inexpressible, then as far as man is concerned, it would be just the same if He did not exist at all. But Jesus said He does exist, He does express Himself and make Himself known to men. Even to say God exists can be misleading for He does not 'exist' as we exist. He 'is'. That is what His name 'I AM' means. Modern man has an option: he can look at the universe and himself and seek an explanation of it all without the idea of God, or he can look at the same facts and with the idea of God read an entirely different meaning into the facts. But such an idea is more than an intellectual assumption; it is rather the discovery of a new dimension, a depth, to use Tillich's pregnant phrase, which involves the believer in an act of commitment. Christianity is a faith, not just a philosophy;

it is a Way of Life as well as ideas about life; it is personal relationships, not just a system of theological abstractions.

3. Faith, then, is the distinctive feature of Christianity, as it is of all personal relationships, for without faith one can never love or treat another person as a person. But faith can degenerate into mere credulity and superstition. Enormous crimes have been committed in the name of God by men of faith. Faith can easily slide into bigotry and fanaticism. Faith can be so blind in its devotion that it inflicts horrible suffering on those who oppose it, and it is experience of religious bigotry that has led secular man to conclude that faith is so unreliable, inconsistent, and dangerous that he is better off without it. Men of faith hold such diverse and often contradictory views, all with such passionate conviction, that the unbeliever can see little virtue in these private opinions about matters which seem to be entirely beyond verification. And since Christians seem quite incapable of solving their internal differences, what reason is there to believe that there is a substantially agreed body of Christian truth in which a man can with any confidence have faith?

4. Must we not recall the great lessons of religious toleration and freely recognize that Christianity guarantees liberty to think? Consequently we must seek, not uniformity but unity in essentials. Men vary tremendously in background and education, character and development. There are still many for whom the orthodox theology makes sense. Such people will respond to the traditional evangelical appeal and find themselves at home in conservative evangelical circles. Because traditional evangelism can speak to their condition in a way that liberal or radical mission fails to do, we want to insist that they ought not to be discouraged or denigrated by other Christians. What they believe has a long and noble history; for centuries it was the way in which men understood the Gospel. It uses the thought forms which had proved effective in past ages. Some of these appear to be unacceptable to increasing multitudes today, but the form must not be confused with the content, and with all its faults traditional evangelical theology contained sufficient Gospel to transform the lives of millions of men. Jesus Himself advanced the simple pragmatic

test—'You will recognize them by the fruits they bear' (Matthew 7:16), and the fruits of the Evangelical Revival have been, and in some parts of the world still are, rich indeed. A considerable part of the Christian strength in England belongs to this school, and it is spreading rapidly in South America and Indonesia.

5. Assuming then that we are prepared to live with the pluralism of modern theology, is there sufficient common ground between the various schools to make mission intelligible? What is common to the traditional and the radical understanding of salvation? The Hebrew conception of Israel's God as a Deliverer or Saviour was the natural outcome of the nation's history. Deeply embedded in their racial memory were the events of the Exodus and their delivery from bondage in Egypt. A little people were prised loose from the grasp of a giant world-power, escaping first into the liberty of the wilderness as nomadic tribesmen, and then to the conquest of lands of their own. Israel's religious genius saw the story of the nation as a series in which infidelity was followed by subjection to powerful adversaries from which came deliverance through some mighty act of God, working through men and women of courageous faith. Old Testament theology is predominantly Salvation theology. Israel's God is the Saviour God who comes to the rescue of sinful, penitent Israel and delivers her from all her enemies whether Egypt or Babylon, Greece or Rome. Salvation is not primarily thought of as individual; it is essentially the salvation of the nation, the rescue and restoration of the people of God. It is firmly of this world, embracing all that we mean by social justice, the equality of all within the commonwealth and the care of all within the welfare state.

6. Hebrew understanding of its Saviour God depicted Him as intervening directly by supernatural acts which were almost magical in their operation. The various accounts of the Crossing of the Red Sea show the process at work. What is not in doubt is that the people escaped their pursuers and were freed from the power of the Pharaoh. What is very much in doubt is how this happened. Was it wind pressure that drove and held back the waters? The timing of the saving act is just as significant as the act itself; indeed, it was its perfect timing

that made the event a miracle of salvation. The fleeing people stood helplessly trapped between the sea and their confident enemies. Then the impossible happened; the waters divided and they walked across to freedom. It happened to them in their situation. All they cared for was that they were free at last and not by any act of their own, save that they had dared to flee from slavery, trusting the God of their fathers. It is no wonder that they flung the story of their deliverance into triumphant poetry. 'The Lord is a man of war . . . Pharaoh's chariots and his host hath he cast into the sea' (Exodus 15:3). This is poetry and myth; it expresses the joy of deliverance and it ascribes directly to God the attributes of a successful general who has destroyed his enemy. It is true as far as it can rightly go; but it is grotesquely false beyond that point. For God is not only the God of Israel whom He redeemed; He is the God of Egypt whom He judges; and both acts are expressions of His loving purpose. The Egyptian horseman, lost in the flood of returning waters, matters as much to God as the Hebrew climbing out on the other side a free man. Even the picture of judge is only very partially true, for the Egyptian soldier was doing his duty as he understood it, and what righteous judge could execute him for that?

7. The Exodus occurred a long time ago. For Israel it was the all-important event, but to Egypt it was so insignificant that it is not recorded in the known history of that people, though some passing reference is made to the appearance of the Habiri, who may be Hebrew tribes. But as the centuries proceed the number of such dramatic and apparently miraculous interventions decreases. There was no parallel act of salvation when the Jews began to return from Babylon after the Exile. The prophet had promised that there would be a miraculous road, smooth and straight, opened for them through the desert, along which they would come in joyful procession. In the event they came back in handfuls to a mixed and disappointing reception. During the long persecution by the Seleucids faithful Jews prayed in vain for a deliverance, but though eventually a quasi independence was won, it was at the cost of terrible suffering. Israel slowly learned that God did not always save when they expected Him to save; that many good

and innocent people perished; that wickedness seemed to triumph as much as, if not more than, righteousness. Doubt began to rear its head and the Books of Job and Ecclesiastes and some Psalms voice the question, Where is God? Why does He not defend His own? Why does He not save the righteous? By the end of the Old Testament there is not only an official Salvation theology, there is also an unofficial sceptical theology which dares to insist that the human story does not reveal an increasing purpose, but exposes an essential meaninglessness, the emptiness of emptiness, the vanity of vanities. It is no use orthodoxy brushing such teaching aside as decadent. It also is Holy Writ and it bears witness to facts that are very evident to modern man. There was no deliverance for the six million Jews who perished in the Nazi concentration camps.

8. In the New Testament these two elements are blended into a new synthesis. There is salvation theology, but it is a different kind of salvation than that of the Old Testament and there is an exposure of the Nothingness far more tragic than the drama of Job. The two are brought together, not in any systematic philosophy, but in a series of pictures which demand commitment, leaving the believer free to work out his own solution to the problems. Traditional Evangelicals have emphasized the salvation theology which they have interpreted often in narrowly individualistic ways, while the liberals and radicals have seized on the social and political elements of the Gospel. Because of their own experience of the Nothingness the radicals cannot avoid questioning the artificiality of orthodox salvation theology. Yet the two belong to each other and complete each other. May it not be that what God requires of His Church today is that each side should learn from the other, and together attempt the new understanding of the Gospel for which the world is waiting?

9. The key figure again is Jesus. In His teaching salvation is not so much a series of acts by which God miraculously intervenes in human affairs but the Purpose which He always and everywhere pursues. Jesus depicts salvation as both an individual and a social matter, but He insists that it must be individually sought. This is the unpopular truth that evangelicalism preserves. Thus God loves the whole world, and

gives His own Son to it, but the apprehension of the gift must be made by each believer individually. No one can do someone else's believing for him, though we can help others to faith. Acts of government can transform society, improving it and making it more agreeable to its members; they cannot create faith or bring men into fellowship with God. Radicals realize that society is changed by political action, and some of them are now urging Christians to go into politics and into other centres of decision-making, particularly in industry and education, so as to ensure that legislation will embody Christian ideals. But one must first produce awakened Christians and a Christian activist is one who believes in Jesus, is captivated by the Christ-way, and who believes in the Fatherhood of God.

10. For in Jesus the two ideas are held firmly together. On the one hand is the sense of absolute identity with God, an identity of will and purpose. Jesus thinks of Himself as a Saviour, not in the sense of one who magically interrupts the normal course of nature to work some supernatural feat, but as a good shepherd who seeks until he finds his lost sheep, or as a poor woman who searches thoroughly every corner of her house for the coin she cannot afford to lose. The pictures are of a search for individuals but the search is also for all mankind. The breadth of this love was finely brought out by Charles Wesley:

Throughout the world its breadth is known,
Wide as infinity;
So wide is never passed by one,
Or it had passed by me.

M.H.B. 77

Jesus speaks of Himself as coming to seek and to save that which was lost. The object is to restore a lost relationship, to recover that which was lying useless, out of circulation like an unused coin, or in danger of dying like a trapped sheep. In the story which we call the Prodigal Son, He depicts two lost sons—one lost in a far country of illusion and the other lost at home in his father's house, unable to comprehend the father's motives. The younger son comes to his senses and realizes his impoverishment: the older brother is truculent to the very end. He wants the Father to be stern and severe, exacting a fitting punishment from the younger son for his folly. Here Jesus seems to be indicting the religious leaders of His own people for their harshness towards those they called fools and sinners. But may it not be that today the secular world is coming to its senses while traditional orthodoxy is far from understanding the merciful motives of God? This suggestion is supported by the other story of the Master's about two brothers, one who promised to work for his father, but did not keep his word, and the other who first repudiated the father's control, but changed his mind and actually did the work. Is not secular man often doing the will of God while religious men talk about it? Any local Christian Church today which takes a census of community need and how it is met is likely to be astonished at the amount of utterly selfless devotion to people in need which is given by those who profess no faith at all, while the energies of Church people are exhausted in maintaining their own buildings and society. The Church seems to be ministering to itself with little time or energy left for others, and to that extent the Church, like the elder brother, seems to be lost as well as the prodigal 'outsider'.

11. The word 'lost' is surely of some significance to modern man. Dillistone describes the chief characteristic of our restless age as 'alienation'. Man seems no longer at home in the impersonal universe. He has no unifying philosophy to give him security. He is exposed to meaninglessness, for he lives in a world that is doomed eventually to disintegrate. His irrational nature is quite capable of destroying him long before life must cease on this planet. Modern literature from Ibsen to Sartre[1] is full of the terrible loneliness of those who cannot communicate what they really feel. They have not the words to express their inner tensions and torments, nor the means of getting through to the consciousness of others who are in equal distress. They therefore continue to destroy themselves and one another. The evidence of current literature supports Dillistone but apparently some radicals do not feel this sense of alienation. They believe that man must save himself and that this is what God wants him to do.

12. Perhaps the fact is that man is both lost and at home in

[1]See Helmut Thielicke, *Nihilism* (Routledge, Kegan Paul, 1962).

his world. Certainly he dominates it now more than he has ever done, and is to that extent more in control of his destiny than ever before. Men who can walk on the moon and who are reaching for the stars must in one sense be aware as never before of the vastness of the universe, but they must also be supremely confident in what they can do with it given sufficient co-operation and resources. The transformation of this planet into a garden paradise free from hunger and want, ignorance and disease is no longer an impossible dream; we know it could and ought to become a reality, if only we would unite and devote ourselves to the problems. But our present inability to co-operate reveals the irrational, fearful, and distrustful element that defeats us both as individuals and as nations. There is a brute selfishness about us, an ability to blind ourselves to the needs of others, a deep fear of what others would do to us if we lowered our guard. There is a resentment against all those who seem to threaten our comfort or security or our accustomed way of doing things, a hatred of those who dare to question our values and conventions. Each of us carries a dream of our own importance, and we are wounded when we fail to win the recognition and appreciation we think we merit. However sociable we may be and in need of society, we nevertheless experience life as individuals, and the world is full of the pain, frustration, fear, and hate of each individual and this is the constant source of human misery and suffering. We are lost in our own home. Both aspects are true, but the misery of the world cries out louder than our exultation at the orbiting of the moon.

13. The Bible word for such a condition is 'sin'. As we have seen, modern man no longer thinks of law as absolute nor of punishment as pure retribution, so that he is repelled when the Gospel is presented as the salvation of sinful wrongdoers from the death penalty, the fitting punishment for their iniquity. These forensic images so far from commending the Gospel to modern minds, raise difficult questions about the way in which the death of Jesus can possibly 'save' men. There is urgent need to restate the idea of sin and once again we turn to Jesus who uses other pictures besides that of the oriental despot dispensing justice. The Prodigal recognized he was a sinner when he

'came to himself'. He suddenly became aware of his true condition of poverty and hunger and realized in a flash of discernment how much he had lost. He came frankly to his father and confessed, 'Father, I have sinned against heaven and in thy sight.' The young man realized that he had spoiled a clean universe and hurt his father. Sin always involves this desecration of the sacred order of life; it is a violation of the good, not just a breaking of a law; it is the staining and corrupting of what was pure and holy. It is not only wrong done to others, it is an offence against what life ought to be and essentially is. That is why guilt always carries with it a sense of uncleanness and why so often the symbolic washing of hands betrays the repressed feeling of guilt and shame so marvellously illustrated in Lady Macbeth's sleep walking. A guilty man feels the need to wash away the stain upon his inner self, which both corrupts him and offends the sacred universe. The obligation to maintain that sacred order which most men seem to feel in their deepest consciousness is the basis of what the Bible calls the Law of God. How this sense of responsibility is inculcated is a matter for psychological study, but its value for society and for the individual himself, is not in question. It can be explained, but not explained away. It is required if the infant is to become a mature adult and so it belongs to the structure of our humanity.

14. Secular man, we are told, no longer feels any sense of what we have just called the sacred order—that conception disappeared finally with the passing of the Middle Ages. Certainly man no longer thinks of it as a theocratic state, a divine organization of which he is part. Nor does he think of moral law as absolute; he traces it to the communal needs of humanity. Society changes and each stage requires modification of the law. But each change is related to one constant principle—the well-being of humanity. Change in itself is a constant feature. Life evolves from simple originals to ever more elaborate and complex forms. The good is not static; it is whatever helps to create and support developing life. Morality is relative, but relative to an ascending hope. Law changes but the good is that which enhances and secures the hope. That new order will always be new, and so it is impossible to define

or describe its ultimate shape, save by adjectives that are really negatives. It will be just—but by that we mean that no man will be wrongfully deprived; we do not know what content justice will then have. It will be egalitarian, but by that we mean there will be no second-class citizens, no underprivileged minorities, no lower castes: we do not know how brotherhood will be expressed, by what new convention and standards men and women will live together. But that hope, the ideal that beckons and which is so keenly felt by the best young people today is in its own right an absolute, or the sacred ordering of things. It is the Purpose that runs through the human story against which every man must measure himself. He may refuse to recognize it, but in his best moments he feels the tug of it and wishes he had responded more often and more fully to its invitation. This is what the process theologians are teaching us.

15. The hope is at work in the present and shapes the future. The technical achievements of today are all part of man's evolution, but every moment a moral choice has to be made—is man going to use them for the betterment or for the destruction of society? We have spoken of this transforming and compelling ideal as the hope, but is not this what Jesus was talking about when he spoke of the Kingdom of God, the divine order that is even now at work and which is to be manifested in the fullness of time, an order which will eventually embrace in one harmonic whole both heaven and earth in a new creation emerging from Him whose purpose is to make all things new? The life of the Kingdom is living in co-operation with that mighty Purpose: sin is living to oneself in isolation from and rejection of that Purpose. Modern man may not feel himself a sinner in the old sense of one who has broken God's laws, but he knows that he and his world are not what they could be and ought to be, and that in some measure he and every man is responsible for most of the suffering and sadness of the world.

16. In popular speech 'sin' usually means certain immoral acts, generally sexual offences; the old phrase 'living in sin' meant the cohabitation of the unwedded. But sin is also our common attitude of limited liability and indifference which is responsible for the continuation of so much human injustice.

Wars, famine, plagues, all could be controlled, but we are defeated by our failure to allay suspicion, overcome innate prejudices and built-in resistances to change. All that conditions us and makes us slow or reluctant to co-operate with the hope must be included in our conception of sin. It involves both society itself which shapes us at every point, and our own psychological structuring, more immediately affected by our treatment in infancy, childhood, and the early years of adolescence. We are what we are, incapable of breaking out of the prisonhouse of our human nature, (too often, inhuman nature) save by a great shift of personality. Normally we remain true to type, with our fears and suspicions and prejudices firmly in command, and it was this normal sub-human reaction that crucified Christ. He was not murdered by demonic sadists or power-crazed tyrants. He was arrested, tried, and condemned in a long-drawn-out process which gave opportunity for men to speak for or against Him or to keep silent. Christ was betrayed and slaughtered by ordinary men, reacting predictably, for sin is the fear, ignorance, inertia and backdrag which tries to defeat the onward surge of the Purpose of the Universe, and sin always inflicts pain and injury on the bringer of hope.

17. The modern radical can understand the death of Jesus as the supreme example of the self-sacrifice required by those who would take the Way of Love. To love is to give oneself for others, to lay down one's life for them. So to the radical Jesus is the great Example and the greatest joy and honour of the disciple is to take the same road and lay down his life for others. The Christian must become the man for others; the Church must die to itself for others not yet inside the Church. All this is needed corrective to the inturned Church and to the introspective Christian, intent on his own salvation, but it does not exhaust what Jesus Himself and His first followers thought about His death. Jesus Himself saw the clash coming and prepared Himself and His disciples, as far as He could, for the approaching tragedy. He used a curious word to describe it; He called it His baptism (Mark 10:38; Luke 12:50). A baptism is an initiating ceremony which admits into a new community. It marks the washing away symbolically of all the old association, and the entrance by a kind of new birth into a new

society. Somehow His death would mark the beginning of a new creation through an ordeal of purification which would wash away the old. Jesus also spoke of His death as a 'cup' which the Father had presented to Him to drink. Everything within Him revolted against the suggestion, but this was the Will He had known and loved all His life asking of Him His life as once it had asked Abraham for his son. This time there would be no other lamb to be sacrificed, only the one Lamb of God. It will be recalled that when Luther and his wife were reading together the story of Abraham she cried out that it was all wrong; God could never ask for the life of a son, 'But, Katie!' said Luther, 'He did!' This dreadful cup was offered because it had cosmic significance; God did not exact it. There was no demand for a ransom, but Jesus gave it.

18. Jesus did not think that God was asking Him to submit to a cruel death simply as a witness to the truth of what He had taught. He thought of Himself as a shepherd laying down his life for his sheep, as one whose death enables many others to escape. The death, if He was willing to die—and the choice was His—was an essential part of the Purpose, or to use our modern term, of the Process by which the whole stream of life was to be purified and redirected. The disciples themselves did not comprehend what Jesus sought so desperately to explain; these were ideas far outside their normal thinking. Crushed and broken by the triumph of His enemies they watched Him die in utter bewilderment and disappointment. They watched while Jesus Himself endured not only the excruciating agony of the nails, but the more terrible spiritual torture of the Dereliction. In that awful moment the life-long consciousness of God evaporated suddenly and He was left alone as He had never known loneliness before. He hung there conscious only of His humanity, a dying man, while the fateful words of Psalm 22 broke from His lips, 'My God, my God, why hast thou forsaken me?' Jesus entered the Nothingness; He experienced that loss of God-consciousness which is the normal condition of humanity. But what by us is scarcely noticed was to Him the final horror. The Saviour God refused to save Him, there was no intervention, no miraculous deliverance. He died as men die. But He did not let go of God. 'Yet will I trust Him, even

though he slay me' (Job 13:15). He died commending His spirit into the hands of God, knowing that His work was accomplished. 'It is finished.'

19. What was finished was not just the ordeal: something had been accomplished which altered the whole direction of humanity, a power had been identified and liberated, a power which generations of Christians have called 'redeeming love'. From the Friday till the dawn of Sunday His disciples huddled together in mute humiliation, fear, and uncertainty. Then came the news, first from the women, that He was risen, that they had seen Him. Modern scholarship has subjected the resurrection narratives to the closest scrutiny, every inconsistency has been noted, they have been demythologized, but what remains is astonishing agreement that whatever happened that First Easter, the disciples became joyfully aware that Jesus still lived, that He could still speak in and through them, and that His mission was now theirs. They were to work His works and to share with Him His risen life within the Purpose. The Primitive Church is quite inexplicable apart from this inrush of creative energy which they called the Holy Spirit. Tongues as of fire, the rushing of a mighty wind are all mythopoeic expressions, attempting to describe that flaming power that transformed the timid bunch of disciples into the fearless apostles of the new faith, a faith which sent men cheerfully on hazardous journeys, to suffering and death to proclaim the joyful mystery that in the death and resurrection of Jesus the paralysing grip of sin on the human heart was broken and men were set free to become followers of the Way, the apostles of hope, the children of God.

20. Just how the death accomplished this salvation is not explained; the apostles were more interested in the indubitable experience than in explanations. Naturally they used the current ideas of sacrifice, propitiation, and expiation and this leads us to our next suggestion for co-operation between Christians of differing theologies. Can we not also, like the first disciples, unite on the fact and leave room for difference of opinion about the explanation of the fact? As Dillistone has shown there are many different approaches to a solution of what precisely happened in the Atonement, and each contains

some insight into the mystery. Surely he is right in reminding us that in tragedy we identify ourselves with the representative man who draws on his innocent head the appalling agonies of irresistible fate. We watch the plot build up, we see the gathering storm, we know the hero will not surrender his integrity and that he will die a terrible death as those vengeful forces remorselessly close in upon him. We come away from such plays not despairing of man's wickedness and pitiful weakness; but through some strange mode of identification we feel cleansed by that suffering, humbly proud to belong to a race that can produce the one heroic figure who dares to die rather than collapse like a coward. We are affected by our personal identification with that representative man, the one who stands as champion for the many. He dies yet in him humanity has triumphed over its own baseness. But no tragedy has ever had the compelling and moving power of the story of the Crucifixion. Without any attempt at effect, minimizing the physical details, it depicts succinctly the tragic representative, who scorned to save Himself. Few can read that story without being moved, and to be moved is to be involved.

21. Tragedy then suggests one approach. The apostles, being Jews, turned naturally to the Law and to the sacrificial system for their understanding. They seized on the ancient conviction that when wrong is done the sacred order is violated, and that before order can be restored some restitution must be made. This conviction is very deeply ingrained in primitive thought. It lingers today in the feeling that some propitiatory gift should be made which costs the offender something. Such a gift not only seeks to please the wronged one and to assure of good behaviour in the future, it is also intended to help the offender to forgive himself, it expresses his own repentance and determination to undo as much as he can and to compensate for what he has done. But what gift can one give to God? The only gift He wants is loving obedience, which is the one thing we cannot give, though we can make spasmodic efforts at it. Now, if a representative man could offer that gift, fully and gladly up to the last demand that could possibly be made of him, would not the whole sacral order be for ever altered by that perfect gift? It is this kind of thinking that led the New

Testament writers to speak about the cleansing blood of the Lamb of God. Demythologized it points again to the perfect obedience of Christ, even to the last demand of death itself, an obedience which has forever justified and consecrated the divine order, the eternal Purpose that was purposed in Christ Jesus. The Fourth Gospel has this in mind when in the words of the Priestly Prayer, Jesus 'sanctifies himself' for what He has to do. He was identifying Himself with the Divine Kingdom, releasing its energies for the creation of the New Heaven and the New Earth, the entirely new and utterly holy universe that is the goal of both Hope and Purpose.

22. The legal metaphors are far from the thought forms of today, but they too when demythologized point to the truth that man has deliberately rebelled against the divine order; he does not want to share his life with God and in consequence man has partially dehumanized himself. Endless error and confusion creep in when we try to systematize the legal picture and begin to ask to whom was the price of redemption paid. The substitutionary theories are fraught with peril just because they force these questions forward. But behind these terrible pictures of the innocent one freely offering Himself as a ransom for the guilty many, is a profound insight. Men do lay down their lives for others, a heroic few can save a nation at the expense of their lives. What the death and resurrection of Jesus did was to release a new energy and to set humanity on its road again in a new direction. Those who believe in Jesus and commit themselves to His Way are energized by the Spirit of God and share as never before in the Increasing Purpose, or as Jesus called it, His Father's Will. This is the heart of the Lord's Prayer, 'Thy Will be done, Thy Kingdom come on earth as it already is in heaven.' Here is the Purpose and the Hope now made manifest and plain for all to see, secured and guaranteed by the death and resurrection of Jesus and in the gift of the Spirit. And here too is release from the crippling sense of guilt, here is pardon and forgiveness, here is welcome for the son who has come to himself.

23. But that death and resurrection can never be understood until we have answered Christ's question, 'Who do you say that I am?' We must go back to our beginning. This Jesus,

who lived so close to God, who was so identified with God, in whom God so obviously dwelt, who was He? Just another prophet, another teacher, another martyr? He was all these, but so much more. Those who knew Him best made the leap of faith and declared that He was God. Again, they could not explain how, but the fact they could not deny. If God was in Christ, if what He taught was the Will of God and the Wisdom of God, if what He did was the power and the mercy of God, what then was His death? Who was it that died? And again the infant Church hurls out its incredible credo, 'God was in Christ reconciling the world to himself.' It was God speaking and pleading in the agony of His Son. God Himself accepting the degradation of execution at the hands of sinful men. God Himself who takes the Way of the Cross. There is no longer any question about to whom was the ransom paid. To nobody because it was not that kind of ransom. It was not a measured compensation, it was perfect obedience and perfect love for sinful man which dies and rises from the dead, because love is stronger than death and sin and breaks their chains. So once again the infant Church sang of the glories of the Saviour God and of the dying Lamb, of Him who was dead and is alive for ever, whose blood cleanses the whole universe, who holds the keys of death and Hades. Demythologized this means that the Purpose is fulfilled in Jesus and in Him the Hope will be realized and that there shall not be one lost good. Because He lives, we shall live also.

CHAPTER SEVENTEEN

Some Thoughts on Mission Today

WE have tried to understand the present crisis of faith in the West so as to discover how in such a turmoil the Church can best fulfil its mission. There is no simple solution, though some Christians are still firmly convinced that traditional evangelism has the only answer. Others, equally sincere, are quite sure that conservative theology has no word for industrialized society which is spreading throughout the world. Between these opposing views are great numbers of bewildered Christians of many shades of opinion, painfully aware that the Church has lost its nerve and wondering whether it really can be renewed for mission.

2. Our first conclusion is that we must learn to live with religious pluralism, recognizing frankly that the Church will and must contain believers who hold widely different views. May it not be that in such rich diversity the wholeness of the Gospel expresses itself, and that the Spirit refuses to be encased within the rational formulations of any one school. He has distributed His gifts and insights to each and we need each other for the full picture. Because we believe this to be so, we suggest that there already exists in our common experience of Christ a sufficient content and dynamic to make co-operation in mission possible, provided Christians are gripped by the realities of their common faith and are prepared to commit themselves to what Christ requires of them.

3. The growing realization of the extent of the common ground is a direct result of the ecumenical movement however unfashionable it may be at the moment. As the Churches have talked together many differences which at first sight seemed insurmountable, on closer examination have turned out to be differences of emphasis and language rather than of principle.

We are learning to respect each other and to see what God has done in and through each other. The conclusion is unavoidable; we belong to one another because we belong to Christ. Some of us would draw the further conclusion that for the sake of Christ and His mission we ought to come together now and continue the theological debate inside the unity we seek. However that may be, the Lund Principle accepted by many Churches, that we ought to do everything together except those things which conscience forbids, would seem to provide a sufficient ground for joint action in mission.

4. United action may at least help the world to believe that our mission is from God (John 17:21) for it is certain that the world has little time for our divisions and no confidence in a self-proclaimed reconciling faith which cannot even reconcile Christian to Christian. We need therefore to explore together the area of our agreement, gratefully accepting what each can contribute. Shared study and planning will take us deeper into the Mind of Christ, for it is not Christ that divides us; the resistance lies in us and our concepts of truth. We do well to heed the warning of the Dutch Catholics that there is a difference between the Living Truth and our formulations of it which ought to change with the unfolding situation. The process theologians remind us that change is the norm of our existence; the universe at this moment sums up all that has gone before; we affect the world by what we are and do; God Himself operates at every point sustaining the whole and giving Himself. So we move into the different world of the next successive moment. Our understanding of truth ought never to be static. The Fourth Gospel says truth is the Living Jesus. When jesting Pilate asked, 'What is truth?' the Answer was staring him in the face, bound and bleeding. He wanted words but the answer is a Life and a Way. We defend our separations in the name of truth, but truth is not theological formulae: it is the Crucified and Risen Lord who fills the universe with the purpose of love. All our truths are under the judgement of the Crucified. He is the common ground of mission, and to deny that common ground is to deny Him however much we claim to speak in His name, and to stand on truth.

5. Missionary effort today is crippled by our divisions and

we believe that the Holy Spirit is prompting us to seek the lost unity of the Apostolic Church which provided so great a stimulus in the expansion of the Church in the first three centuries. We are ashamed that we can give no guarantee that a convert received by one denomination will be equally welcomed into another. Anything like global planning is impossible, even though national and international missionary conferences do their best. In industry trends are carefully studied and the models to meet the projected needs seven years hence are already on the drawing board. But the fragmented Church, whose united strength is far greater than the most colossal industrial combine, is unable to utilize its resources in an integrated strategy of mission. Yet the population explosion makes such planning imperative. We know that by the year 2000, barring plague or nuclear war, the world population will double to 7,000 million. The explosion will occur mostly in non-Christian lands, so that the ratio of Christian to non-Christian will fall dramatically. In 1900 there were 571 million Christians, about 36 per cent of the world population; in 1964 there were 925 million Christians, but they were only 29 per cent of the total. By the year 2000 they will be only 20 per cent. These estimates reckon as Christian the entire population of the so-called Christian lands, but the assumption is unrealistic, for in the West the number of practising Christians is steadily falling, so that by the end of the century the Christian proportion may be very much less than 20 per cent. Yet the Churches have scarcely awakened to this challenge and our denominationalism prohibits the rational deployment of our resources that coherent mission demands.

6. Any comprehensive global planning ought to take into thoughtful consideration the remarkable expansion of the Pentecostalist Churches in Latin America and of the Faith Missions in hitherto unevangelized areas. Based on strong fundamentalist theology these movements enlist missionaries in increasing numbers, while the older denominations have difficulty in maintaining their missionary force. Undoubtedly there are sociological factors which account in some degree for their astonishing success, but political deprivation is by no means the whole explanation. These missionaries are driven

by a strong love of Christ, a living faith in the guidance and power of the Spirit and a consuming passion for souls. They rely heavily on the 'promises of God' recorded in Scripture. Their experience of 'call' to mission is as decisive as their conversion. This observation raises the disturbing question, Is there a connexion between authoritative call and effective mission? Must the missionary know himself to be 'sent' by God? Certainly a profound sense of call can sustain a man through the darkest hours of strain and temptation. But in an age of doubt when the whole validity of religious experience is questioned, what substitute, if any, is there for the self-authenticating moment of encounter with God?

7. Traditional evangelism expects and encourages this kind of response, and mission, so understood, is still wonderfully rewarding not only in remote mission fields but in some situations in this country. In many towns there are packed Churches of various denominations where evangelical preachers are drawing crowds of old and young from all sections of the community. We must recognize that there are people who respond to this presentation of the Gospel; it is the way they come to Christ. For those who can accept it, it is wonderfully satisfying; they learn how to pray, how to read the Bible and how to use the gifts given by the Holy Spirit. They learn how to bear witness to their faith. Those who so scathingly criticize the evangelicals must offer an equally effective alternative.

8. Yet the fact remains that in Western Europe the great mass of the population is unmoved by the appeal of the evangelicals. For many people traditional theology is incredible. Devoted Christian workers in the artisan areas have sought by every means to 'offer Christ' but with little or no success. The failure caused radicals and liberals to conclude that old ideas of mission as forays into enemy territory must be abandoned; the Church must no longer call men to itself, but become the Servant Church, content to go out to wash the feet of the world, to care for the aged, the lonely, the handicapped, and to enter the many avenues of community service open to the volunteer today. Some ministers, sick at heart with the failure to evangelize, have immersed themselves in social work. They have described their relief from intolerable strain when they

realized that God was not expecting them to win souls in an age like this, and that mission was service. Freed from the nagging constraint to evangelize they could give themselves in humble obedience to Christ in His ministry of compassion. By friendship and sharing they could perhaps attract people to fellowship with Christ in the Church. Only those who have been reared in a strongly evangelical tradition, who have been told 'evangelize or perish', who have been drilled in the necessity of 'aggressive evangelism' know how unrelenting is the pressure on the spirit and how burdensome the sense of failure. To such workers the new ideal of mission as service has come with immense relief, as if Christ Himself had said, 'Come and I will give you rest'. The easy yoke, the light burden is to go out in love, to all mankind, assured that God Himself was not asking for more.

9. Such expressions deserve sympathetic attention because they come from workers in the front line, not from scholars writing at a distance. These men and women are trying to grasp what mission today really means. They do not generalize about 'secular man', they talk to him. He is the car worker, the housewife, the shopkeeper, the typist, the lay-about, the turf accountant, the ex-prisoner, the doctor, the policeman and the milk roundsman. They see secular man not as a 'soul' to be saved, nor as a faceless abstraction; he is the neighbour next door, the man on the bus, in the street or at the next bench. If mission is to begin at all, it must begin with him in his situation here which is very different from remote mission fields where the missionary addresses people for whom the supernatural presents few difficulties. There the idea of a God who speaks, sends, intervenes, who is pleased or angry, who judges and punishes is quite credible. But the West uses a very different frame of reference. Technological man turns to medical aid and to the sanitary engineer to fight plague, not to prayer and incantation. The problem of the missionary here is how to word his mission, how to explain his own sense of call, if it has survived. Here he must ask himself in what way is God still a Sending God if he is not transcendent and if religious experience is of doubtful validity? For if, as some radicals have suggested, mission is now reduced to the categorical imperative

'You must love your neighbour as yourself' we seem to have arrived at an ethic entirely free from all religion. But is it the Gospel?

10. Such considerations are forcing us all to re-examine our Christology and it is always a healthy sign when Christians are driven back to look at Jesus again. The same age-old question confronts us, Who is He? As we have seen, those who knew Him best were compelled to make two apparently contradictory assertions—He is truly man and He is truly God. The Church struggled for centuries to preserve and express these convictions and the Creeds are to be understood, not as an explanation of the mystery of Christ, but as defences against the twin errors that would make Him either solely human or solely divine and so destroy the Apostolic Faith. The astonishing affirmations of the Creed, however strange in modern ears, summarize the Church's experience of Christ. It is Christ who has made God known to us and He is the key both to what humanity and divinity really mean; just as He is the life of the Church. The Church is not a society keeping the memory of its hero green like the Burns Societies of Scotland. It has no life of its own, it dies without Christ. The experience of the Living Lord known in the fellowship of the Church, the life which He supplies in sacrament and prayer is the life of God and the guarantee of that future which such a love as His must ensure. Because He lives, the believer knows he too shall live, not less but more than he lives now, for the gift of Christ is always more abundant life. And faith as we understand it is the commitment of the whole personality to that apprehension of Reality we meet in the Fact of Christ. The Christian does not arrive at Christ from abstract ideas about God; he arrives at God because of what he sees in Christ. 'He has made Him known.'

11. Theology and mission both spring from experience and that is why the facile devaluation of religious experience by some radicals needs to be checked. Admittedly feelings can run to excess and emotionalism is a poor basis for faith, but Christianity is quite incomprehensible apart from the fact that men have all down the ages encountered God in moments of discernment and committal. Whatever light psychology may throw on the mental processes, the fact remains that for the indi-

viduals concerned these great moments have been the turning points in their lives and not infrequently in the life of their nation. To brush it all aside as unhealthy and illusionary is quite unscientific, and to assert that modern man is incapable of it is also a dogmatic assertion that ought to be closely scrutinized. It may well be, as the process theologians are telling us, that modern man is looking for experience in the wrong place and failing to recognize it where it is actually happening. Because God is the Ground of all Being, because He is the Creating Spirit every intuition and apprehension of and response to the glories and beauty of the universe felt by every nature lover is an experience of God; every creative impulse of the artist and the poet and every inspiration that grasps a deeper truth are all experience of the life of God. We are victims of language when we externalize God and then say we cannot find Him, for He is waiting to be known.

Thought answereth alone to thought,
And soul with soul hath kin;
The outward God he findeth not,
Who finds not God within.
(M.H.B. 281) FREDERICK LUCIAN HOSMER

12. But perhaps the most common experience of God in which every man has surely shared is in those impulses to put aside our own comfort and interest and to go to the aid of someone who needs help. Jesus is emphatic that in such moments, whether we know it or not, we are ministering to Him and working with Him. Our age is more concerned to help the underprivileged than any in the past and one of the new techniques of mission must surely be to help people to discern God and to recognize His constant presence in all their experience. We live only in, through, and by Him. He is not utterly remote, He is within. The experience of awakening and renewal are often felt as if they were infusions or injections of power from outside, but they are rather the recognition by the deep self that God is its life, the collapse of the barriers of fear and false pride, the washing away of sin. Whether we call it acceptance, surrender, encounter, identification, awakening, conversion, second birth, illumination, will depend upon our

religious vocabulary and theological stance, but all these are attempts to describe the indescribable experience of God. Such experience supplies the motivation for mission, for he who knows himself to be called knows also that he is sent and he knows what the message is. But if every man can know God in this direct self-authenticating way, in whatever form the experience may take, why is not every member of the Church aflame with mission?

13. For it is now clear that if mission is to be undertaken on the massive scale demanded by the world situation it must become once more a vast lay movement. The deprivation of the laity and the exaltation of the clergy are both offences against the Body of Christ for in the Body all members are equally valued though their functions differ. Even the older authoritarian Churches are realizing that the Lay Apostolate is an immense reservoir of untapped talent and energy and that its voice must be heard not only in worship but in the decision-making courts of the Church and above all in mission to the world. The layman lives and works in that world, he knows its language and its pressures and he has much of importance to teach the Church. Why then is he so silent, especially in witness to the world? The clerical leadership of the Church, once it had formulated this question concluded that it was because they had not given the layman the training he needed. He had been fed on pious homilies and moral anecdotes; he had not been equipped for mission.

14. In the early attempts at lay-training it was assumed that the clergy knew the answers to the world's need and that all that was required was a short series of lectures on elementary theology, a smattering of sociology and a few practical hints on how to counsel enquirers. Those so equipped were then commissioned and sent out. It was further assumed that because they were laymen they would be received where the clergy could not easily penetrate and that they would speak in language that the non-churchgoer would understand. But the witnesses quickly returned dismayed and confused. Their superficial knowledge of the faith was quite unequal to the questions and criticisms they encountered in the pubs and clubs. In the subsequent post-mortems they learned that their

trainers did not have very convincing answers either. Some began to wonder why it was ever imagined that a layman after a three-month crash course in mission should be thought capable of taking on the secular world, when full-time professionals were so obviously out of touch with that world and had so little understanding of its life and thought. Some concluded that the Church's idea of mission was so unrealistic that it did not know what it was asking of its laymen. Indeed in several cases as the course proceeded the laymen began to drop out; they could see what was expected of them and felt either unequal to the task or unwilling to engage in so unrealistic a venture.

15. These initial failures taught some valuable lessons. It was soon realized that the Church did not possess any spiritual *élite* who had the answers and who could train and equip the laity for mission today. Even training itself can no longer be thought of as a series of lectures imparting knowledge but must be a process of sharing, of learning together in small groups in which the members challenge and influence each other. Learning through group dynamics and non-directed group activity establishes a very different relationship between the minister and the group. He is no longer the teacher, the paternalist-authority, but one among the others equally subject to criticism and to the processes of group-examination and self-realization. He may go as the 'resource person', the man with specialist knowledge who is there to be questioned, to supply information. The consultant hovers on the outskirts of the group without himself becoming involved directly in their exploration of the subject and of each other. Those who go through this experience describe it as similar to the technique of the early Methodist class-meetings, and as a valuable school for the maturing of personality. It is also advocated as a superb method of mission since it is not difficult to set up groups for all kinds of projects in which non-Christians are willing to co-operate. In the intimacy of such groups the Christian faith can be explored together. And there is considerable evidence that people who would never go to Church will gladly join a group meeting in a private house and are quite ready to talk religion and to share in practical programmes of study and work.

16. In such training it is the group itself which makes the agenda. Information is required but it can only be absorbed and utilized when it relates to the needs and interests of the persons who want it. Thus the 'resource person' or consultant takes the place of the teacher. This is a dangerous role to play for it could create a class of impersonal non-committed minds, floating banks of information who are not really involved in the struggle to relate knowledge to life. The one safeguard is to insist that the resource person is himself an ordinary member of another group, in which he submits to the pressures and exchanges of group sharing. There are obviously great values in this method, but there is some risk of it developing an esoteric terminology of its own, and by conditioning its members to frank confession and mutual criticism turning what is essentially a therapeutic device into an addiction, a dependence on the group which could be unhealthy. But where these dangers are recognized and avoided the group, working party, or workshop, as it is variously called, does gather up the resources of the group, helps them to do their own thinking, to plan and execute their own programmes. There is plenty of evidence that moribund churches have been revitalized by the decision to set up working parties to think through together the various problems of the church in its own neighbourhood. The self-survey of resources often arouses a church for the first time to the real facts of its weakness and its foolish waste of its resources: the survey of the community around the church also discloses unsuspected needs and opportunities for service. Often, but not always, the group begins to match the need with service. The time comes when the facts are plain, the opportunities of service and contact are known and the laity have to decide what they are going to do about it all. Sometimes this leads to a great response, but by no means always. The challenge of mission is not always accepted.

17. The house-group may also become a unit of mission when specially-made films presenting the faith can be fed into private television sets, a development we are likely to see in the not too distant future. The impact of the film has never been properly evaluated, but as the proposed University of the Air suggests there are many people who are willing to study at

home directed by relayed lessons. If the Churches can agree together in the production of the best possible material for the exposition of the Gospel then a whole new avenue of mission is opening for us. Such, at least, is the vision of Lord Rank and Film House Fellowships may soon be in operation.

18. Groups are thus one of the main agencies of modern mission and they need careful shepherding. Where they become unrelated to the Church, they can hive off and very easily become the victims of heretical ideas and misguided enthusiasms.[1] The links with the Church must be strong and there is need both for regular meetings of group-leaders and for guides and study papers to keep them fully abreast of the rapid developments in Christian thought and method. Such material is best prepared in answer to specific need rising within the groups and quickly relayed to the centre. It may well be that an important function of the new British Council of Churches Committee on Mission and Unity will be to provide the necessary joint theological research. It should also be remembered that groups will probably be short-lived for membership quickly changes in our mobile society and techniques and programmes must be adjusted accordingly. In any case it is better to discharge a group when its limited work is done and to form a new one with a somewhat different membership for the next job. This keeps interest alive and broadens fellowship. Many busy people who could not possibly commit themselves to permanent membership are ready to give themselves for a limited period, and they have much to give which would otherwise remain unused. They have also much to receive. There are specialist groups as well as residential, for it is possible to gather working parties and groups ministering to the needs of the various occupations and professions which divide modern society into self-conscious social units often desperately conscious of their isolation and the pressures upon them. But recent surveys suggest that the residential grouping is still by far the most determinative of the factors in modern society and mission must be primarily directed to where people live. The organization of mission requires that the work and the policy

[1]See Neville B. Cryer and Ernest N. Goodridge, *Experiment in Unity* (Mowbrays, 1969).

of the groups should be constantly evaluated by what in effect becomes a core, or executive, or a team-ministry of clergy and laity. Thus the structures of the renewed Church begin to emerge.

19. For we reject that form of radicalism which denigrates the Church and prophesies its imminent collapse. We think such an attitude completely misunderstands the dual nature of the *Ecclesia*. From a human point of view the Church is a company of very fallible folk, but it is also a supernatural society, the Assembly of those called by God to be His people, fed with His life and guided by His Spirit. The Church is always under judgement and its organization and structures must change to meet the changing scene but it remains the Body of Christ and will live as long as it lives in Him. Any idea of mission apart from the Church is doomed to failure and will die like any other severed branch. The special ministries which are trying to reach into industry, education and the social services, depend on the despised Church for their existence. The worker-priest may maintain himself by his own labour, but his mission is seriously limited and in grave danger of distortion unless he himself is firmly rooted in the life of the Church and is nourished and comforted by it. Sector ministers who believe that the Church does not understand the needs of the secular world are especially tempted to regard the ties of Church as an encumbrance. They need the special care of the Church to sustain them in their exposed position.

20. Industrial Mission is revealing the complexity of the problem of mission today. It began some twenty-five years ago when some keen churchmen discovered that it was possible to get inside the factory gates and to present the Christian witness. Industry, which made it plain that it would not tolerate rival denominationalism, was ready to receive an ecumenical team. The work originally started by local ministers and clergy has developed and now in many industrial areas there are ecumenical team ministries of full-time chaplains. They have given much time to the study of the needs and strains of industrial society. Some have suggested that the original part-time chaplaincies should be discontinued on the grounds that the personal counselling which is their main work ought to be done

by the paid full-time welfare officers of the firms and that busy ministers with churches to look after cannot give the time or thought to the problems of industry that the work demands. We believe this view to be mistaken on both counts. The Gospel is primarily a message to people and there will always be a place for pastoral care in the mission of the Church. Indeed the warmth of the support industrial chaplaincy enjoys is due to the appreciation of this personal work by both management and labour. The part-time chaplain is the living link between the local Church and the local factory. But the problems of industry are not going to be solved by full-time chaplains for that calls for industrial and sociological training which industry is itself struggling to provide. What industry wants from the Church and what the Church ought to give is insight into the Christian doctrines of man and society, work and leisure. The role of the full-time industrial chaplain as we understand it is to feed the insights of the Gospel into industrial society and to feed back to the Church the new conceptions of society that industrialization creates. They too are link men. It is also an important part of their work to co-ordinate, advise, encourage, and recruit the part-time chaplains in their region. But it is the duty of both full- and part-time chaplains to help the Christian layman to become the active agent of mission, for it is the layman, not the chaplain, who is the worker, the foreman, the under- or middle-manager. He is the one who feels the pressures, who is threatened by redundancy, whose decisions may cost him his job. He needs pastoral care and support as well as theological and sociological instruction. Industrial mission will really get under way when the Christian laymen are equipped and supported by the Church as a whole. The small groups of self-conscious Christians who meet in factories for prayer and Bible study make little impact on their fellow workers. What we have in mind is that mission will mean the conscious and sustained effort of the Church to arouse and equip its millions of laymen to become the people of God in industrial society. At the moment we are but scratching the surface. Industrial mission is only one aspect of the total mission of the Church but we are convinced that it must be ecumenical and Church-based. It must grow out of and be constantly nourished and corrected by the worshipping community; when it is tempted to isolate itself it is in serious danger.

21. Thus the Church is beginning to realize how immense and complex is the effort to arouse the People of God to their commission. It requires much more than a resolution in Convocation or Conference, for it involves nothing less than the complete renewal of the Church and the reversal of all those forces of decay that make for the present drift from faith. Nor is it only the laity that need 'retooling', the ministry too is increasingly aware of its unhappy isolation and ineffectiveness. The Methodist Church for instance, proposes to recall its ministers every ten years for an intensive course on the social and theological changes affecting the Christian mission. Lay training also must become a permanent, not a spasmodic, feature of the Christian life. Understanding and commitment go together: only when the facts are known does there come a sense of responsibility and without responsibility there can be no impulse to mission. But at the moment the Church is very confused and has little idea of how to set about the process of renewal.

22. Renewal ought to flow from Christian worship, but unfortunately traditional forms of worship all too often fail to produce either understanding or commitment. Because for many people worship seems so unreal and so remote from life, it repels rather than attracts, and is said to be boring. Attempts to make it intelligible and interesting led to the liturgical movement which tries not only to clarify the objectives of worship, but to help every worshipper to participate in what is happening, for worship is an act of conscious communication with God and the elements of worship should provide for the full expression of that relationship. Attempts to liven worship by the introduction of guitars and drums must be seen as correctives to the Victorian domination of the organ; the new hymns with their references to steel, concrete, and aeroplanes are attempts to relate worship to the actual conditions of modern life, their mostly noisy tunes with their strong and rapid beat are in reaction to the slow and sonorous tunes of the last century. The addition of poetry readings and dramatic presentations to the reading of Scripture are attempts to show

that the Spirit has been speaking outside the Bible and the Church and has new things to say to us. The Sermon in particular has come in for sharp criticism and alternatives such as question-and-answer periods, dialogue instead of monologue, brains trusts and teach-ins have been tried. But the liturgical reform movement remains very much a minority concern for there is still considerable resistance to change. Curiously enough when young people are asked to draw up their own form of service, they often produce something very traditional. Those who do experiment have realized that new forms of worship take more time and energy to prepare than do the traditional forms and they can very easily become more abysymally boring and trivial than what they are intended to replace. They are also beginning to understand that in nineteen hundred years of experience of worship the Church has gathered many treasures which should be used, not discarded. Live worship depends on the content of the service and the spirit of the worshippers.

23. It belongs to the confusion of our day that some young ministers no longer see any purpose in the 'care of souls' and are turning from the pastoral office. The idea that a pastor should be a spiritual guide seems to them to be a false trail leading to a useless mysticism. They insist that only in community service is Christ to be known. He is already outside the Church in the strain and sorrow of modern life and we serve Him best when we serve others and forget all about such old fashioned words as 'souls'. Again we would yield to none in proclaiming that the Christian must seek the redemption and the renewal of society, but he goes to it offering not simply himself, but the transforming power of God. He may have to express this in new ways, but if he is to deliver his message, sooner or later he must sit down and tell what Christ means to him. He must know how to speak about God, he must be able to articulate his own experience, and to offer the fellowship of the Church and it is the Church's business to equip him for his mission.

24. So we are learning that there is no short-cut to mission, no magical formula which will revitalize the Church and transform its ministry and laity into a militant army of spiritual

warriors, fully equipped for mission. We can understand how frustration and despair at the weakness, intransigence, and failure of the Church can vent itself in caustic criticism and frantic demands for reorganization which merely reshuffles the structures. But this is to begin at the wrong end. We cannot renew the Church, for though we are its members, we are not its life. God Himself is the Renewer (Revelation 21:5) and it is His Spirit that makes dry bones live (Ezekiel 37). Pentecostalism has much to teach us for the Church has suffered fearfully from its neglect of the doctrine of the Spirit. He is and always has been the Creator Spirit who takes and unfolds the things of Christ and leads the Church into new truth. We believe that He is working within the Church today in all its unrest, humiliation, and self-examination. The near despair that now inhibits action must be resisted for what it is, a temptation to turn away from the source of our life and the centre of renewal. Thus one of the urgent needs of the hour is to pray with expectancy, with the faith that relies not upon ourselves but upon God, and consequently to place ourselves at the disposal of God. Whether or not we can now believe in theophanies and magical interventions, we believe that the Father will not refuse the Gift of the Spirit to those who ask (Luke 11:13).

25. The Gift of the Spirit has preceded nearly every great revival of the evangelical type. It has also preceded other creative movements in the life of the Church. Unfortunately too many Christians have been reared in forms of spirituality and worship which have not yielded what they promised. It is not enough to ask people to recollect the presence of God without telling them how this is done. Some have vainly tried to locate God in the dark recesses of the soul. What we need is training in how to realize the immediacy of God, how to sink deeply into our total experience of life and sense His presence at every moment and in every situation. Our study of religious experience suggests that mission will begin to pulsate when groups of members awaken to the life of God within which their own life is lived, and when they open themselves to the Spirit by both the reception of new ideas and by deeper commitment to His known will. If there are things amiss in our own lives we must face them and put them right before we can

go on mission, and this is why the message of repentance and forgiveness can never be absent from mission.

26. New forms of mission will then develop from within the group itself and they may well conceive it to be their first duty to help others to discover the Living Ground of all Reality who fills the whole universe and speaks His eternal word of love and renewal in Jesus. This may mean a new approach to society and to individuals. We have wondered whether many Christians have been unable to discern the immediacy of God and the power of the Creator Spirit because Western theology has so stressed the Fall and the Atonement that they have assumed that God can only be experienced by penitent sinners. The reluctance of so many laymen to engage in mission may be due to their innate distaste of presenting the faith in these terms; they are embarrassed by the thought of invading other people's privacy in order to induce a consciousness of sin. We may have to begin much further back, as Jesus often did, with the picture of God as a father waiting for his sons to come home, a host waiting with his feast all ready for invited guests who fail to come. Mission is the opening of blind eyes to light, the discovery of unimaginable treasure in the field of daily work. The treasure is God Himself, the light is Christ, the Father's house is the Kingdom. In the light of Christ we learn what darkness and sin is, but we begin with the light that still shines in the darkness and which the darkness will never quench. Old spatial and regal images which now create mental obstacles to faith must be corrected by ones which disclose the waiting Father, the Christ who knocks at the door of every man. Once such discernment begins the Christian must be prepared for a lifetime of conversion and renewal, not just for a once-and-for-all experience. He must seek that daily penetration of the inner self by the Spirit who seeks to transform the believer more and more into the image of Christ (2 Corinthians 3:18). It is the business of the Church to call men to be saints, to produce Christ-like character, nor must we be deterred because the search for holiness has sometimes been fearfully perverted by bigotry and fanaticism. Mission takes into the world the humility, the sweetness, the courage, the longsuffering, the peace and joy of Christ's Spirit-filled followers, for the world

does not and cannot of itself produce the fruits of the Spirit.

27. Mission, we believe, must spring from the activity of the local Christian community. They are the people of God, His witnesses. In each neighbourhood Christians of all denominations must begin to come together for the sole purpose of asking themselves how they can be the People of God to the people around them. Mission may create the unity we seek. While it may begin in the deep concern of one Church we must be anxious and ready to join hands with others and be willing to share all our resources. But the local mission must be linked to the regional need, for society today is increasingly developing zonal characteristics as a counterpoise to distant national and global integration and centralization. There is need for District, Diocesan, and regional planning for mission, in which the special needs of the area are appreciated. But the mission is one. Perhaps the most hopeful sign today is the realization of the British Council of Churches that mission is one of its permanent responsibilities and that it should unite all local and regional enterprises and programmes into a comprehensive strategy for mission today.

28. Finally our conclusion is that when we are through this present crisis of faith, when we have restructured the Church according to our new insights, when we have re-expressed the great truths of the Gospel, we shall find that the Church is still recognizably the Church, the People of God, that the Gospel is still recognizably the Gospel of God in Christ reconciling the world to Himself, that however and whenever man experiences God it becomes in the end a salvation experience leading to the goal of Christian perfection and that the Gospel requires the redemption of society. The present turmoil is a time of refining and sifting; elements now seen to be false to Christ must be eliminated and neglected truths, especially the truth of the activity of the Holy Spirit, must be restored to their central place. Man may have come of age, but he is still a son of God called to adult responsibility in the partnership God has offered from the beginning of time. Change belongs to the very nature of the universe, but it is not accidental, it is gathered up into the Eternal Purpose by which all things will be reconciled in Christ. Reconciliation is costly beyond all measure, and

Christ on His Cross speaks the full and complete word of reconciliation and now welcomes us into the fellowship of His life, suffering, and triumph. We begin to mission when we begin to forgive, as we ourselves are forgiven and when we tear down barriers of ignorance, hate, and fear which separate us from our fellows. We begin to mission when like Philip (John 1:46) we can talk about Jesus and say to our unbelieving friends, 'Come and see!'

INDEX

I

SUBJECTS

INDEX

II

PERSONS

INDEX

III

SCRIPTURE REFERENCES